MILITARY

8·50

Jeanne Uphill

1993

# F SECTION, SOE

# F SECTION, SOE

## THE BUCKMASTER NETWORKS

Marcel Ruby

LEO COOPER

LONDON

First published 1988 by Leo Cooper Ltd.,

Leo Cooper is an independent imprint of the
Heinemann Group of Publishers, 10 Upper Grosvenor Street,
London W1X 9PA

LONDON   MELBOURNE   AUCKLAND

ISBN: 0-85052-6809

Printed in Great Britain by
St Edmundsbury Press Ltd, Bury St Edmunds, Suffolk

TO MY WIFE

# —— CONTENTS ——

## ——— FOREWORD ———
## by Jean Pierre-Bloch[1]

No one is better qualified to write this book than Marcel Ruby, author of numerous works on the French resistance and winner of the *Comité d'Action de la Résistance* award for literature. It is also a timely book. An epic saga of the British secret service agents and SOE's Buckmaster groups, it makes a thrilling story.

At a time when many writers, glossing over the horrors of mass deportation, are trying to impose their own ignoble version of resistance history, it is salutary to recall the days when France was struggling to repel the Nazis and their accomplices in the Vichy régime. For this is the story that should be told. The first steps towards an organized resistance in France were taken by SOE. Many of us, among the first SOE agents, were unaware of what was happening in London, thanks to de Gaulle's reservations about the British. In 1941, as far as we were concerned, the men who fell from the sky had been sent by de Gaulle, and that was all that mattered. But Marcel Ruby demonstrates how those early agents, both French and British, opened the door to a better understanding, so that London had a clearer idea of what was going on in France, and vice versa.

At that stage of the war, many of those who later proved their worth in the resistance were either counselling prudence or flatly refusing to offer us the slightest help. For them, Nazi Germany had won the war, was on the way to world domination, and we had better just accept it.

But as we proved, even in those early days, there was a movement towards resistance in France, doing all in its power to help the British in their lonely stand against Hitler.

Once again, let us thank Marcel Ruby for his lively and accurate account of the Buckmaster groups and their exploits.

---

1. Former minister, MP and chairman of LICRA, as well as one of the first agents in the Buckmaster networks.

# ——— INTRODUCTION ———

All secret service agents, or so the general public fondly imagines, are supermen like James Bond. They live wildly exciting lives, unravelling machiavellian plots, courting death at every turn, performing feats of prodigious daring in defence of vital interests. Equipped with sophisticated weapons, they belong to a world of violence, alcohol and lovely women. And they always win.

The reality is very different. It often exceeds in dramatic intensity anything that cinema has been able to invent. The secret agent, man or woman, who undertakes such work is seldom prepared for the pitiless war in the shadows. With precious little else to help them, they must rely on their own courage and common sense to fulfil the impossible tasks they are set. They must watch themselves at every turn. But they are only human. They know what fear is; they know the constant anxiety of living in enemy territory – where, nevertheless, they sometimes find real, true friendship and bravery. Sometimes even love. Sometimes prison, torture, deportation or death . . .

Winston Churchill's orders to SOE and the Buckmaster groups were brutally simple: 'Set Europe ablaze!'

And so, under the leadership of the legendary Colonel Buckmaster, men and women of exceptional strength of character threw themselves into the savage fight, their enthusiasm undimmed by all the risks.[1]

In the secret war, truth really was stranger than fiction. This book shows how honest citizens transformed themselves into redoubtable terrorists. How

---

1. Despite a general reticence born of genuine modesty, the author has managed to acquire the personal eyewitness accounts of these remarkable exploits from (among many others): Jean-Bernard Badaire, Peter Churchill, André Courvoisier, Benjamin Cowburn, Jean Pierre-Bloch, J. M. Régnier, J. Rousset, the three de Vomécourt brothers, and Pierre Vourron.

Surviving members of the Buckmaster groups, and the families of those who were lost, form the core of the FNLR (Fédération Nationale Libre Résistance – 'Amicale Buck' as the group is known), whose president is Jean-Bernard Badaire. All of them have offered me their total co-operation. I hope that this book will offer them sufficient proof of my gratitude.

they made parachute landings by night, duly equipped with a cyanide pill – just in case. How the reception committee was often missing – or replaced by a German one. How three courageous brothers, then a handful of agents, managed to weave a veritable spider's web of resistance groups over the whole country.

How each group was organized: the logistics (utterly reliable people who hid arms, money, addresses of those responsible for local operations); the clandestine radio operators (whose role, apparently modest, was in fact essential – and terribly dangerous – for without them the agent was isolated and useless); and, of course, those who were directly responsible for taking action in the field.

How the agents were relentlessly pursued by the Gestapo and its allies, French collaborators. How they fell into traps, as at the Villa des Bois in Marseilles, or into the hands of Mathilde Carré ('La Chatte'), whose exploits were the subject of a recent film – but who was finally used to hoodwink the Germans. How they fell victim to certain *passeurs*, those whose duty it was to lead them along the escape lines but who led them instead to imprisonment in the Spanish camp at Miranda; or were betrayed by people seeking to save their own necks or by others actively working for the Nazis. How certain highly regarded people made a pact of honour with the Germans – and later paid the price for their mistake. But also how the imagination, cool heads and astonishing ingenuity of people like Ben Cowburn often served to outwit the enemy and his accomplices.

How the handful of Buckmaster groups managed to destroy vital economic and military targets – usually by means of plastic explosives – like the metal-pressing plant at Fives-Lilles, the propellor works at Ratier, the wireless factory at Ronchin, the Ducatillon oil refinery at Willems, the sluice at Roubaix, bridges, intricate machinery, trains carrying fuel or munitions, giant cranes, railway equipment, the main transformer for the submarine base at Bordeaux, etc., etc. How the famous Peugeot works at Sochaux, turning out cars and trucks and also tank turrets for the Wehrmacht, were put out of action with the knowledge and help of their owner, Robert Peugeot.

And above all, how Buckmaster's people provided arms, training and active guidance to the maquisards and resistance workers, notably following the Normandy landings when they managed to delay a German tank regiment on its way to the battlefront. The reader may well be surprised to find some familiar names cropping up here.

From the SOE doctor interned in Buchenwald concentration camp, to the dainty elegant figure of a young Hindu princess who became an SOE heroine, shot in the back of the head at Dachau, the story of the Buckmaster groups could well be turned into a whole series of thrillers or spy films.

Marcel Ruby
1 May 1985

Suddenly appearing as if from nowhere, old Curly was already running towards us, making frantic gestures.

'My god, where have you been?' he yelled. 'They've been waiting for you for an hour, circling round and round. What the hell were you doing?'

'But it isn't time yet,' we protested. 'We said midnight or one o'clock, and it's only what – eleven twenty now.'

'Time or not, they're here. And at that altitude it'll be a miracle if everybody in the country hasn't spotted them.'

Moonlight flooded the clearing in front of us, about nine hundred metres by three hundred. Beyond it stood the forest, covering the horizon; for some reason I found this reassuring, perhaps because its shadows offered a refuge from the moon's floodlit stage.

The aircraft – one of ours, of course – was still circling overhead. We set to and laid out the huge white paper cross which Dupuy had brought. Curly stationed himself at one end, Dupuy at the other, with me in the middle, each clasping a flashlight. The aircraft came straight over us but they didn't drop anything. What was happening? We had given all the right signals.

We waited so long I began to get worried. 'Hey, Dupuy,' I called softly, 'you don't think . . . ?'

'It could be an enemy plane? Yes. Put your torches out.'

We had just switched off our flashlights when three parachutes left the aircraft above. At last! We ran towards the nearest man who had already landed in the middle of the clearing and was getting out of his harness. As we approached he stood up, gun in hand, shouting, 'Who's there?'

I gave him the password and he lowered his gun. Dupuy joined us with the second man, who was pointing at the trees. 'Our friend has got stuck,' he said.

We found the third man at the edge of the forest, somewhat scratched but safe, and began to guide them towards the road. There was no time to lose.

'It's not over yet,' one of the parachutists said. He spoke excellent French and I took him for a Gaullist officer. 'You're supposed to be getting three crates of weapons and two radio sets.'

But the aircraft had vanished.

'We weren't told about that,' Curly said. 'It probably isn't meant for us. Anyway, the plane has gone now. The best thing we can do is look after these fellows. And it won't be all that easy, getting them away. That plane of theirs was droning round and round for hours and the alarm's probably been raised already. We'll have to get them hidden as fast as possible.'

He was right. And so the two parachustists who were going with Curly gave us the bundle of 500 letters (written by refugees in London to their families in France), as well as their revolvers and two million francs in 1,000-franc notes which were urgently needed in Marseilles.[1]

This dramatic scene described by Jean Pierre-Bloch took place not in June 1944, on the eve of the Normandy landings, but way back in October 1941. Barely a year after the German invasion and occupation of most of France, intelligence agents were already flying out from England and making parachute drops onto French soil, to be met by French patriots. And so, even then, despite the Gestapo and Vichy authorities, there were obviously close links between France and Britain. These men and the weapons and funds they brought would help the bitter struggle against the occupying forces and collaborators.

How was this possible, so soon after the greatest defeat in French history? Who were these men rallying to the cause, backing the gallant French resistance in its fight against an enemy who then seemed so invincible?

Colonel Buckmaster's SOE was still unknown. And yet . . .

1. Jean Pierre-Bloch, *Le Temps d'y Penser Encore* (Jean-Claude Simoën, Paris 1977).

# —— PART I ——

## SOE AND THE
## BUCKMASTER NETWORKS

On 19 July, 1940, Hitler made a triumphant speech at the Reichstag in Berlin, boasting of his victories and proclaiming that the Third Reich would last a thousand years, that England would soon be defeated. Magnanimously he offered to end hostilities 'as a victor speaking in the name of reason'.

On the same day, 19 July, 1940, Winston Churchill started SOE. In a brief handwritten memorandum to his War Cabinet he said that SOE's function was to 'co-ordinate all action by way of subversion and sabotage against the enemy overseas'.

This was the reply of the old British lion to the adventurer who had forcibly seized much of Europe and who dreamed of dominating the world.

Now it was up to the British War Cabinet to organize SOE, appoint its chief – and get the French involved.

# — 1 —

# SPECIAL OPERATIONS EXECUTIVE

Winston Churchill, the father of Special Operations Executive, summed up its mission in an eloquent phrase: 'Set Europe ablaze!' SOE was born there and then, an original concept and an ambitious one, in response to a threat unknown in Europe since the days of Napoleon I. It was also something of an ad hoc enterprise, the structure of which would have to be modified and adapted in the light of lessons drawn from the first active operations.

Assembled on 22 July, 1940, the British War Cabinet rejected Hitler's offer. In a broadcast speech, Lord Halifax, the Foreign Secretary, 'brushed aside [Hitler's] summons to capitulate to his will' and confidently asserted: 'We shall not stop fighting until freedom is secure throughout the world.'[1] It was a brave assertion, for Britain's armed forces – apart from the Royal Navy – seemed almost insignificant by comparison with Germany's.

At the same meeting, the War Cabinet approved Churchill's memorandum; thus SOE was officially born on 22 July, 1940. It was placed under the authority of Dr Hugh Dalton, Minister of Economic Warfare.

At the end of May, the Chiefs of Staff of the three services had sent a joint report to Churchill. Britain, they said, 'stood alone and at bay', and her only chance against the might of Germany was either to destroy Hitler's war potential by massive aerial bombardment (although there weren't enough aircraft) or to 'stimulate the seeds of revolt within the conquered territories'. Hence the Prime Minister's decision to create a special organization that could carry out sabotage operations and stir up subversion.

SOE's objective was all the more urgent at a time when British intelligence had lost its main sources of information following the Nazis' conquest of western Europe, and particularly as a result of the Venlo affair. Venlo was the little town on the frontier between Germany and Holland, where on

---

1. Quoted in E. H. Cookridge, *Inside SOE* (Arthur Barker, London 1966).

9 November, 1939, the SS had lured senior British intelligence agents into a trap and arrested the Chief of Continental Operations, Major H. R. Stevens, and his deputy, Captain S. Payne Best. The situation became even worse in May 1940 when the Germans, having invaded the Netherlands, discovered a suitcase containing all the papers relating to British informants; scores of people were arrested, both British and Dutch. In fact, such was the plight of British intelligence that they were obliged to ask SOE agents to collect military information for them, which wasn't SOE's job at all. SOE was asked, for example, 'to discover the progress of German research in V-rockets, the pace of German armament production, the location of German warships in Western ports', etc.

Colonel Sir Geoffrey Vickers, Deputy Director-General of Economic Warfare from 1942 to 1944, has said on this subject:[1]

> The Enemy Branch of the Ministry of Economic Warfare was engaged from 1942 to 1944 almost exclusively on intelligence work which the Services needed for strategical and operational planning, but which their own Intelligence Directorates were not organized to supply. We had to do the work almost entirely with civilian personnel. It is highly abnormal that the Services should go outside their own Intelligence Directorates for information and advice needed to plan operations.

The problem was that British intelligence now had only a few dozen agents in German-occupied countries, and their resources were stretched to the limit.

This situation helps to explain the rivalry for control of SOE which was claimed by the Secret Intelligence Service, the three armed services, the Foreign Office, the Ministry of Information and the Ministry of Economic Warfare. Finally Churchill appointed Dr Hugh Dalton, Minister of Economic Warfare, after Dalton had told him that he needed a free hand 'to use many different methods, including industrial and military sabotage, labour agitation and strikes, continuous propaganda, terrorist acts against traitors and German leaders, boycotts and riots'.[2] Dalton would remain in overall control of SOE until February 1942, when he became President of the Board of Trade and was succeeded by Lord Wolmer (later Lord Selborne).

After the war, Major-General Sir Colin Gubbins was to describe SOE's task as being essentially 'to encourage and enable the peoples of the occupied countries to harass the German war effort at every possible point by sabotage, subversion, go-slow practices, *coup de main* raids, etc, and at the same time to build up secret forces therein, organized, armed and trained to take their part,

1. Quoted in Cookridge, op.cit.
2. Ibid.

only when the final assault began. . . . In its simplest terms, this plan involved the ultimate delivery to occupied territory of large numbers of personnel and quantities of arms and explosives.'[1]

The first organizer to be parachuted into France, in May 1941, was Pierre de Vomécourt, one of SOE's heroes. In his opinion. 'The ultimate goal was to provide the French with the means to share in the liberation of their country, but the immediate objective was to thwart the enemy's war production in France – by disrupting the transport and delivery of raw materials, sabotage at the work place, deliberate errors in the administration and planning of munitions production, etc.'

These various definitions of SOE's mission, some of which were not revealed until after the war, are indicative of how original, diverse and effective it was. SOE was a unique organization formed in unique circumstances. Its success or failure would depend to a large extent on the way it was run and on the men who were running it – notably Colonel Buckmaster.

After the fall of France, Britain's military deficiency reduced her options to economic and subversive warfare.

Churchill was closely involved in the development of his new creation, and took a particular interest in its progress. It is significant that the very day after it was formed, on 23 July, 1940, he sent the following note to the War Secretary, Anthony Eden (later Lord Avon):

> It is of course urgent and indispensable that every effort should be made to obtain secretly the best possible information about the German forces in the various countries overrun, and to establish intimate contacts with local people, and to plant agents. This, I hope, is being done on the largest scale, as opportunity serves, by the new organization under the Ministry of Economic Warfare.[2]

The Prime Minister's support was decisive, especially in the early days. Indeed, SOE met undisguised hostility from the War Office, where it recruited some of its best men; from the Air Ministry, which had to supply aircraft for SOE missions (at a time of dire shortage); and from the Foreign Office, whose ideas were often diametrically opposed to those of SOE. It was Churchill, too, who decided to dissolve the War Office's research section and give it to SOE instead.

As for the legendary Intelligence Service (SIS), this was in fact a very complex organization, run since October 1939 by Colonel Menzies. One of its departments at that time was Section D, headed by Lieutenant-Colonel (later Major-General) Laurence Douglas Grand, which was subdivided into two sections: SO-1 and SO-2. SO-1 was to be responsible for subversive propaganda against the enemy in time of war, while SO-2 would concern

1. Quoted in Cookridge, op.cit.
2. Ibid.

itself with acts of sabotage and the training of saboteurs. When SOE was formed, however, Churchill ordered that SO-1 and SO-2 should be integrated into the new organization. Later SO-1 would be split off to become the Political Warfare Executive, independent of SOE, under General Dallas Brooks.

As the first recruits to SOE, Churchill appealed to men who had already proved their worth. This initial nucleus included men from SIS, from the RAF, Royal Navy and the Army, and also some experienced civilians.

Each SOE branch was designated by the initial of the country where it was working; for example, SOE 'Y' for Yugoslavia, SOE 'F' for France, etc.

On its formation, SOE was installed at St Ermin's Hotel in Caxton Street. But these premises soon proved to be too small, and SOE's French Section moved to 62/64 Baker Street, of which Cookridge writes:[1]

> Those who have known that grey, five-storey building, with its dark narrow hall, the 'Briefing Room', the 'Map Room', with its benches and blackboards, and the wobbly lift hesitantly ascending to the small plainly furnished office rooms, will remember it with nostalgia.

Meanwhile, SOE's top brass moved to 82 Baker Street, a large building nearby known as Michael House and belonging to Marks & Spencer. Michael House backed onto a little side street, and SOE staff – rarely wearing any kind of uniform – went in an out without attracting attention. Only a modest plaque of black marble indicated the presence here of an official organization: 'Inter-Services Research Bureau'.

In obedience to the Official Secrets Act, which forbids any mention of anything relating to national defence, and further ordered never to use the organization's official name in private conversation, SOE's agents, officers and administrative staff kept the secret so well that its existence long remained unknown even among high-ranking civil servants. (Among themselves SOE's staff called it 'the Racket'.)

Churchill agreed that the War Office should supervise recruitment and that SIS should run the security checks on all potential agents.

When the time came to appoint SOE's first directors, the Prime Minister sought advice from his old friend Sir Claude Dansey, an expert on the Secret Services. The task was a delicate one, for the job would entail organizing and training SOE agents in all the countries occupied by the Germans and Italians. Dansey recommended the appointment at the head of SOE of Sir Frank Nelson, a former officer of the Indian Army, a specialist in intelligence and a one-time Conservative MP.

Nelson brought in a few SIS men whose qualities he already knew and

1. Cookridge, op. cit.

appreciated. Thus Colonel F. T. Davies was put in charge of training and Major (later Colonel) George Taylor was appointed to organize the first overseas sections and planning operations. Geographically, Nelson invited Captain (later Colonel) Bickham Sweet-Escott to run the Balkans and Middle East sections, Brigadier Colin Gubbins the East European sections (Poland and Czechoslovakia), and the banker Charles Hambro – a close friend of Churchill's – the Scandinavian section. He entrusted the organization's finances to a chartered accountant, John Venner, who remained in the same post throughout SOE's entire existence. As Chief of Staff, Nelson brought in Major Taylor, with Sweet-Escott as his deputy; the latter then left the Balkans section to devote his time to Western Europe. Charles Hambro later became Nelson's deputy.

In 1942, Dr Dalton, who had been made President of the Board of Trade, was replaced as Minister of Economic Warfare by Lord Selborne. Selborne arranged for Nelson to leave, and thus Charles Hambro, knighted in 1941, became head of SOE with Colin Gubbins as his deputy and, in September 1943, his successor.

As the author E. H. Cookridge points out, Brigadier (later Major-General) Gubbins was a man of exceptional qualities and 'he needed these qualities in good measure when dealing with the motley collection of bankers, dons, lawyers, journalists, film directors, schoolmasters, artists, wine-merchants and "foreigners" from a dozen European countries.' And, adds Cookridge, a specialist in SOE affairs, 'Applying his boundless energy, Brigadier Gubbins gave SOE spirit and substance; and in his subordinates roused the enthusiasm so direly needed in adversity.'

As a final note to SOE's administrative set-up, it should be mentioned that on 5 October, 1943, SOE was brought under the control of the Allied Commander-in-Chief, Europe – though in fact remaining directly responsible to Churchill – and that in July 1944, after the Normandy landings, SOE was transformed into 'Special Force Headquarters' under combined Anglo-American and French command; all the F Section agents run by Buckmaster then came under control of the French General Koenig.

In the first few months following SOE's creation in July 1940, there were just three operations and all of them ended in failure, as M. R. D. Foot remarks. On 1 August, a boat taking three French SOE agents (Victor Bernard, Clech and Tilly) from England to Britanny ran into a German convoy and was forced to turn back under fire. On 11 October, a further two Frenchmen working for SOE were taken across by motorboat, but again failed to land ('reason for failure as obscure as identity of agents', notes Foot). And on 14 November, a French agent due to be parachuted into France refused at the last minute to go (Foot points out, objective as ever, that this was the only incident of its kind in four years of operations).[1]

1. M. R. D. Foot, *SOE in France* (HMSO, London 1966).

The first active operation was in March 1941. Jointly arranged by the Free French and SOE, 'Operation Savannah', as it was codenamed, was launched in the Vannes area, in the south of Morbihan province, and its aims were high.

The Vannes-Meucon aerodrome was a base for certain elite squadrons of the Luftwaffe, which dropped flares to mark out British targets for bombing raids by heavier aircraft and less well-trained crews. They were guides, in fact, for the waves of German bombers looking for targets. The idea behind Savannah was to ambush two buses that took aircrews from their quarters to the airfield every night, a journey of several kilometres undertaken without special security measures. Any disruption to this elite company was obviously desirable.

As yet SOE had no one ready, so they asked the Free French for a team. General de Gaulle agreed and a commando unit of French volunteers was formed under Captain Bergé, including Sub-Lieutenants Petit-Laurent, Forman, Le Tac and Renault.

But there were problems. De Gaulle refused to let the team use the Free French fishing boat *La Brise* for their return journey because previous authorization had not been requested. For his part, the Chief of Air Staff took a poor view of the RAF being asked to transport saboteurs in civilian clothes, though in the end he gave in. Finally the Admirality agreed to provide a submarine to bring the men back.

But these obstacles had caused such a delay that when the operation finally took place, on 15 March, the Germans had tightened their security arrangements and started transporting their crews in groups of two or three in light vehicles. When the Savannah team reached France, therefore, the mission was impossible.

Their return, too, was fraught with difficulties. On the night of 5 April, the submarine HMS *Tigris* was wallowing in very heavy seas off Saint-Gilles-Croix-de-Vie, and only Bergé and Forman could be taken on board.

But the mission had not been a complete failure. Back in London the men were able to supply a fund of useful information, particularly about de Gaulle's popularity in France. In fact, as Foot says, 'SOE formed RF as a second main country section to work into France, specifically in co-operation with the Gaullist headquarters. The rival F Section remained apart; not anti-Gaullist, simply independent.'[1] This was no mean consequence for an operation deemed to have failed.

There were now three SOE sections for France: F Section, which had no contact with the Free French; RF Section, which did work with the Free French; and DF Section, specializing in escape lines. Such a situation, one imagines, did not exactly help the prevailing climate of Anglo-French relations, especially with de Gaulle being so furious with SOE for recruiting Frenchmen.

1. M. R. D. Foot, op. cit.

Operation Fidelity was organized by SOE's DF Section, that is to say the escape line section. On the 25 April, 1941, two agents were landed on the Mediterranean coast in the first successful sea operation: E. V. H. Rizzo (codenamed Aromatic), a civil engineer, and Albert Guérisse, a doctor.

With the help of some Pyrenean smugglers, Rizzo was to set up a formidable escape line, the second largest of all, known as Group Edouard or Group Troy. Guérisse, who was using the name Pat O'Leary, was arrested the day after his arrival and imprisoned in Marseilles. But he soon managed to escape, and later set up the excellent escape line, Group Pat. From April 1941 to March 1943, when he was recaptured and sent to Dachau, he helped more than 600 Allied servicemen return to active service – a magnificent achievement, paid for by one man's sacrifice.

The next operation was codenamed Josephine B. In the spring of 1941, the SOE chiefs were planning an attack on the power station at Pessac, near Bordeaux. This was considered a worthwhile target because it supplied power to the German submarine base at Bordeaux.

On the night of 11 May, 1941, three Free French officers were dropped near Bordeaux; Sub-Lieutenants Forman (who had been involved in Savannah), Varnier and Fraichin. Like Savannah, this was an active operation planned by SOE's RF Section, the one liaising with the Free French. All went well until they found that a high-voltage electric fence had been installed on top of the boundary wall and that the Germans had mounted a heavy patrol to keep watch. The operation was called off.

But the Josephine B team refused to give up. Hiding their explosives in bracken, they made repeated trips to inspect the target. Soon they noticed that the Germans were reducing their patrols and that a single guard was left on night watch. The operation was relaunched for the night of 6 June. At Forman's request, the three-man team was joined by Joël Le Tac, who had also been on the Savannah team. Le Tac scaled the power station's wall, carefully avoiding the high-voltage wire, and managed to open the gate for his companions. The explosives in their magnetic containers were attached to the eight main transformers and linked to incendiary bombs, which would set fire to the oil in the transformers as soon as they exploded. It all took less than half an hour.

The four men then sped off on bicycles, pedalling furiously as the first explosions went off. It had been a good night's work: six of the eight transformers had been totally destroyed. Pessac's power station would be out of action for a year – with major consequences for the German submarine base at Bordeaux. The sabotage team, meanwhile, made an uneventful return to Britain via Spain.

And so, despite the somewhat erratic early stages, a handful of determined men had rapidly turned SOE into an effective weapon. The arrival of an exceptional man as Chief was now going to give it fresh impetus.

# — 2 —

## COLONEL BUCKMASTER

In September 1941, there was a major reshuffle of SOE's senior staff. H. R. Marriott was succeeded by Maurice Buckmaster as head of French Section, and Marriott's deputy, Thomas Cadett, resigned shortly afterwards to join the Political Warfare Executive.

Marriott had officially left for reasons of health. This is confirmed by Buckmaster himself in his book *They Fought Alone*. But the historian M. R. D. Foot reports serious disagreements between Marriott and his immediate superior, Hugh Dalton, at the Ministry of Economic Warfare. Marriott resigned, says Foot, 'in the false belief that he was indispensable; Sporborg[1] had to tell him he was not.'[2] In an official minute, Dalton, a socialist, complained about 'underlings playing reactionary politics'.[3] It is possible that he meant Marriott.

Whatever the truth of the matter, Buckmaster became boss of SOE's French Section in September 1941 and stayed there to the end.[4] Thanks to him, the organization found a new impetus.

Major Maurice J. Buckmaster had been a member of SOE since March 1941, five months in fact, first as Information Officer and later as acting head of the Belgian section. He was already 'one of the crowd' therefore, when he became head.

Passy describes him as 'a tall, thin man, rather round-shouldered, speaking French well'. A former pupil of Eton College and scholar at Magdalen College, Oxford, he had been a brilliant student. Later he went to Paris as a

---

1. H. N. Sporborg, a London solicitor, was in charge of SOE's affairs in Northern and North-Western Europe. In May 1942 he replaced Gladwyn Jebb as principal private secretary at the War Office, with special responsibility for SOE.
2. M. R. D. Foot, op. cit.
3. Quoted in Foot, op. cit.
4. When Buckmaster took command of F Section, his team at Baker Street comprised just eight people. One year later there were twenty-four, almost all of whom had taken part in missions in France.

reporter for the newspaper *Le Matin*, where the leading figure was the well-known journalist Stéphane Lausanne. At the age of thirty he changed course and went into business, becoming a manager with the Ford company in France. He stayed there from 1932 to 1936 when he was promoted to a managerial post in Britain.

In 1938 he joined the reserve forces and went on an SIS course at Minley Manor with the rank of Captain. The following year he landed in France with the British Expeditionary Force, serving in the 50th Division under Major-General Martel. During the German offensive he fought at Ypres (he was mentioned in despatches following the fierce battle there), Béthune and Arras. He was among the last units retreating to Dunkirk, and one of the very last to be shipped out, on 4 June, 1940. He considers himself to have been very fortunate. 'I was lucky,' he told me. 'My commanding officer said I might have had to stay at Dunkirk because my French was so good that if I'd been caught I could have passed myself off as a Frenchman.'[1]

Three months later he went to Dakar with Admiral Cunningham's fleet, aboard HMS *Devonshire*, to support de Gaulle's ill-fated expedition. On his return he was posted to the Intelligence Corps, but later rejoined his original division just as it was leaving for Egypt as part of the Africa Campaign. Buckmaster was not too happy about this – he didn't speak much Italian – and tried to get another posting. Then, he says, 'I was lucky enough to meet a general I knew, who would end up a field marshal [General Templer]. He told me that he thought I might suit an organization which he didn't know much about except that it had something to do with helping the French; knowing that I was a great Francophile and that I'd spent some time in France, he suggested I should join them. That's how I started at SOE, on 17 March, 1941.'[2]

This, then, was the man who in September 1941 became head of SOE's French Section. From now on he would devote himself entirely to this all-important work. As he told me personally: 'The point is that those years, from 1941 to 1945, were enormously interesting and demanding. We worked eighteen hours a day. We slept whenever we could – if we couldn't, we went without sleep altogether. Our life was totally devoted to SOE.'[3]

The secret was so well guarded that even his wife didn't know where his office was. Buckmaster tells an amusing story about this: 'My wife hadn't known where I worked for four years. It was our dog – which I sometimes took to the office when she couldn't look after it – that gave the game away. My wife was taking the dog for a walk one day and it suddenly turned left, towards my office. 'What are you doing?' she said. Then, following the dog, she saw the plaque on the wall and she understood.'[4]

1. Personal interview with author, 9 December, 1981.
2. Ibid.
3. Ibid.
4. Ibid.

When he took over at SOE, Buckmaster found it sadly lacking. As he explains, 'For the first time in modern history. Britain was cut off from the Continent by enemy forces, so that we could not land our men there. As a result we had to find some way of encouraging those who were opposed to the occupation. But it was absolutely essential to avoid any spontaneous rebellion. We had to co-ordinate the efforts of various resistance groups while waiting for the right moment to land. As de Gaulle was in England, all the French, everyone of French origin, rallied to him and not to other organizations. In other words, I could recruit anyone so long as he wasn't French. I couldn't recruit the French when they were automatically joining de Gaulle's forces. So I was particularly anxious to find anyone British or Canadian who could speak French like a native. This wasn't as easy as it sounds; after all, it isn't every Englishman who can speak French fluently and without an accent and pass for a Frenchman in France. At first we looked for people who weren't French nationals, and it was only in Mauritius that I found some suitable people, with British passports and French as their native tongue.[1] . . . I had problems with the Canadians as they had such frightful accents, so we had to invent an imaginary background for them, to account for the way they spoke, which wasn't always so easy. They had to learn the backgrounds that had been invented for them until they actually thought they were these imaginary people and not themselves. As you say in France, they really had to get into the skin of these characters.'

When he took over, Buckmaster had only about a dozen agents at his disposal, including administrative personnel and staff. He took scrupulous care to ensure that they knew what they were doing when they volunteered for this unconventional warfare. As he said himself: 'We were always telling them, "You are volunteers, we aren't ordering you to do this; but we're offering you a chance to do something more interesting for the war effort than simply drive lorries or fly planes. If you want to take the job, that is entirely up to you. You'll be doing this or that . . ." Obviously at that stage we didn't tell them exactly what they'd be doing.'

Later on Buckmaster had less trouble finding English volunteers who spoke good French. From mid-1942 onwards he was allowed to recruit women; altogether he enrolled forty. And in 1942 SOE started to recruit Frenchmen and women in France itself, especially those who had already helped SOE agents on active operations.

SOE's problems were compounded by other affairs relating to the progress of the war. The BCRA, commanded by and comprising only French

1. Churchill, harassed by de Gaulle, had ended up agreeing that Frenchmen and women arriving in Britain should not be asked to join SOE. But some French refugees already in Britain decided to volunteer for SOE straightaway, rather than join Colonel Passy's BCRA (Bureau Central de Renseignements et Action). Buckmaster also recruited Britons who had lived in the French colonies, French-speaking North Africa and the Seychelles. Recruiting among those newly arrived from France remained difficult for the first two years, and was chiefly confined to those of dual Anglo-French nationality.

nationals, always took offence at British agents' activities on French soil. Politics, too, often cast its shadow on SOE's relations with the other organizations. At the very beginning Churchill had categorically stated that 'de Gaulle and his handful of followers could not claim to be an effective alternative French government', and he continued relations with the Vichy government right up until May 1943. Roosevelt, for his part, never acknowledged de Gaulle as the true leader of France.

In his memoirs Churchill wrote: 'De Gaulle felt it to be essential to his position before the French people that he should maintain a proud and haughty demeanour towards "perfidious Albion", although an exile, dependent upon our protection and dwelling in our midst. He had to be rude to the British to prove to French eyes that he was not a British puppet.'[1] As for de Gaulle himself, he fought to prevent his agents falling under the British yoke and to keep the British from controlling certain resistance groups. He even went so far as to accuse SOE of trying to undermine the French resistance. But the situation improved when Churchill appointed Sir Claude Dansey as Deputy Director of SIS French Section, and, in this capacity, chief liaison officer with the BCRA. Moreover, SOE's RF Section helped the BCRA and Gaullist leaders in their efforts to unify resistance forces in metropolitan France.

It was a very different matter with the Americans. Negotiations with Admiral Darlan, at the time of the Allied landings in North Africa, and attempts to replace de Gaulle with Giraud produced a lasting animosity between de Gaulle and the Americans. This all affected SOE's arrangements – for example, with regard to the recruiting of agents, supplying arms, control of radio transmissions, exchange of information, and so on.

In my interview with him Colonel Buckmaster maintained that he personally had got on well with Colonel Passy (Dewavrin) and the BCRA – but this is not borne out by others who were involved. Buckmaster said:

> My relationship with Passy was excellent. We each respected the other's need for secrecy over operations. If a rescue mission had to be mounted, I always told Passy, and he did the same; and we always helped each other whenever we could. On the whole, we tended by mutual consent to keep our operations quite separate, but I was always told if there was going to be a Gaullist operation so that I didn't send my people to the same place too. We did have problems deciding which of us could use the very limited air transport at our disposal, for we never had enough planes. The trouble was that de Gaulle thought – or claimed to think – that our section got priority treatment where air operations were concerned, which wasn't true. I had nothing to do with it; an

1. Churchill, *The Second World War*, Vol. I (Cassell, London 1949).

operation was arranged by the RAF according to how secure it was, what plans had been made and all the other relevant factors. The RAF never even knew whether it was a Gaullist operation or one of mine. SOE and the BCRA worked separately, independent of each other, but from time to time we were able to work together because of good relations at the top. What's more, the Gaullists had a liaison officer at our HQ and I had frequent meetings with him. We were great friends, very close. But he worked for de Gaulle and I worked for Churchill.

For his part Colonel Passy, head of the BCRA, gave due recognition to Buckmaster when he wrote: 'Latterly I was often obliged to argue with the staff of this section [SOE], especially with their chief, for our ideas and our methods were often very different. But although their work was sometimes at variance with the resistance movement's plans, or clashed with French interests, it was certainly no less effective than ours – more effective, in fact.'[1] Such was Passy's compliment to SOE.

Colonel Buckmaster, then, was the man who created and inspired SOE in France, to such an extent that the French usually referred to his groups as 'the Buckmaster networks'. And it was he who enrolled Frenchmen and women, including some very remarkable people like the de Vomécourt brothers.

1. Passy (Colonel A. Dewavrin), *Souvenirs, Volume III: Missions Secrètes* (Plon, Paris 1951).

# — 3 —

## SOE AND THE FRENCH

There is no better illustration of the pioneering role played by some of the French in setting up and running SOE operations than the achievements of a man like Pierre de Vomécourt. And it is worth mentioning that his recruitment to SOE was a direct consequence of General de Gaulle's refusal to let this man, who only wanted to serve his country, carry out his original intention.

Pierre de Vomécourt belonged to a family that had rendered great service to France. His great-grandfather had been tortured and killed by the Prussian invaders in 1870. His father, at the age of fifty-one, had volunteered for army service in 1914 and was killed early on in the First World War. His elder brother Jean was at school in Britain in 1917; lying about his age, he joined the British air force and was shot down in aerial combat (seriously wounded, he was given a war pension by the British government). Too young to fight in the First World War, his younger brother Philippe completed his studies at the Roman Catholic Beaumont College, near Windsor, and served in the British Territorial Army.

In a written statement he sent to the author in January, 1983, Pierre de Vomécourt shows that he was one of the first to tackle the vital questions raised by SOE's creation and operation and remained active until he was captured on 25 April, 1942. His testimony, as one of the SOE's first and most important agents in France, is of outstanding value in helping us to understand exactly how French citizens were turned into SOE agents, how the first groups were set up, what action they took, and the conditions under which they worked.

I was the first SOE group leader to be parachuted into France.[1] Of my immediate circle of colleagues, only one is still alive today

---

1. The first SOE agent to be parachuted into France was radio operator Georges Begué (codenamed Georges Noble), on the night of 5 May, 1941. But Pierre de Vomécourt was the first group leader (*chef de réseau*) to be sent to France, on 11 May.

Lucien Ambrosini – though perhaps I should include Benjamin Cowburn, who arrived in France in September, 1941, on a special operation. But he didn't join our group except when we needed to communicate with London, and we worked quite separately. It was only when we had lost touch with London for several months, and then when we were betrayed, that our association became close.

As for my personal involvement, I had been attached to a British Army regiment as Anglo-French liaison officer up until 17 June, 1940, when I received orders from French High Command to leave. The regiment was being shipped out from Cherbourg, along with the rest of the division to which it belonged, while I was told to join my fellow liaison officers and work out a way of getting to Bordeaux. It was while we were having lunch, deep in discussion, that we heard Marshal Pétain on the wireless, his broken voice telling the country that an armistice had been signed and the fighting was over. Not waiting to finish my lunch, I rushed off to rejoin my unit at the docks, thus leaving France on the last ship out of Cherbourg. I landed in England on 18 June, 1940 – a glorious tranquil summer's morning, in marked contrast to the tumult I had just left.

Some weeks after arriving in England, I was horrified, not to say distraught, to hear that two young Frenchmen had been shot near Nantes, for cutting telephone wires; their death was intended as a warning to the nation. If such courage and patriotic devotion still existed in France, I thought, what else could be done in the way of practical sabotage to hinder the German war effort?

I eventually managed to get in touch with Major de Châteauvieux, head of the Deuxième Bureau [de Gaulle's intelligence unit]. He expressed interest in my ideas for sabotage, which by now I'd had time to refine, and we got on very well. He told me he would call me again when he got back from a short trip, so that we could pursue the subject. But he never returned. (When I reached Paris at the end of May 1941, I saw the dreaded red and black wall posters announcing that one Captain d'Estienne d'Orves of the French navy had been executed with some of his comrades. I knew that this meant Châteauvieux was dead – the gallant, friendly man I had met in London.)

I had also managed to contact someone in British Intelligence who showed even more interest in my ideas; the subject was already under discussion, I was told, but it might be better to develop my ideas in close co-operation with the Free French. They further encouraged me to ask the French authorities, when I went back to them, for a quick decision; otherwise the British would go it alone.

This was in December, 1940; London was being bombed nearly every night and the outcome of the war was still very uncertain. Finally, I met Passy (Dewavrin) and his deputy, Manuel. Passy, who had recently replaced d'Estienne d'Orves, showed a similar interest in my ideas and told me he would discuss them with General de Gaulle. Some days later I was invited to meet Monsieur Gaston Palewski, who asked if I would be prepared to make a parachute drop into the Unoccupied Zone as the General's political representative. I refused, saying that I did not possess the necessary qualities for such a mission. Two months later the British, tired of waiting, had started to set up their own organization, SOE as it would be called, and I received a letter asking me whether I was still of the same mind as at our last meeting. At this stage of the war, therefore, de Gaulle apparently gave no priority to the kind of action envisaged by the British and myself.

SOE parachuted me back to France on the night of 10/11 May, 1941. As far as I know, the first Free French parachute drop did not take place until the full moon of September that year.

There thus arose a regrettable duplication in France between the SOE network and the BCRA 'active' section (purely Gaullist). This duplication sometimes caused problems and feelings of resentment. But in my own experience, it was enough just to tell anyone wanting to fight the Germans that help would be coming from London – without specifying SOE or BCRA. In those terrible days it seemed pointless to quibble over details.

Only those who actually lived in Britain in 1940–41 can understand quite how short the country was of all kinds of armaments. In our over-hasty training course, for instance, they had to be content with showing us how to load and unload the newly introduced Sten gun – for which they still had no ammunition! They did let us have a dreadful old Tommy gun, though, to practise with. For the time being, that was all they could give us, except the plastic explosives which were so easy to handle. With such a widespread shortage of weapons, it would obviously be months before sufficient quantities of arms could be sent to France. As a result we had to improvise, making do with whatever means we could find of slowing down the production of armaments for Germany. It was much as I had always expected.

In May 1941, during the first full-moon period, Georges Begué was parachuted into France, landing near Châteauroux. He was a radio operator, and within two days he had radioed his safe arrival and given the address of a 'letter-box' where he could be contacted,[1] all of which was arranged with the help of Max Hymans[2] and Jean Pierre-Bloch.[3] Then it was my turn. I landed on 11 May, in the same area, while on following nights Roger Cottin landed in Britanny and Noël Burdeyron in Normandy. The following month Antoine Dupuy arrived, heading for his home in Maine-et-Loire. Thus we each had our own specific area.

Apart from Paris and the surrounding area, I had also been given a more general task: to see if there were enough resistance bands in France, and whether they were sufficiently coherent and vigorous, to justify the risk of Britain sending aircraft and precious munitions to revitalize and support their efforts. This seemed to me all the more important in view of what I had discovered for myself about the current state of affairs in England; even in six or nine months' time it would be hard to arrange priority clearance for equipping the French. If I thereby ran any extra risk of detection, or involved myself in unusual or even unacceptable activity by normal standards, that was just my hard luck.

I had decided to return to France under my own name, with papers showing that I had been demobbed in North Africa; my delay in getting back to France could be explained by the fact that I had first wanted to see what was happening there. On the other hand, Cottin and Burdeyron had false identity cards and had each been given the address of a safe-house, as well as a password, so that they could get help once they were settled in. In theory it was a perfectly good idea. In fact, however, in both cases, the owner of the 'safe-house' turned them out and threatened to denounce them to the Germans! With false papers and without local help, it was impossible to obtain a ration card or coupons to buy clothing, shoes and so on. Moreover, they had no contact apart from the safe-house!

They soon spent the money they had been given – ridiculously little, in any case, since life on the blackmarket was very expensive – and finding nothing better to do, first Cottin and then Burdeyron eventually turned up in Paris to join me. Which was how I came to have two such fine associates.

It seems extraordinary that SOE, now hovering on the brink of

1. The chemist's shop owned by a man called Renan, SOE's first letter-box in France.
2. The former socialist politician and long-time friend of Cadett, who had spent many years in France as a journalist (and who would return to France after the war as the BBC's correspondent).
3. Author of this book's Preface, whose story will be told later on.

its debut, had no liaison at all with British Intelligence which had been involved in French affairs for years. It was to prove a costly mistake. SOE knew literally nothing about life in France since the Occupation, not even the cost of living or the restrictions that had been imposed. This nearly led to my being arrested the very morning I arrived. I had, obviously, been parachuted 'blind': in other words, there had been no indication lights for the aircraft, no reception committee for me. As the blackout was in force throughout France, it isn't surprising that I should have been dropped about eight kilometres from the intended spot. But I eventually found a road and signposts showing placenames that I recognized, and at last I reached a little station on the line to Châteauroux. Noticing a few people entering a café opposite the station, I went in too, being absolutely frozen; it was 5.30 in the morning and I had had no sleep. I asked for a cup of coffee laced with cognac. 'It's our day without,' snarled the café owner.[1] Seeing that I didn't understand, he said it again. I didn't want to cause a fuss, so I just mumbled: 'Oh, I see . . .' But I'd been spotted already. As a precaution, I left the train one station before Châteauroux and went the rest of the way on foot. Just as well! I heard later that at Châteauroux station the police had been scrutinizing everyone who arrived by train. The man at the café had telephoned them to say he had heard an aircraft circling that night – and that this clown, who didn't know what 'day without' meant, had just caught the train. That's how much SOE knew about what was happening in France.

I finally reached my brother Philippe's home, Bas-Soleil, at Brignac-la-Plaine, near Limoges. Knowing I could trust him completely, I immediately enlisted my first recruit.

Before moving on, it is worth pointing out that in May, 1941, Britain was virtually in a state of siege, that the USSR was Germany's ally in the partitioning of Poland, and that America's entry into the war was still hypothetical. But even at this dark hour, a handful of determined men and women were joining the resistance.

I put Philippe in touch with Georges Begué so that he could be in direct radio communication with London. This was how the first parachute drop of arms and explosives was arranged that June. It was only a small delivery, just two cases, and it was made near my brother's place. Another, slightly larger drop was made at the same time at Villamblard in the Dordogne; this was arranged by Georges Begué and Pierre-Bloch. All it amounted to,

1.  In France at that time cafés, etc, were only allowed to sell alcohol on alternate days.

in fact, was a small sign of encouragement from London; Britain was still suffering all sorts of shortages, and there were no significant drops until nearly the middle of 1942, after my February trip to London.

I met Max Hymans and Jean Pierre-Bloch a few days after my arrival. Pierre-Bloch was to take on Périgord, while my brother looked after the Limoges region as well as Clermont-Ferrand. I then went to Lyons where Henri Sevenet[1], the son of some family friends, put me in touch with René Piercy[2] and his wife; the three of them formed the core of the Lyons network.

At René Piercy's suggestion I went to Vichy and met someone who worked on the allocation and distribution of paper supplies, paper having been effectively rationed and under strict control. This man was soon supplying, among others, General Cochet in Clermont-Ferrand – and the General was organizing the distribution of anti-Pétain tracts throughout the whole of unoccupied France. Inevitably, he ended up being arrested by the Vichy authorities, for his name was very well known and would have encouraged the faint-hearted; after all, he was one of the most brilliant senior officers in our air force. In the same way, we sometimes managed to help the well-known local newspaper *La Montagne*, which published a clandestine issue from time to time, refuting the lies that appeared in its official editions.

Once my friends and I had set the wheels in motion – and after losing some of our first recruits who were still somewhat undecided, opportunists wanting to see which way the wind blew, as well as Pétainists patiently awaiting word from the Oracle himself – I next made for Paris, crossing the Demarcation Line on foot and pushing my bicycle across the fields. The bicycle, a recent acquisition, would have been difficult to find in the Occupied Zone; there was no better way of getting around Paris than on a bicycle, for the city was virtually empty of traffic except for vehicles belonging to the Germans or to any collaborators who had been given petrol. No better way, either, of spotting possible surveillance. The moment I reached Paris I sent for my brother Jean in Pontarlier, as it was easier for him to get permission to leave the 'red zone' and visit Paris on some pretext or other than for me to visit him. Like Philippe, he didn't even hesitate. He took control of his own region, Franche-Comté,

---

1. Henri Sevenet went on a training course in England in 1943 and later helped to set up the Black Mountain maquis, of which he became the leader. He was killed in the final skirmishes before the Liberation.
2. Piercy was denounced, arrested by Barbie and died in a concentration camp.

which would be important as an escape route to Switzerland, as well as Nancy, where our family had come from.

Jean told me about the Marquis de Moustiers,[1] one of the few politicians who had opposed legislation granting full powers to Marshal Pétain. De Moustiers, an old friend of the family, had homes both in Paris and in Franche-Comté. By virtue of his position he was chairman of the Marle Collieries and director of numerous industrial firms, and he knew scores of engineers and technical experts who would be useful to me. Through him we successfully recruited dozens of specialists, as capable as they were daring, who worked in German-controlled industries as well as in a vitally important organization which co-ordinated and distributed the supply of raw materials to factories all over the Occupied Zone. As their numbers increased, these agents gradually turned the organization into what was probably the most effective hindrance to the flow of goods to Germany – and this lasted throughout the course of the war! It was all very simple. A factory on their black-list would receive the raw materials it had ordered, but only after a tremendous delay, which confused the assembly lines; or else the materials did not meet the required specifications; or sometimes the materials were even supplied in excess, thus depriving a factory elsewhere.

De Moustiers arranged for me to meet Gourdeau, the Sarthe MP, who in turn introduced me to the two Besnier brothers, one a teacher in Vaas and the other in Le Mans. Thanks to them, we were never short of ration cards! They rapidly set up a little group of relatives and friends, including Jules Hérin, a farmer (who ended the war as a major in the Free French army), and someone who worked for the railway board at Le Mans station. The Besniers also arranged for me to meet Captain Floch, who had organized a group of 'smugglers' to help people cross the Demarcation Line. Floch, who had once been a military engineer, knew where the army had left its explosives when it was retreating. He was thus able to help the Besnier group when they blew up a munitions train in the marshalling yard at Le Mans – probably the first such train to be attacked in France (July 1941).

I had high hopes of Floch, an expert technician, and his stock of explosives. Sadly, however, a few days after the train had been blown up, I heard that he had been arrested for his smuggling activities; someone had informed on him, apparently. He was sent to a fortified camp in Poland, and died there. We were left once again without a trace of explosive in the Occupied Zone, for

1. Arrested in 1943, de Moustiers died in a concentration camp along with one of his sons and his son-in-law. Another of his sons, arrested at the same time, was the only one to survive.

Floch hadn't known me well enough to trust me with the secret of where he kept his stock. We did have a small supply in the Unoccupied Zone, thanks to the parachute drops at Philippe's and at Villamblard; but I hadn't had the time to arrange transportation between the two zones. At that time, it was none too easy to cross the Demarcation Line. To go by train you needed a pass, which was closely scrutinized. It was the same if you went by road, when all lorries were searched (unless you did as my brother Philippe did once: he was travelling with a farmer in a lorry-load of beehives, complete with bees, only the bees were less numerous than usual for one corner had been used as a hiding place for explosives. No one felt the urge to search the hives!).

The easiest way to cross the Demarcation Line was to go by night and keep to the fields. But the Germans sent out frequent patrols, often with dogs, so it was wiser to seek help from a local 'smuggler' who knew both the terrain and the Germans' routine. The danger, if one was caught, was not so much the few days or even weeks in prison as the ever-present possibility of making a mistake during questioning, which would be noted and recorded by the police. This was a risk one dared not take. It was months before I found someone to make me an *ausweiss*, or travel permit, for use on trains crossing between the two zones.

It was through Landry, a senior politician, that I came to know Antonini, who was at the time Joint General Secretary of the French railways, and right-hand man of Louis Armand, the chairman, who ran the 'Railway Resistance'. This encounter resulted in a flurry of activity that considerably interrupted rail traffic taking goods to Germany and Italy. Accurate replicas were printed of labels that were stuck on goods-wagons to show their destination. Then, whenever a railway worker belonging to the resistance spotted an 'enemy' wagon in the marshalling yards, he would change the label for one showing a different – though technically feasible – destination, and the wagon would go wandering off, from station to station. One wagon, for example, left Germany with a load of submarine engines destined for repair in Saint-Nazaire, but was finally discovered back in Germany after more than a month's excursion. Philippe made a speciality of this kind of sabotage, working closely with 'Railway Resistance' agents in various parts of France.

It was in July or August, 1941, a few weeks after I had met Antonini, that I suffered one of the greatest disappointments of my life. One day Antonini sent me an urgent message, asking me to call in and see him, whereupon he gave me the timing, route and formation of a train on which Goering was to travel the next day. The train would be led by a special locomotive with a line-clearing attachment, and it would consist of three carriages, so we would have to mine the track itself and control the explosion from a distance, to make sure it occurred just as Goering's carriage went past. But I had neither the explosives nor the detonators for such a job; I didn't even have a radio to tell the RAF about the train. It was heart-breaking!

Working as always with whatever local support we could find, we had recruited a number of engineers and specialist technicians at the major factories where trucks were produced for the Germans. In those days the trucks all went to the Russian front. Our job here was particularly awkward: the trucks had to leave the factory and go a good enough distance without trouble, but then suffer a breakdown, preferably in one of the engine parts that would be hard to repair on the spot.

My brother Jean, meanwhile, was working with his team to damage the canal locks, the canals being used to transport munitions, from Le Creusot for example. At the same time he was making raids on the sort of factory using delicate machine tools or making items that would be damaged by contact with water, such as electrical goods. Once the guard or guards had been silently disposed of, the factory would be deluged with floods of water from its own fire hydrants. At the Peugeot plant in Monbéliard, some of his friends managed to acquire several bicycles for him, bicycles being almost impossible to find and virtually the only form of transport. And of course, we all continued to search out the brave, enterprising sort of people working in the planning departments of major industries. Taking advantage of every little opportunity, they would arrange for the wrong materials to be sent to the assembly floor, which would thus be rendered idle for hours, days or even longer.

This was the sort of activity, not involving weapons or explosives, that we developed with the aid of many imaginative and daring individuals. Slowly but relentlessly, it spread across the country like an oil stain, steadily increasing up to the time of the Liberation. And this was the way so many Frenchmen and women – mostly anonymous – took part in the fight to free their country.

By the end of 1941, apart from Philippe and René Piercy in the Unoccupied Zone, our organization included: Jean, in the Lorraine/Franche-Comté region; Burdeyron, with his four groups in upper and lower Normandy; Cottin and the two northern groups he had found, one of which extended into Belgium; Charles Brune,[1] doing well in the Chartres area; Tony Dupuy, busy in Anjou; Jack Tar (Jacques Legrand)[2] who already had a small network going in Britanny, with Janine Picabia in Paris; Lucien Ambrosini, who was successfully recruiting among Corsican circles and particularly among the police and Sûreté (what a source of information they provided!), as well as carrying out various tricky missions for me; and finally Pierrat, a former journalist, busily preparing newssheets that were published somewhat irregularly.

On a completely different level, two notable individuals had given me a message to deliver to London as soon as I could get back there. Monsieur Gourdeau, a man who had given me some useful contacts in the Sarthe area, asked me to go to Paris one day to meet Monsieur Ribet, a leading barrister who was defending President Daladier in the case at the Riom Law Courts. Monsieur Ribet wanted to know if it would be possible to convey to the BBC the true facts of the case, which had been suppressed in French reports; several people, including Marshal Pétain, had been accused of failing to defend the country with all the means at their disposal (France did have her own armaments, despite later claims to the contrary). But the case was halted under orders from Pétain and it never resumed. Daladier was doing his best to escape, but he needed a plane, a Lysander, to fly him to England. He did not intend to raise any political issues on the BBC; he simply wanted help in leaving France and a chance to tell the BBC what he had not been allowed to tell the world from the witness stand in the Cour de Riom.

On my return from London (March 1942) I was able to assure Doctor Mazé, Secretary General of the Radical Socialist Party, that someone from London would shortly be in touch with Monsieur Genébrier[3] to arrange a plane for Daladier's escape. Unfortunately, as I later discovered, a last-minute hitch prevented the escape. Some have suggested that it was Daladier who made an eleventh-hour decision not to go. This is not so. I hope

1. Charles Brune was appointed Minister of Public Works shortly after the Liberation, and later became Minister of the Interior.
2. *Pierre de Vomécourt writes:* 'Jacques tried to arrange my escape from Fresnes with the help of a French priest, the prison almoner who professed to be one of our supporters. But he betrayed Jacques, just as he had betrayed others. He was shot after the Liberation, but Jacques never returned.'
3. René Genébrier, a local government minister, recently published a book called *La France Entre en Guerre* (Éditions Philippine, 1982), setting out a number of facts that Daladier had wanted to make known. As the leading member of Édouard Daladier's cabinet, Genébrier kept Daladier in touch with the outside world throughout his imprisonment, until the Germans deported him to Germany.

that one day Monsieur Genébrier, who lived through every minute of this episode, will tell us the details.

Monsieur Léon Noël, the French ambassador, who was a supporter of ours and whose son was in my group, asked me one day to go and see Monsieur Michel Clemenceau, son of 'Tiger' Clemenceau. He too wanted a Lysander sent over to facilitate his escape, for he was seventy years old at the time and though very fit – remarkably fit, in fact – some things were getting a bit beyond him. He wanted to speak on the BBC and use his not-inconsiderable reputation to encourage more of the French to join the resistance. In London I had sent his personal message to Churchill, via the usual channels. Towards the end of my stay in London, more than three weeks later, I had a meeting with Mr Eden and asked him what I could tell Monsieur Clemenceau. Eden replied that there were certain problems still to be resolved. But by the time I was captured, on 25 April, I had still had no answer to give Clemenceau. He was arrested shortly afterwards, and imprisoned in Germany until the end of the war. It is interesting to speculate what sort of influence Clemenceau would have had, by comparison with Pétain, if he had been able to make a broadcast.

From June 1941, when I arrived in the Occupied Zone, until September, I had to cross the Demarcation Line every time I wanted to send a radio message to London – too often for my liking! I had to keep London constantly informed, for if I was arrested all sorts of things we were setting up would have fallen through.

Round about 15 September, André Bloch arrived in Paris to act as my radio operator in the Occupied Zone. Unfortunately André Bloch happened to be Jewish and this was all too obvious in his appearance. To send us Bloch was yet another example of London's incredible ignorance of the realities of life in occupied France. Less than a month after he arrived he was denounced as a Jew by one of his neighbours. When the Germans came to his house to arrest him, they howled with delight to find his transmitter. Expecting merely to arrest a Jew, they had found themselves a radio operator!

About a month later, André Bloch was shot, without having talked. He was indeed a courageous man, a loyal comrade with tremendous personality.

I dashed off to Châteauroux so that Georges Begué could warn London of André Bloch's loss. I arrived just as Begué himself was rushing to leave Châteauroux, as his contact at the 'letter-box' had been arrested. Georges was able to transmit one last message to London from the house of some friends near Loches (the home of Henri Sevenet's mother), then left for a safe-house outside Marseilles – where he fell into a trap, almost at the same time as Jean Pierre-Bloch. I heard this from Philippe, who had nearly been caught there too.

During the wait that ensued, we all found ourselves totally out of touch with London. I still think of those four months with feelings of astonishment and sadness that we should have been so completely cut off. No matter how terrible SOE's internal problems – and it seems they were indeed serious – they shouldn't have led to the SOE chiefs forgetting that a handful of agents had been left in enemy territory without any means of communication, without any resources at all. It was quite beyond my comprehension. Yet it could have been so easy, so straightforward to send a courier into the Unoccupied Zone to warn my brother Philippe we were temporarily out of action. At the same time the courier could have brought us funds, for my personal finances were dwindling dangerously with all the expenses involved in my rapidly developing network. But no one ever came.

It worried me, this silence from London, especially as I was under very great pressure from our recruits and even more pressure from the members of already existing groups with whom we had made contact. Quite plainly, they wanted to know when they could expect all sorts of help from London. But I had nothing to offer them save promises. Given the munitions shortage in Britain, we couldn't rely too much on there being any parachute drops in the immediate future; even when communications with London improved there would be delays finding suitable places to make the drops.

On top of all this I knew that in one sense my mission was accomplished, as I had proved that there was indeed a resistance movement in France and that it did need support. In fact it wasn't just the resistance groups in the Occupied Zone that needed help; I now knew of the existence of underground groups in the Unoccupied Zone as well. I had met Henri Frenay and through him it would be perfectly simple to approach the main groups in Lyons and the surrounding area, like the 'Marie-Madeleine Alliance' and so on, not forgetting René Piercy's group. I was sure I could convince the British, despite their own needs, that sending arms to us in France would be one of the best moves they could make.

Finally, as soon as I had managed to make another trip to London, I would have to return with the necessary funding for a number of plans that I had been turning over in my mind. I had already begun to pave the way for some of these plans. For example, Jack Tar (Jacques Legrand) and his team – mainly composed of women – were already making discreet enquiries to see if there were any doctors who would be prepared to offer secret medical assistance if anyone needed it. It was equally important to have a few nurses we could count on, as well as two or three safe-houses in suitable locations in Paris and the surrounding area; but this would have to wait till we were sure of getting the necessary finance. I had also arranged for observers to check the German routine for searching vehicles that were crossing the Demarcation Line, for I had discovered a way to get blank passes (*ausweiss*) made up for couriers wanting to reach the Unoccupied Zone. It had gradually dawned on me that we would be able to transport people and explosives if only we could buy up some small haulage company which the Germans had approved for deliveries back and forth between the two zones. The idea was put into effect later in the war – but not by me, for obvious reasons.

As time passed and still there was no word from SOE, I began to realize I ought to find a group that was in contact with British Intelligence, so that I could send out an SOS call. Finally, at the end of January 1942, an international lawyer, Michel Brault, told me about an intelligence network called Interallié, to which he belonged and which was in radio communication with the intelligence services in London. One of the founders of this network, a Pole, had been captured along with some of the agents, but the co-founder, a woman by the name of Mathilde Carré (codenamed La Chatte, 'The Cat') had escaped the raid with her transmitter, along with other agents, and was continuing her work.

My first message was for Room 105 at the War Office, telling them I urgently needed to make contact again and asking whether, in view of the dearth of radio operators, I should continue communicating via this new indirect route. The reply was affirmative. For greater security I asked for money to be made available at the Canadian Consulate in Vichy. Their response was that I should get in touch with someone at the US Embassy in Vichy. As a result, I later met Colonel Scow, the military attaché, and he duly gave me a package. By now I was thoroughly reassured about this new means of communication with London. I then asked SOE to come to the Chartres area and pick me up by Lysander, for I had found a perfect landing spot – thanks to Brune – the bearings of which I passed on to them.

But there was some confusion over the rendezvous details, transmitted to me via Mathilde Carré, and I was unable to make a departure. As a result, by the end of January my suspicions had begun to grow. Then came the La Chatte affair.[1] Mathilde Carré admitted to me that she and her transmitter, and a few other Interallié agents, had not in fact escaped the Germans' raid but had agreed to work for them. Thus all the messages from or to London had been passing through German hands. It was obviously a terrible blow. That same evening, quite by chance, I was due to see Cottin and Benny Cowburn, and I told them about the role Mathilde Carré was really playing. . .

[*The three men decided to use La Chatte to disinform the Germans. Pierre de Vomécourt continues:*]

During this uncertain, rather nerve-racking period, we did not remain idle. First I asked my brother Philippe to come and see us and told him of our plans. I arranged a meeting with Mathilde Carré in a café, with Philippe at a nearby table so that he could photograph her in case she changed sides again. Then Philippe went to Vichy, to see Colonel Scow and ask him to warn London that Interallié was working for the Germans.[2] But I knew it would take ages for the message to reach Britain from Vichy via Geneva and Washington; yet we had to move fast, as London was continuing to ask Interallié for intelligence and their requests were revealing British plans to the enemy. This was how the Germans found out that the British were interested in Saint-Nazaire's defences. It cost many men their lives in the commando raid on the port, which harboured an enemy submarine base. I urged Cowburn to make one of his 'routine trips' in the south-west, and he managed to push on right into Spain. He was in Barcelona when he heard that I had finally reached London. I had in fact left towards the middle of February, on a small English sailing boat which I had boarded off the Britanny coast.

Before leaving, I had reorganized a network of people who knew about Mathilde Carré's treachery. With everyone fully aware of the situation, we carefully singled out any of us who might be known to the Germans from the context of messages that had been sent to London, or directly from Mathilde Carré to whom we had entrusted our messages. All of those who were not known to the enemy then became part of what I called the parallel group. Cottin, Burdeyron and I went to enormous lengths to

1. This will be discussed in a later chapter (see p. 164).
2. At the same time Philippe warned the Piercy network in Lyons, telling them to avoid Paris at any cost.

conceal our contacts with them from the Germans, and none of them was arrested because of the treachery against us. Although the Marquis de Moustiers was arrested one year later, that was a result of another operation. Brune, Antonini and many others were never captured. Mathilde Carré and the Germans never had a clue about the existence of the parallel group.

While I was out of France, we had agreed that my signals from London should be passed to Cottin via an Interallié agent, one of those who had undertaken to work for the Germans at the same time as Mathilde Carré. Cottin knew this, of course. Fully aware of the circumstances, he knew he could not believe any of my signals although he would have to pretend that he did. From London we thus managed to divert German attention to targets in which the British had no interest whatsoever, to implicate known collaborators, and much else besides. The Germans were therefore hoist with their own petard. The disinformation trick had worked out really quite well.

On reaching London I met Buckmaster, and then Marriott and Cadett, who told me they had left SOE and that I should report to General Gubbins as well as Buckmaster and their aides. When this round of meetings was over I had several more meetings with Lord Selborne, Minister of Economic Warfare, and Gladwyn Jebb as well, and later with Anthony Eden, the Foreign Secretary. Finally I was summoned to an interview with the Chief of the Imperial General Staff, later Lord Alanbrooke. I impressed on him the vital importance of arming the French resistance as soon as humanly possible, and managed to convince him that the resistance, although only small at the time, really did exist and that it was in Britain's own interests to help us. Perhaps my pleas had some effect, helping to bring about the day when parachute drops were resumed and gradually increased in frequency (July 1942).

I had intended to return to France, secretly of course, and a few days later to take delivery of a transmitter and two or three helpers. The latter would act as couriers for Cottin, Burdeyron, etc, to help them resume communication with all their contacts. Then one fine day all who were known to the Germans would vanish from their homes to reappear in England, leaving the Germans facing a vacuum.

Unfortunately, the transmitter never came, and only one helper. I therefore sent a courier to the new 'letter-box' in the Unoccupied Zone, to get things moving in London; I might have been spotted on the streets and the Germans would have started worrying about the long training course in England which I was supposed to be attending. But my courier was arrested at the Demarcation Line, and the Germans realized I had returned without warning Cottin via the German-controlled transmitter. They immediately arrested Cottin and all the people they knew about. None of them knew where I lived. Unfortunately, a man by the name of Wolters suddenly started bargaining with the Gestapo and told them he was due to meet me the next day at a certain café.

The day, 25 April, 1942, I was sitting in a café opposite the one where we were due to meet, and I saw Wolters arriving. There was no one following him. I waited for a while: still nothing suspicious. So I went across and joined Wolters at his table; he gave not the slightest hint that anything was wrong as I sat down beside him. We had just started talking when three men appeared in front of us, guns in their hands. 'German police. Hands up!' Yet again, my lack of transmitter had cost me dear.

The above testimony supplied to me by Pierre de Vomécourt, virtually uncut, raises several interesting points. To begin with, it demonstrates the rather haphazard nature of the early SOE networks, although it is true that Pierre de Vomécourt himself was able to rely on trustworthy members of his own family right from the start. It reveals the first moves, the problems and the successes (achieved with modest means but plenty of courage); the setbacks and acts of betrayal; the British failure to understand the realities of life in France or the potential of the resistance; the dire lack of transmitters, arms and other equipment – a chronic problem which caused complaints right to the end. This testimony provides an excellent overall picture of what the SOE networks in France were like, and what they did, right up until April, 1942 – in other words, up to the time Pierre de Vomécourt was captured, just before the Germans moved into the Unoccupied Zone on 11 November, 1942.

It also reveals what the great tradition of service to one's country had meant to generations of Frenchmen and women.

An 'active' network like Buckmaster's can only comprise volunteers, men and women of the utmost courage. But luck has its part to play too.

We have seen how Pierre de Vomécourt took his decision without a moment's hesitation, and how his two brothers Philippe and Jean willingly followed him into perilous adventures. But Pierre de Vomécourt had managed to leave France before the Occupation, with the British unit to which he was attached as interpreter. It was a harder job to recruit people actually in France during the Occupation. The following stories will help us understand how such recruits and other supporters were enlisted.

The first story is that of Jean-Bernard Badaire.[1] In 1939 Jean-Bernard Badaire lived in the Dordogne, a boy of only sixteen. He came from a military family which for three generations had supplied the French army with outstanding officers. He aspired to the same career. He dreamed of going to Saint-Cyr military academy. But his dream would not be fulfilled until many years later – after he returned from the concentration camp.

His father was lost in action in 1940. Was he captured? Was he killed? His wife and children knew all the horror and anguish of waiting to hear the worst.[2] The fall of France was bitterly resented by people of such patriotic spirit. They listened anxiously to BBC broadcasts – and thus heard General de Gaulle's appeal on 18 June. Stirred with a young man's passion, Jean-Bernard spread the news of this appeal for optimism and action to everyone he knew. He was a Gaullist from the very start, and a Gaullist he would remain. He decided to make for England, but his mother – who shared his sentiments – asked him not to leave; in his father's absence, she said, he as the eldest son was head of the family.

Jean-Bernard therefore continued his studies, particularly mathematics, ever hopeful of being accepted for Saint-Cyr. But he had made up his mind: he joined the resistance. In May, 1941, with Pierre Accart (who was executed by the Germans in 1944), he formed a group of like-minded students. These young people, refusing to admit defeat, gathered for deep discussions on the situation in France and the rest of the world; they daubed slogans over the walls of houses belonging to pro-Vichy partisans and collaborators; boycotted all lectures and parades that supported the Germans or their French friends; recruited other young people; and generally flung themselves into a most effective civilian resistance movement, distributing pamphlets (which they wrote themselves) and clandestine newspapers as well. Leroy-Ladurie says that the group eventually reached a membership of 200–300. Jean-Bernard also managed to make contact with other resistance groups, equally short of arms, though these units tended to be more interested in politics than action.

But it was action, and action alone, that interested Jean-Bernard and his friends. In 1943 he took part in several sabotage operations in the province of Loir-et-Cher. At the end of 1943, however, something happened that was to have a decisive effect on his life: he met Philippe de Vomécourt, head of SOE's Antoine group (the Ventriloquist network). De Vomécourt had heard about the activities of these young people led by Jean-Bernard, and he

---

1. Jean-Bernard Badaire is president of the Fédération Nationale Libre Résistance (Amicale des Réseaux Buckmaster). He was formerly the orarganization's secretary general for more than thirty years. As second-in-command of the Antoine group, which was led by Philippe de Vomécourt (who died in 1964 at the age of sixty-two), he became de Vomécourt's deputy a second time when war was over, tracing all who had been members of the Buckmaster networks. He is also the group's national treasurer.
2. Badaire's father, it later transpired, had been captured by the Germans and imprisoned in Oflag 10B.

enlisted him officially in SOE and appointed him second-in-command of the Antoine group – a remarkable advance for such a young man. He also gave Jean-Bernard the job of enlarging the group and contacting all the little unarmed groups that were springing up everywhere, especially those who were refusing to work for the German war effort. Jean-Bernard ensured that these groups were kept in touch with de Vomécourt, who was himself in regular contact with London via wireless. They formed reception committees; they arranged for parachute drops of arms and equipment for various official and unofficial groups, including the maquis of Nivernais, the Indre, the Forest of Orléans (under Marc O'Neil) etc. From then on the attacks became more frequent, sabotaging railways and various strategic targets, along with ambushes and general guerrilla warfare.

It was Jean-Bernard who was responsible for this rapid increase in clandestine activities. Up till now he had favoured small units, armed and determined, preferring to create a secure ring of five to eight well equipped, well trained individuals, so that it would be easy to reach them in a hurry if the need for action suddenly arose. But this stage of the resistance was over, owing to the influx of volunteers and young people who were refusing to be conscripted into the German war effort. Jean-Bernard was horrified by the tragic fate of senior pupils at the Henri IV high school, about twenty of whom had formed an underground cell in the Ferme du By, in the Loiret region. He had been in touch with them, but before he could supply them with arms the cell had been discovered; every last one of them was killed by the Germans.

Obviously the maquis was important, rallying the rebels and showing the Allies and rest of the world that at least some French citizens were resisting the Occupation. But these loose bands of people were particularly vulnerable to enemy raids, for they were easily spotted and infiltrated. Significant losses were caused by betrayal, which was much less of a problem in small independent units. In 1944 Jean-Bernard told de Vomécourt of his fears: 'There are just too many of us,' he commented.

His anxiety was not unfounded. He was arrested by the Gestapo on 13 July, 1944, at four in the morning, in Châteauneuf-sur-Loire, probably as the result of someone's betrayal. He was taken to Orléans prison and tortured.

The case of Jean-Bernard Badaire is typical in that it shows how a group of young people, led by one determined boy, could form themselves into a resistance group. It further shows how such a group, uncertain of its future, could be taken in hand and integrated into an organization as important as SOE. From then on, this group's activities became part of the operations launched by Interallié's leaders.

Our second story concerns the socialist MP, Jean Pierre-Bloch. During the First World War he had been captured by the Germans but managed to escape, and was later awarded the Croix de Guerre with two bars. Following the German invasion of 1940 Pierre-Bloch had fled with his wife and children to Villamblard in the Dordogne, where he made a living from *foie gras*. But he visited Léon Blum in prison and was in touch with other members of his party who belonged to the resistance and who, in 1941, were trying to organize themselves, to publish some pamphlets and a clandestine newspaper. He undertook to run the resistance in Limoges and the Dordogne, in partnership with his friend Max Hymans, the former Government minister, MP for Indre, and member of the International League Against Anti-Semitism. On 6 May, 1941, Hymans had been sent a radio operator from London. He had been looking for involvement in some real action for months, without finding the opportunity. Then one day, writes Pierre-Bloch:[1]

> I found a message from Max Hymans waiting for me in Villamblard: 'Come and see me, I've something to tell you.' I dashed off and caught the Périgueux-Paris express. Max was waiting for me on the platform at Châteauroux station. Spotting me from afar he yelled:
> 'Hello there, old man – I want to introduce you to my sister-in-law!' Then, taking my arm, he whispered: 'It's Jacques, one of the top men in London. He arrived last night and he's waiting for us.'
> I was thunderstruck. My mind whirling with thoughts, questions and sheer astonishment, I hardly said a word on the way there. In the main square of Châteauroux, opposite the Faisan hotel, a tall good-looking young man was standing waiting for us, apparently unbothered by the blazing August sun. Max introduced us:
> 'Pierre . . . Jacques . . . You've got a lot to talk about – I'll leave you together.'
> Jacques and I then took a long stroll through the quiet streets of Châteauroux. As we walked he started to explain.
> 'I've come to look at a special matter – landing sites for parachute drops of arms and men. I need you to help me.'
> 'I am at your service,' I told him, 'but there's so many things I want to ask you. Do you know de Gaulle?'
> 'Yes. Are there any suitable sites in your area?'
> 'I'll have to look. What sort of man is he?'
> 'Oh, he's quite remarkable. Do you think you'll be ready for

1. *Le Temps d'y Penser Encore* (Jean-Claude Simoën, Paris 1977). The 'Jacques' who is mentioned here was Jacques Vaillant de Guélis. Son of a French father and English mother, at the age of thirty-four he had been a liaison officer with the British Expeditionary Force. Captured by the Germans, he managed to escape and returned to England where he was immediately sent to SOE by General Brooks, who knew him. He had recently been parachuted into France when he met Pierre-Bloch.

drops in the Dordogne soon? We've got everything ready at our end.'

'I think I know a site for you. What are they saying in London about troops coming over here?'

'We'll send you transmitters, arms, sometimes men . . .'

Finally we both burst out laughing. 'We can't keep. talking about everything all at once!' he said. 'I'll give you all the news you want but then we must study the question of sites. But there's one thing I must say before we go any further. You will be risking death, if not worse – you must know that.'

'Yes, I know,' I told him. 'But I'm prepared.'

'Don't give me your answer straight away. Now I must go. We'll meet again at 11 o'clock, if that's all right with you, at the Place de l'Église. Think about it carefully – you can still say no.'

Whiling away the time before this romantic rendezvous, I dined alone at the Chat qui Fume, deep in my own thoughts. It suddenly struck me that I might be under surveillance. I looked around, but there was nothing suspicious. I ate very fast. I couldn't sit still. I went out and started wandering through the streets.

I was at the rendezvous half an hour early. In the moonlight, this provincial town had taken on a strangely unreal air. I strolled along in the shadows, more excited than if I had been about to meet my lover.

At exactly 11 o'clock, I saw Jacques coming down the road, a cigarette in his mouth (an English cigarette with its characteristic odour) and a book under his arm. I hastened to assure him: 'I've made up my mind. I've already missed once chance and I'm not going to let this one go. I'll do it!'

He shook my hand warmly, then we set off again, ambling slowly along, smoking his delicious cigarettes and enjoying the beautiful night . . . We had soon agreed what was necessary for the parachute drops. It was all arranged. All we had to do now was visit the actual dropping zones.

'Can you come and see them yourself?' I asked.

'Certainly,' he told me. 'I'll be coming to Villamblard exactly a week from today. By the way, you need a codename. What do you suggest?'

'Let's say Gabriel. My wife's name is Gaby.'

'Right. I'll ask for Gabriel then, and say that it's Jacques calling.'

I returned to the Faisan alone, and after a sleepless night caught the train home. There I told my wife all about the new plans. She approved entirely and gave me her whole-hearted support. Our next step was to look for reliable people in the area. After some discussion we settled on Dr Dupuy, Mayor of Villamblard, a man of great spirit and a traditional socialist. He immediately agreed to help. Thanks to him I met a local farmer, Rigoulet, who was willing to work with us and who had been with the resistance for several months already. My wife nicknamed him 'Curly'.

Jean Pierre-Bloch was henceforth a member of SOE. Chance and his own courage had just plunged him into the start of a tremendous adventure.

Our third story involves André Courvoisier. In 1939 Courvoisier was called up as a radio operator, a corporal with the 4th battalion of the 208th Infantry Regiment. Following the hard fighting of the German offensive in May 1940, while his unit was on the retreat Courvoisier was captured. But he managed to escape on 29 December, 1940, just before he and his fellow prisoners were due to be sent to the German POW camp at Pont-Saint-Maxence. He reached Lyons and joined the resistance. Here he gives a brief account of the way he was recruited:[1]

> In Lyons I first found work with a transport company in the Rue de Marseille, then I became a driver-mechanic in the heavy goods vehicle department of the Chemin haulage company in the Rue de Vienne; and I finally ended up as foreman and supervisor of the electric kilns as Établissements Plauchu, 281 Rue de Créqui.
>
> However, wanting to join the Free French army, I was looking for someone in Lyons who could help. But it was a vain search. I didn't know Lyons and had no contacts there, not being a member of any political party or any religious or secular association. It was simply for love of my country that I wanted to offer my services again. So I was delighted to meet Dr Jean Rousset following an introduction from a mutual friend, Madame Granger.
>
> At his house Dr Rousset greeted me very warmly and gave me instructions on how to reach North Africa via an escape line set up by a former diplomat who had retired to the Côte d'Azur. He also suggested several precautions, and advised me to take at least 10,000 francs to pay for my passage on the ship that would take me on as a member of crew. I told him I would even agree to be the humblest deckhand if necessary.
>
> But when Dr Rousset discovered that I had been a radio operator in the army, he strongly advised me not to leave France; it was my duty to stay, he said, and if I really wanted to fight the

1. From a document dated 2 March, 1968.

Germans there was interesting work right here. In true patriotic spirit, I agreed, despite a feeling of repugnance that I would have to become an 'outlaw', not in uniform. He told me I would soon hear from certain people claiming they had come 'from the Doctor' – a phrase that later became the password for people visiting me from SOE.

Indeed, a few days later, in early September, 1942, I had a visit from two British agents at the place where I was staying – 9 Rue de la Méditerranée. One was known as 'Dominique' (Brian Rafferty) and his companion was 'Eugène'. They had been sent to me by Virginia Hall, an American journalist, confusingly known to SOE's Buckmaster networks as 'Marie' and to the Free French resistance as 'Germaine'.

During their first visit, these two British officers assured me that they were working for General de Gaulle's cause, as I had been insistent about this; but I was unaware of all the complications and rivalry between the various intelligence, sabotage and espionage services, not to mention counter-espionage. To us in France, whose only wish was to serve our country, there was but one enemy – and we would oppose him by every possible means.

Dominique asked me to look after a serviceable old Tanker transmitter, which had just been dropped for us, and also to find various places in and around Lyons from which to make transmissions. Even though he did not conceal the fact that it would be extremely dangerous, and that I would have to be armed whenever I moved around with the transmitter and actually made my broadcasts, I agreed to make the first one from my house. He slapped me on the back, remarking that this was the way to make progress.

In fact I had soon started transmitting from the Rue de la Méditerranée or from 279 *bis* Rue de Créqui where I worked. I also had a visit from two other British agents, who stayed at my place while I kept watch for them – they were being pursued. Before they left the following morning, one of them – 'Tommy' – gave me his revolver, an 8mm Saint-Étienne.

I usually met Eugène and Dominique either at my lodgings or at the Place du Pont tram stop. We never met in cafés. I had to arrive before them, so that I could see them coming and set off ahead of them while they followed at a distance. I carried the transmitter set in a toolbag to hide its excessively smart beige leather case. I later got my landlady to make a black cover for it so that it wouldn't be so noticeable.

But I generally moved the set several hours before making a transmission in order to be more relaxed by the time we met. My employer had got me an *ausweiss* for travelling at night, which allowed me to move around using my own identity.

I ought to point out that I never received any money from anyone, either at this stage or later on. Besides, the British agents never had enough money themselves, nor enough food or tobacco coupons, though I often managed to spare them some of mine, allocated to me as a 'conscripted worker', and I also used to buy coupons on the black market, being an employee at Plauchu's. I may add that the two Englishmen never offered to reimburse me for these coupons. I would never have let them, of course, as I was making a pretty good living (about 4,000 francs a month).

I found more places suitable for making transmissions in the Rue Boileau, Rue de Marseille, Avenue Henri-Barbusse and a house in Saint-Romain-au-Mont-d'Or. But in December, 1942, I lost all contact with SOE, nor could I go to Dr Rousset as he had just been arrested the previous month. And, as I had feared, Dominique was captured too, near Dijon. Realizing that things were getting dangerous, I hid the transmitter set at home until contact with SOE was re-established.

Meanwhile, back in August 1942, I had met someone from the Combat movement, a well educated young man of about twenty-three. His name was Pascal Plessis,[1] he said, and he asked me to look after the storage and distribution of various clandestine newspapers, some back-issues of which he showed me. I was only too glad to help, so he arrived one day with bundles of *Combat*, *Franc-Tireur* and later, about January, 1943, *Coq Enchaîné*, which I delivered to addresses in the 7e Arrondissement and surrounding districts.

I never mentioned this sideline to my British friends in case they tried to stop it. If I had had to tell Pascal that I couldn't carry on with this undercover job, without being able to explain why, I would have looked a proper con-man in his eyes. For the same reason I refused to transmit signals from a radio set built by railway workers at Oullins – which was what they asked me to do when they came to me at the Rue de Crécqui one day in September, 1942. I had to turn them down without being able to tell them I was working a British transmitter.

We used to keep the bundles of underground newspapers that Pascal brought in the bicycle shop owned by old Lassère, at 5 Place Gailleton. Then, whenever he wanted, Plessis would come and collect however many copies he needed, leaving the shop by way of Passage Fleurieu while I went via Rue Laurencin or the

1. Pascal Plessis's real name was Paul Girin. He was arrested a few days before the Liberation and executed by the Germans in Loire province.

Quai Gailleton. In those days Plessis had a room at 9 Place Colbert, Croix-Rousse, which was a safe-house for resistance members visiting Lyons. The house had a secret exit leading to Rue Imbert-Colomès, and thence to several alleyways so one could get down to Place Terreaux without attracting too much attention.

Pascal Plessis introduced me to a young man called Raymond. Quite tall and exuding good health, Raymond gave me the nickname 'Nicotine' because I used to smoke so much then. Our first and subsequent meetings were always at a café in the Place de l'Abondance. This dynamic young lad, aged twenty-five or thereabouts, was interested in the military side of things. He was planning a spot of bother at the Bron aerodrome and he wanted me, armed with a gun, to take up a position on the airfield's northern boundary. I promised him that I would cycle out there and take a look. But all too soon we had met for the last time. Around 15 November he began to think he was being followed, and Pascal told me he was worried, advising me to take precautions too.

André Courvoisier's account shows what an important part luck played in the proceedings. Intending to go to North Africa to join the Free French, it was entirely by chance that he met Dr Rousset, working for SOE, and was in turn recruited as a local radio operator for SOE.

It is worth noting that, against all the rules requiring agents to take care, André Courvoisier – then a young man – simply could not resist involving himself in other resistance operations at the same time. Understandable, of course, in a young man thirsting for action, but highly dangerous to the affairs of an SOE network – which surely had priority.

Another first-hand story of how SOE recruited people comes from Jean-Marie Régnier. Called up on 2 September, 1939, Jean-Marie Régnier joined the 81st Battalion, Heavy Artillery Division, and thus experienced the 'phoney war' against the Italians in the Modane Mountains. He was demobbed on 24 July, 1940, at Bourg-en-Bresse, and returned to his home in Lyons.

From 1941, when he met Jean-Pierre Lévy, Régnier became involved in the distribution of clandestine resistance newspapers, a task made easier for him by the fact that he was employed as a commercial traveller. This is his own account:[1]

> Until 1941 my duties as a resistance worker and opponent of the
> Nazis and the Vichy government . . . consisted of distributing the

1. This is taken from his own evidence commissioned for the *Histoire de la Guerre, 1939–1945* (CHR, no date).

clandestine newspapers of that time: *France-Tireur, Coq Enchaîné, Combat, Libération, Petites Ailes* and *Témoignage Chrétien*. It should be said that these papers were issued very irregularly, for obvious reasons.

I was a representative for several companies, including a perfumery business, the Récamia laboratories at 107 Rue Pierre-Corneille. Monsieur Joseph Marchand, the owner of the perfumery, was a great friend of mine. Well aware of his feelings as a true Frenchman, and knowing his political views, I gave him a few of the underground newspapers each time a new batch came in. I ought to mention that Marchand would much have preferred an active role but at that stage he had to be content with information. However, we began to hear rumours that there had been parachute drops in the area.

In May, 1942, Marchand told me that he himself had been asked to distribute a considerable quantity of copies of *Coq Enchaîné*. Delightedly I realized that he had been so eager to help that he had managed to join the Coq Enchaîné movement.

At the beginning of June, 1942, Marchand asked me if I could find a house or some safe place where ten or twelve people could hold a meeting, which would be attended by two officers from the British secret service, and I told him I would start looking straight away. In fact, I already had a place in mind, a family-run guest house in the Rue Puits-Gaillot, on the fourth floor. I had seen the sign, 'Pension Trianon', and I knew the owner, a man of Basque origins by the name of Pierre Lairé. So I went to this guest house to see Lairé and asked if we could use one of his dining rooms one evening for a business meeting. He agreed at once. The meeting was thus arranged for the day Marchand had suggested.

We assembled before the meeting at a high-class bar in Rue-Puits-Gaillot which was often used by the Lyons silk dealers. The meeting was attended by the following: the two SOE officers, Alain and Nicolas; Marchand himself; Louis Pradel, the future mayor of Lyons; Séran, who had been badly wounded in the 1914–18 war and was a former administrator in the Rhône local government; Hotton, who came from Lille and was the Lyons area representative for some clothing firms in the north; a young chemistry student from the Brotteaux district whose name I don't remember (but whom I had the pleasure of meeting again when Châlon-sur-Saône was liberated, by which time he was a second lieutenant in No 1 Army Group); and myself. That makes eight people present. But I fear I have forgotten two people, as I'm sure I remember there being ten of us. The meeting finished just in time for the last tram, for in those days there was no question of driving around in motor cars. People had bicycles if they were lucky, and there weren't many of those on the market. At this meeting, the main subject was what preparations needed to be made for receiving parachute deliveries of arms.

The evening ended for some of us at Louis Pradel's flat in Cours Vitton. It was a very friendly party, I remember, and among those present were Alain and Nicolas (the two SOE officers), the young student, myself – and Séran and Hotton, too, I think. It was only now that I discovered Nicolas was one of the two men who had recently made a parachute jump at Anse. . . . Afterwards, I gladly offered to go with Nicolas and show him the way to the Rue Burdeau.

When we parted company, at the end of the Rue Burdeau near the Rue de l'Annonciade (he obviously didn't want me to know exactly where he was living), he asked me to meet him at the Place des Terreaux around noon the next day.

I met him as arranged and took him to Marchand's home at 2 Quai Perrache, where we had been invited to lunch. During the meal we learned something of what Nicolas's mission entailed: firstly, to take over from Alain who had been ordered back to England as soon as possible; and secondly, to contact various resistance groups so that supply drops could be sent to them and they could be told what preparations were needed. At the same time he was to carry out – or find others to carry out – London's instructions for special missions and sabotage operations of mutual interest to both Britain and France.

Nicolas soon became a regular visitor at Marchand's flat in Quai Perrache, and a good friend of the Marchand family and myself. I remember that the takeover from Alain proved to be something of a problem, Alain being none too keen to leave Lyons and especially his friends in the local resistance. One day, Nicolas asked me to go with him to a meeting he had arranged with Alain in Louis Pradel's office at Établissements Bouvard, in Rue Dugas-Montbel. Louis and I soon left them alone together, for their discussion was highly confidential – as well as somewhat heated, Alain being loth to take the orders Nicolas had to give him. . . .

From then on [continues Jean-Marie Régnier][1] there was a close relationship between Nicolas and the resistance activists; together they organized reception committees for parachute drops, and arranged for arms and other supplies to be distributed to various

1. Evidence supplied 20 March, 1983 (CHR).

underground units, mainly in the Coq Enchaîné movement. Later there were also parachute drops for the Franc-Tireur organization.

But the activities of Nicolas and his friends had been causing quite a stir in the Rhône-Alpes region – and alas, some people were captured, active members of various groups and cells in this large area. We found out, through friends in the Lyonnais police, that the Gestapo were circulating wanted posters with descriptions (fortunately inaccurate) of Nicolas, Marchand and myself, and offering a substantial reward to anyone who could provide information leading to our arrest.

Nicolas immediately radioed this news to London. Their reply came back: cease all activity and await instructions to arrange our departure and escape to London.

The instructions did not take long to reach us. Nicolas and Marchand were to contact someone in Paris by the name of Gilbert (he turned out to be a double agent, for which he was summoned to stand before the Cour de Justice after the war), and Gilbert would arrange for a plane to pick them up somewhere around Angers. As for me, I was to make my way back to London via Spain and Gibraltar. Nicolas wanted to get me away on the plane as well, and asked me to go to Paris with them. But the meeting with Gilbert fell through.

So – back to Lyons. Nicolas arranged for me to meet Lucien, head of the group running the local escape line. It was agreed that on Sunday, 1 August, if my memory serves me right, I should go to the Tête d'Or park and there, at the entrance facing Rue Tête d'Or, I would meet a woman whose description he gave me along with the usual means of identification. We both arrived on time and, trying to act naturally, started strolling along the park's avenues. It was nine or ten in the morning, and the park was very quiet as this woman gave me the final details for my departure. The following day, Monday, I was to go to Perrache station and catch the train for Perpignan, leaving at 0707 hours; I would have to change twice, once at Nîmes and again at Narbonne. She gave me my ticket and told me a seat had been reserved in a second-class compartment. Then she said: 'Take a good look at me. I'll be dressed in the same clothes, waiting for you outside Perpignan station when your train gets in. Then, without saying a word, you will follow me until we meet the head guide who is to take you across the Pyrenees. I warn you, during the journey through Spain to Barcelona, you will be responsible for two young men, both under twenty years old, and another man of just under thirty who is a reserve officer in the air force. All three of them will be on the same train as you when you leave for Perpignan. While the head guide gives you your instructions in the park to which I'll take you, I shall return to the station to fetch these three men, whom you must deliver safely to the British Consulate in Barcelona.'

I won't go into the whole story, the severe test of physical and mental stamina and all the vicissitudes entailed in that journey from Perpignan to Barcelona. But my three companions and I did eventually manage to reach the British Consulate; it was guarded by Spanish police, but we went in separately at five-minute intervals as we'd been told. This was on a Sunday, about 10.30 in the morning – almost a week after our departure from Lyons.

Two consular officials were expecting us, having had word of our escape to Barcelona from the British Embassy in Berne, Switzerland. After a few minutes' wait in a drawing room, I was the first to meet the vice consul, a most charming young man who spent fifteen or twenty minutes questioning me. My alias for the journey had been John Rampard, O'Flaherty's son ('O'Flaherty's son' was my codename in resistance circles).

I spent about a week in Barcelona, staying in a luxury hotel which was very agreeable. But I had to be careful that the Spanish police didn't catch me as I had no identity papers whatsoever.

At the British Embassy in Madrid the welcome was somewhat cooler. I stayed at a hotel which was used by French nationals on the run from France. After the war I learned that the hotel's owner had been a double agent, and that he also worked for the Germans, who were very influential in Spain. But the three or four days that I spent in the Spanish capital, attending to all the necessary formalities for acquiring a passport and visa, were very enjoyable. As far as the Spanish authorities were concerned, I was a Canadian airman shot down in France, and I was aged only nineteen and a half – one had to be under twenty, the age at which conscription began, if one wanted to go to England; such were the necessary conditions for getting a passport (a false one, very well made). This document helped me pass both the police and Customs at Algeciras and I crossed into Gibraltar without trouble.

I met a very courteous welcome at the British Consulate in Gibraltar, of which I still have very happy memories. I was there for two days with Marcel Gamant-Singer, a friend who had followed me from Perpignan. Then, at 9.30 on the evening of 21 August, 1943, we were flown out on a military aircraft heading for Bristol. The plane was on a regular daily service from Cairo to Bristol via Gibraltar; it was used by British Army officers in Egypt and the Middle East who were going home on leave.

We arrived at Bristol at dawn the following morning, 22 August, exactly three weeks after leaving Lyons. After the hot dry climate of Spain it was a delightful change to see the freshness of the green and fertile countryside in this lovely part of the world . . .

Once again it was a chance meeting with one of SOE's agents that had led to a member of the French resistance joining SOE, for Jean-Marie Régnier had been brought to England for special training. SOE was noted for recruiting only people whose backgrounds could be thoroughly checked; and only then were they given training and finally sent back to France to accomplish their all-important work.

Our final example of SOE's recruitment process comes from one of their best agents, Benjamin Cowburn. 'Ben' or 'Benny' to his friends, was then aged about thirty-three, an Englishman who had spent many years in France as an engineer in the oil industry. When war broke out, he had volunteered for the armed services and then joined SOE, whereupon he was sent on a training course one class behind Pierre de Vomécourt and Roger Cottin.

Cowburn's experiences give us a good insight into how a British agent set about organizing a secret network in France. In his book *No Cloak, No Dagger* Cowburn relates what happened after he was parachuted back into France.[1]

I started by trying to get a small group together. Back in London I had not been given any contacts; so, very cautiously, I looked up a few pre-war acquaintances. To avoid the risk of being recognized I used to wait for the man I wanted outside the place where he worked, then went up to him in the street. I made my choice on the basis of integrity and character alone – a man's political opinions were irrelevant to me – and this method never let me down. A former Anglophobe or pacifist, so long as he was honest and brave, could turn out to be an excellent recruit. The usual response when the man saw me was: 'Hey, I thought you'd gone back to England! Where have you been hiding since the Armistice?' When I explained why I had come to see him, he would react at first with astonishment; then he'd want to know all the details, and finally he'd ask what he could do to help. We would then agree to meet at his home, one day when there was no chance of my bumping into any relatives or friends who might be too talkative. In this way I soon found myself being welcomed into several homes.

Talking to these old chums was a great help to me in assessing the current situation in France. In the Occupied Zone, people

1. Published by Jarrolds, London 1960.

seemed to see things quite differently from those living in the rest of France. In the Occupied Zone the Germans were everywhere; collaboration here was therefore regarded as synonymous with treachery. Industry and business was in enemy hands, with managers appointed by the Germans. Many of their workers took advantage of all the red tape to escape their duties as far as possible . . .

Here perhaps I should say a few words about my specific objectives. While living among my French friends and apparently sharing their way of life, I was secretly to prepare the way for sabotage operations, using supplies and weapons that I had to keep in safe hands. These safe hands were to be those of French men and women who, refusing either to collaborate or to sit around miserably, preferred to hit out at the enemy despite all the risks they knew they would run. It was my privilege and honour as a special agent to find and recruit such people.

Our initial task was to look for suitable parts of the countryside where supplies of weapons and explosives could be dropped by parachute, and then arrange hiding places. Later on, when HQ had chosen a target and settled on a particular plan of attack, we would have to make the actual bombs and deliver them to those who would carry out the raids.

It was every agent's job to recruit people for hiding and transporting equipment and for direct action. He also needed to find couriers to carry messages, for it was advisable not to trust the postal service (to contact London, of course, he could use a transmitter). The recruits needed to be willing, intelligent, determined and above all discreet. That last quality was the rarest.

My own method consisted of asking my Parisian friends if they knew anyone reliable who lived in such-and-such a town and who had good contacts thereabouts. If my friends could suggest someone, I got them to put us in touch. I usually found these meetings intensely satisfying. As soon as the new recruit understood who I was, he would look me in the eye, give me a hearty handshake and say, 'You can count on me. What shall I do?' It was the oath of allegiance. I would then take him under my wing and we'd arrange a date for another meeting.

During this second encounter I would ask him to find out if there were any local farmers who might help us during parachute drops. He would mention one or two whom he trusted and we would then set off for the country – usually on bicycles, unless my new friend's job entitled him to travel around by car to visit the local farms. This was the case with certain contractors, for example, as well as timber merchants or business representatives selling agricultural machinery. Gossip spreads fast in the country; privately owned cars were rare and easily spotted, and it was essential that our visits did not provoke any curiosity. On reaching the farm where we hoped to make another recruit, my companion would announce that he had brought a friend; whereupon a bottle and glasses would be produced, in accordance with traditional country notions of hospitality, and we would launch into small talk about the weather with various members of the man's family. As soon as he could, my companion would take our host aside for a short whispered conversation; they would both return and the farmer, looking me straight in the face, would seize my hand and shake it vigorously. Another bottle would then arrive – a special one this time – and we would raise our glasses in a toast: 'Here's to health and victory!'

Then I would ask the farmer if he knew of some suitable spot where parachute drops could be made, telling him our ideal requirements: a clearing about 100 metres long, surrounded by woods to provide cover, as far away as possible from roads and railway lines, and preferably on quite high ground so that the reception committee's lights could not be seen from neighbouring hillsides. Yes, he would show us a suitable spot.

Did he knew where supplies could be concealed? But of course; in his own house, that would be best. He had the perfect hiding place already.

Could he find reliable men to help him on the reception committee and to handle the supplies that were dropped – men who could hold their tongues? Certainly; his eldest son, his cousin and two boyhood friends would be glad to help, he could answer for them.

We would then go off to look at the place he was suggesting. If the first site was not entirely satisfactory the farmer would take us a little further on to see another site, which this time suited our needs perfectly. Once that was settled we could return to the farm. Our host would assure us that we could speak freely in front of his own family, for they knew how to keep a secret, but if Madame X his sister-in-law arrived, we would have to change the subject fast as she was as gossipy as a magpie!

I sometimes asked the man if any of his family or friends could supply precise information on a particular target, which I would describe to him; and he would promise to sound out some engineer or employee with access to the place. Then I would stay the night and, if this hadn't happened already, be presented to his family. Only his wife would be let in on the secret; the children would not be told.

It was invariably a very emotional occasion for me when I met such a hospitable family. After all, I was a spy, a secret agent, a vagabond, a soldier but not in uniform, engaged in clandestine warfare and hence fair game for the hunters; I was also an officer in the British Army, facing the same dangers as so many others of my countrymen. But I didn't have any family in France and from a personal point of view I was risking only my own skin; if I were pursued I could hope to escape. It was very different for my French hosts. They were bound by no oath of military allegiance, yet they were running at least as many risks. If things went wrong, not only the man but his wife and children too would be exposed. If the Gestapo got involved, his home and family would be totally defenceless.

Everyone knew that the punishment for helping a British agent was death, not to mention the previous stages of interrogation and torture. And yet I rarely saw fear in a young mother's eyes. . . .

The next day, my host would call on several people who he thought might help, then report back to me. Some of them would have refused, others would have agreed. I would then appoint him my lieutenant in the area and give him a short lecture on how to build up a group, stage by stage – a group that would be ready for action at the critical moment. And I would stress the importance of secrecy, our sole means of defence.

Such were the first steps. They were not always successful, of course; but considering that throughout our recruiting campaign we approached only those who were vouched for by someone else, we had very few disappointments.

This, more or less, was how SOE's agents began to organize a network of little groups across the country. In time these groups were to grow in size and effectiveness. Sometimes they merged. We also happened to come across some 'ready-made' groups. Some of the French had already banded together, but without any precise objectives, just hoping that they would one day meet someone in touch with London who could give them instructions and weapons. One of our recruits was in the process of sounding out a friend when he met the following response: 'This is exactly what we've been waiting for! I'm already a member of a resistance group. It really only exists on paper at the moment, but our chief has always told us we would link up one day and then be able to see some real action.' This happened as the result of a meeting in a café, during which a basis for further action was decided upon. Some of these 'prefabricated' groups had already performed acts of sabotage, some more successful than others. From time to time we came into contact with a Communist group. (Generally speaking, the Communists wanted nothing to do with us, though they were willing to accept our explosives and weapons.) Agents were advised to take extra care whenever they approached an existing group, as it was often difficult to check the group's origins or discover whether it had already become known to the Germans. (I refer to the period between 1941 and early 1942.) A group formed at this early stage had to be built up in such a way that it could continue for years without being 'blown'. It therefore had to work on a restrained scale, and to remain restrained so that the chief could personally supervise overall security; and, as far as possible, the group had to be composed of only the most reliable people. The incorrigibly talkative were a constant danger.

These five very vivid accounts provide us with a better explanation that any systematic analysis of how SOE recruited new members in France, whether it was through the actions of French political personalities such as Jean Pierre-Bloch; or through a former army radio operator like André Courvoisier; or through a chance encounter between a British agent and a French patriot like Jean-Marie Régnier; or even through the 'snowball' process revealed by Ben Cowburn.

Before a new recruit could be given the necessary instruction to turn him into a trained saboteur or group leader, it was important to check that he was not an enemy spy. Hence the special precautions which the British took, here described by Jean-Marie Régnier:

> When I arrived in London I got the greatest shock of my life: a police van was waiting for us on the platform itself. I had had to make the journey from Lyons to London to learn, for the first time in my life, what it was like to travel in a black maria.
>
> During that journey from the station to the Patriotic School, looking out of the van's barred windows I was very struck by the number of shattered buildings, completely destroyed by German air raids. We drove through London for quite some distance before reaching our destination.
>
> The Patriotic School was a vast austere building of two storeys, located more or less in the centre of a large park full of trees and lawns, near London's Wandsworth Common. I later discovered that this great house had been built as an orphanage for the daughters of naval officers and that before the war it had been called the Royal Patriotic School. In 1940 or '41, the military authorities had requisitioned it for the duration of the war.
>
> After the reception formalities we were taken to the canteen for

a late breakfast – it was about ten or ten thirty in the morning. This was a typically English affair: porridge (stewed oats), fried potatoes and tea with milk. Then we were installed in a very military-looking dormitory with bunk beds.

As I wandered around the corridors, sitting rooms and grounds, I realized that this was a holding camp for men of various nationalities, though by far the majority were French.

Early that afternoon I was taken to an office where a British officer was waiting. He greeted me very politely and introduced a lady who was, he said, an official secretary. Then the interrogation began, a session that would last until tea-time, about four thirty.

In the course of that first session I had to give precise details of my background, my parents and family, and as far as possible my two brothers' life histories too. I was asked where I had lived from birth to the age of five, then between the ages of five and ten, and again between ten and fifteen; to give the names and descriptions of people I'd known in childhood and adolescence, schoolmasters and teachers, and – where my memory allowed – distinguishing features of those people. The secretary took it all down in shorthand.

The evening meal in the canteen gave me a chance to talk to some of the other French people, who had come from all over France and reached England by various different means. Some had been at the Patriotic School for several days, others for several weeks, and one – a taxi driver from Paris – had been there for three months; he must have been bluffing his way through interrogation and, not having told the truth, had been caught out in subsequent sessions. He was furious . . .

After an uneventful night in the dormitory we got up and had breakfast.

Between eight thirty and nine o'clock I was taken back to the same office as the previous afternoon; but the officer had changed and so had the secretary. Yet again, at the age of thirty-two, I found myself having to explain every tiny detail of my life up to the moment I arrived at the Patriotic School.

The British secret service archives must still be stuffed with paperwork relating to all the Frenchmen who were subjected to these interrogations. Perhaps that was what they intended.

The following morning I had to start all over again, giving a detailed history of my life up to the stage of fifteen. This was the third interrogator I had seen, though the secretary was the same one who'd been at the first session. There was yet another session that afternoon, and like the day before this lasted till tea-time, four thirty to five o'clock. Again going into great detail I had to describe my life from the age of fifteen to the moment of my arrival at the Patriotic School. This last session was conducted by a fourth interrogator, but they were always the same two secretaries.

My stay in this strange camp was prolonged by forty-eight hours when I suffered a bad attack of angina. The sanitorium was in a block of barracks that had been built at one side of the vast park. I went there twice a day for treatment, morning and evening. After my fourth visit, by which time I was feeling much better, I wandered around curious to see what went on in this great park surrounded by electrified fencing and military guards. Suddenly I was startled to be confronted by two sentries, both aiming their bayonets at me, who very fiercely made me understand that I was out of bounds and must now be marched off to the guardpost. Here I found myself in the presence of a very calm and dignified officer, who ordered an unarmed solider to accompany me back to authorized parts. That was how I realized I was in fact a prisoner – as was everyone else at the Patriotic School.

The following afternoon I was taken to a different room and introduced to a British Army colonel.

With me in a comfortable armchair and the colonel seated behind a beautiful desk, the conversation opened with an exchange of views on the progress of the war, the state of the resistance in France and what potential I thought it had for the future.

Then it was time for business. He told me that I had been 'passed through Customs' and was now free to do as I pleased on British soil; if I wished, I could pursue my studies or seek a job in commerce or industry, or even live off my income if I had any in England.

My reaction was to tell him in no uncertain terms that I had come to England to achieve my one ambition: to serve in General de Gaulle's army, if possible with the paratroops. In response he told me that I had been asked for by Colonel Buckmaster's unit.

I told him I knew nothing about Colonel Buckmaster's unit (the British officers I had met in France and worked with on resistance operations had never mentioned their Chief's name to me – quite rightly, of course) except that I assumed it was British; and being French I couldn't do anything but join de Gaulle's army.

He indicated that he knew about my work in the resistance, and how I managed to travel around in the German-occupied zone, and hinted that I could play a more useful role for the Allied cause if I were to join the special services. When I repeated my wish to enter the French army, he asked if I knew about the BCRA. I said no. He then explained that the British Prime Minister, Winston Churchill, had 'allowed' (the word annoyed me, and I let him see it) de Gaulle to set up and run an organization rather like Buckmaster's SOE, and that I could, in the interests of our common cause, ask to join the BCRA. We finally agreed that at tea-time the next day I should return to the office and meet the BCRA's recruiting officer, and he would make the arrangements for this meeting.

The following afternoon I was duly taken to the office where a major in French army uniform was awaiting me. He greeted me very cordially and introduced himself as Major Carpentier, recruiting officer for the BCRA. He was very friendly and started talking about the Lyons area, where he knew a bit about the various clandestine groups and some of the group leaders and members. He was interested in the general discipline and morale of this Lyons network.

In those days, political opinions were seldom expressed. Our main aims were to kick the Nazis out of France, destroy the Vichy régime, and put a new Republic in its place. But the major suddenly interrupted the conversation.

'You do know, don't you, how lucky you are to have been asked for by the British? Let me tell you why. We have managed to form the BCRA but our means are limited. The British occasionally let one of our secret service officers join their training courses for a week or so. When we think our people have been sufficiently well trained for special duties, the British arrange for them to be parachuted back into France – or whatever we consider best. So our men are sent to places that we suggest, to carry out missions that we have planned, with the promise of arms being parachuted to them later. Unfortunately, these parachute drops often fail to materialize. The British tend to put more trust in the people they have trained themselves. I would therefore advise you to accept their invitation, and join Colonel Buckmaster's SOE French Section.'

I must admit that this advice went against all my own instincts and intentions, and I immediately told him so, though I could hardly express open disapproval of an order that had been so elegantly presented.

'Listen,' he went on, 'it isn't all that easy to join SOE. You'll undergo a pretty unpleasant week at the training school, or "madhouse" as they call it. By way of compensation you'll find yourself living in a beautiful mansion set in lovely grounds.

'I am asking you to do your best in the various courses and tests, though you may find it very hard at times. The staff officers are trained psychologists; they won't tell you if you have passed the observation or organization tests, whether intellectual or physical. If you fail, you'll have to return to regular army service, or join de Gaulle's army, and you will be discreetly followed by British officers who may or may not let us know what they think of your abilities to fight the Germans.

'But if you succeed, as I hope you will, you won't know until you find yourself among a group of twelve or so trainee officers, and about to leave for an intensive but very interesting course at a special school somewhere in the north, probably in Scotland. Once again, I ask you to do your very best in all these tests. After the parachute training – only five jumps in one week, while you have a nice easy time somewhere near Manchester – it is possible, if you've done well enough, that you'll be selected for the group organizer school near London.

'Then, following two months on another interesting course, you will be parachuted back into France with a radio operator on a very imporant mission. Arms and other equipment will be dropped later if you need them. And remember, the weapons that you will have used to help the resistance liberate our country will be recovered later by the French army, which will be in dire need of them to re-arm a brand new army . . .'

When the BCRA major had gone, I returned to the office to see the English colonel. He congratulated me on having promised the BCRA officer that I would join Colonel Buckmaster.

Jean-Marie Régnier's story makes several interesting points. It gives us a good idea of the rivalry and the co-operation between SOE and BCRA; it also reveals the seriousness with which the British undertook the job of first selecting and then training their agents.

Most of the recruits were amateurs; if they hoped to accomplish their missions – and survive – they had to be turned into experts in clandestine warfare. They had to learn how to set up a command post, enlist their own recruits and organize other support, particularly for liaison; how to organize reception committees for agents and all kinds of equipment; how to plan and carry out various forms of sabotage, and consequently how to handle arms and explosives with all the familiarity of an expert. Many of them also had to know how to use a transmitter-receiver set, a veritable umbilical cord to Buckmaster's HQ, which might just prove a life-saver in an emergency.

As the war went on, these special training schools became more numerous.[1] The school for Buckmaster agents was at Wanborough Manor, near Guildford in Surrey. Built in 1527, the manor had belonged to the Earls of Onslow since the seventeenth century. The school was run by Roger de Wesselow, an officer in the Coldstream Guards. Like all the SOE training schools it was strictly guarded by military police (see the incident mentioned above by Jean-Marie Régnier, p.51) and was serviced by 'Fanys' - women, generally from an upper-class background, who acted as military auxiliaries. The Fanys, who were not allowed to leave the ground or even communicate with their families for months on end, provided all sorts of services, from doing the recruits' laundry to secretarial and typing duties, or working as accounts clerks, radio operators, etc.

During the first stage, the 'pupils' were generally followed very closely and their behaviour and reactions carefully studied. For example, they were offered drinks to see what effect alcohol had on them. In his interview with me Colonel Buckmaster said they were sometimes woken up suddenly in the middle of the night, to discover whether they cried out in French or in English; and if they used English it was considered a grave failing, a sign that they needed to undergo further training. Moreover, the only language permitted at the school was French.

For those who had lasted out this far, the second stage concentrated on a stringent course of training in physical fitness. As Colonel Buckmaster told me himself, 'Those who managed to pass what was called the "trial" were next sent to Scotland, for hard physical training – such as crossing a hillside without being seen, making imaginary attacks on a house without raising the alarm, living off the land by catching salmon and so on. They had to be totally self-reliant. At the end of it all they had to submit a report, and we examined these reports very closely. One of the men said one day: "When I get back to France I'll be a tax inspector – so why must I crawl around Scotland like this?" "You just wait," I told him, "you'll find out soon enough when you get there." And in fact he ended up having to flee to Spain; he had to cross the Pyrenees in the middle of winter. As he admitted later, "I was very glad to have gone through that training."'

At the end of the second stage, the recruits still had one further hurdle to face: a special period of training that was meant to 'make Frenchmen of them'. Here Buckmaster was to profit from the services of an exceptional young woman, as Cookridge reports:[2]

> The complex task of devising and supervising the transformation
> of John Smith into Jacques Dupont was meticulously and

1. Altogether, SOE's special schools turned out some 7,500 men and women for work in Western Europe and 4,000 for Central and Southern Europe. But according to Cookridge (op.cit.), 'The hard core of officers sent to Europe during the first three years of SOE operations (until the spring of 1944) did not exceed about 2,000.'
2. Cookridge, op.cit.

brilliantly executed by Vera Atkins, a WAAF Squadron Officer who had joined the French Section soon after Buckmaster assumed command. She was Buckmaster's Intelligence Officer, but this designation covered a multitude of duties. This young and highly intelligent women has been described by some as 'cool, extremely competent and analytical', by others as 'the real brain of the French Section'. To this it may be added that she was also the heart of the section. She gave nearly five years of her life to the French Section and one wonders what the efficiency of the Baker Street Office and the fate of many agents would have been without her.

She collected every scrap of current information about life in wartime France. In her orderly mind she stored an encyclopaedic knowledge of all regulations concerning the day-to-day life of the agent – about work, travel, curfew, food rationing, police registration and so on. The forged documents were supplied by the SOE secret laboratories, but Vera always managed to add a few most useful credentials; a few 'family' photographs, some old visiting cards, a letter from a friend or an old flame – things a man might carry in his wallet and which would enhance his imaginary identity when his pockets were searched. She produced these things from her own private and mysterious sources, and she also produced French tailors' tabs, Metro tickets, French matches and other 'theatrical business'.

But, above all, she was a perpetual source of information which she presented 'with a smile as remote as it was seraphic'. Vera Atkins participated in the agents' briefing sessions on the last day or two before dispatch. Every agent had his or her Conducting Officer who kept a fatherly eye on the candidate during the training, regularly visiting him or her at the Special Training Schools, and usually spent the last few days together with the fledging agent at the 'finishing school' and at the Holding Camp. In addition to her many other duties, Vera Atkins also often fulfilled such assignments.

How did the would-be agent behave at the dinner table? Did he, as a Frenchman would, wipe the gravy with a piece of bread and eat it with gusto, or did he, in proper English manner, leave a few chips or *petits pois* on the plate, and carefully align his knife and fork at 'half-past six'? Of course most of the students had some experience of French manners, but refreshers had to be offered in such realms as French cuisine and wines. On occasions the Conducting Officers would take their wards to Soho restaurants; a favourite was the Coquille, where even the wartime French cuisine reminded them how to behave like Frenchmen.

Final briefing sessions were held at Buckmaster's private briefing apartment at Orchard Court in Portman Square. This was not his home but a small flat provided for by SOE for this special purpose.

The few modestly but tastefully furnished rooms had a convivial atmosphere which assuaged agents on the eve of perilous journeys. Here Colonel Buckmaster, Jacques de Guélis, Vera Atkins, Bourne-Paterson and 'Gerry' Morel talked with the agents, not as their superior officers, but as friends proffering last bits of advice.

This apartment at Orchard Court contained two special features: a butler named Park and a black-tiled bathroom, complete with an onyx bidet, features memorable to all visiting SOE officers.

Park had been a bank messenger in the Paris branch of the Westminster Bank, and he had a prodigious memory. He knew every agent by his pseudonym and made each one personally welcome on arrival. His cheerful countenance was beloved by all. His tact averted many awkward meetings between men who were not supposed to see each other. Buckmaster discouraged agents from meeting each other in the field and the best way to do that was to avoid possible encounters in England. Park would spirit people from room to room.

'Of course people did meet each other,' Buckmaster recalls, 'and we were not silly about forbidding it – our agents were far too intelligent to need petty regulations of that kind – but there was one thing which was absolutely going against orders, that was to tell anyone where one was going. There was a particular danger of this when two agents met in the apartment and knew that they were due to be sent off at the same time.'

The Conducting Officer, who had been largely responsible for the supervision of the training of the agent and had to compile the final report on his accomplishments, escorted him to the airfield and stayed with him until the very moment he boarded the aircraft.

He made the final check of the agent's equipment, even went through his pockets for British cigarettes, money, or a forgotten bus ticket. And his final duty was to give the agent the tiny poison pill, his own personal emotion concealed by a casual remark: 'Well, old boy, I'm sure you won't ever have to use it.' Colonel Buckmaster, whenever his time allowed, used to accompany his agents to the airfield; he often gave them a personal memento, a pair of cuff-links or a cigarette case, bought from his own pocket. . . .

But the meticulous care with which the Section officers had arranged his training, supervised his progress, briefed him for his mission, was of course not at an end. Indeed, once the radio link had been established, a flow of instructions and advice emanated from Baker Street to the man or woman in the field. . . .

Vera Atkins played a prominent part in maintaining contact with agents in the field. At the height of the activity, signals from the radio posts in France were handled by the W/T station near Sevenoaks by a large team of Fanys. The coded messages were usually brought by dispatch riders to Baker Street. They were decoded, and Georges Begué and Vera Atkins checked all incoming and outgoing messages. Often signals arrived badly scrambled and even hopelessly undecipherable. But even if the decoding officers threw up their hands in despair, Vera Atkins, applying her razor-sharp intellect and knowledge of agents and operators and their personal foibles, would try again and usually succeed in making sense of a seemingly incomprehensible or fragmentary signal. . . .

Vera Atkins introduced a special sideline to the 'official' system of personal messages. From time to time she used this means to inform an agent about his home life and family. Such messages had to be prearranged either before the agent left or by preceding Morse signals. Some of the agents' wives were expecting a birth when their husbands had to leave; most agents had brothers or close relatives serving in the armed forces. When Vera Atkins received news from an agent's family (the relatives were, of course, never told of the agent's whereabouts), she would flash it over by means of a personal message. Thus Vera preserved the sanity of many SOE men, often cut off from home and families for a year or more. Not for nothing did men in the field call Vera Atkins their 'guardian angel'.

It took four or five months for a recruit to comple the transformation from honest citizen to redoubtable warrior – even longer for a specialist such as a radio operator. Under the auspices of this most extraordinary organization, SOE, and commanded by a most exceptional man, Colonel Buckmaster, the agents who had attended the special training schools were now despatched to France, to sabotage the enemy war machine and to help French citizens in their ultimate fight for liberation. It was an ambitious mission for this handful of volunteers.

To recap: on the night of 5 May, 1941, the first agent of SOE's F Section,

Captain Georges Begué, alias George Noble, was parachuted into the Unoccupied Zone with a radio set.[1] F Section was now in action.

In Part II we will see how SOE groups were established in one particular region, the Rhône. Part III will deal in greater detail with SOE's affairs in France as a whole.

---

1. Georges Begué was SOE's first radio operator in France. From then on, thanks to his achievements, all radio operators – or 'pianists' as they were known – took the name George as their codename, each followed by a different number. Begué naturally was 'George One'. It was he who later devised messages for the BBC to broadcast each evening, intended to reach SOE agents and members of the resistance directly, and thus reduce the number of clandestine radio transmissions.

# ── PART II ──
## S O E   I N   A C T I O N

Georges Begué's arrival in France marked the real start of SOE's operations there. Four days later he was followed by Pierre de Vomécourt (codenamed Lucas), the first SOE group leader in France, who landed near Châteauroux and soon enlisted his brothers Philippe and Jean. The three de Vomécourt brothers, Begué and Roger Cottin – codenamed Albert, but often called 'Roger les cheveux blancs', Cottin made a parachute landing on 13 May, 1941[1] – thus formed the first group of SOE agents in France. The five of them then hastened to set up other groups: Begué in Limoges (the Ventriloquist group), Philippe in Châteauroux (Antoine, later Saint-Paul), Pierre in Paris (Gardener) and Jean in Pontarlier (Autogiro).

They kept in touch with London via George One in Châteauroux, who transmitted their signals on his bulky suitcase-type radio set, either from the home of Renan the chemist or from that of Fleuret, a garage owner (codename Espadon).[2]

The first arms drop was made near Philippe de Vomécourt's home at the time of the June full moon. This was another significant landmark: for the first time since the fall of France, Frenchmen were being sent arms to fight the Nazis!

From now on the SOE networks would rapidly spread across the whole of France. And as we have seen, it wasn't long before Jacques de Guélis – operations organizer for SOE's French Section – had arrived from London to inspect their progress for himself.

To illustrate the way SOE agents laid the foundations in France, and their first sabotage missions and clandestine lives, we may choose Lyons as our example, the 'capital of the Resistance'.

---

1. Born in France of British parents, Cottin was a tall hearty fellow despite his prematurely white hair, and had travelled all over the world as a representative for one of the big Paris perfume houses. After the fall of Dunkirk he had reached Britain on one of the last heroic little ships which evacuated the British Expeditionary Force.
2. Fleuret was later captured and executed.

# — 1 —

## LAYING THE FOUNDATIONS

Pierre de Vomécourt began by setting up a group in the Rhône. He entrusted the running of this group to René Piercy, helped by one of Philippe de Vomécourt's men, Henri Sevenet. This little unit would very rapidly expand – but before we follow its fate, we ought first to examine how such groups were run, how they came into being and what their aims were.

An SOE network generally was built up around three agents, of whom at least one – the leader – and more usually all three had undergone special courses at the British training schools: the leader himself, the radio operator and the arms instructor. Sometimes the leader was a radio operator as well, and the radio operator occasionally doubled as arms instructor. This unit would be joined by other resistance workers recommended by groups already in operation or suggested by reception committees, as was the case with both Courvoisier and Régnier.

Having safely landed in France despite anti-aircraft fire, these two or three agents knew they would be hunted down by hundreds of Abwehr officers, German secret police, Gestapo and French collaborators. In fact, of the first hundred agents sent to France between 1941 and the end of 1942, only about thirty managed to keep working right up to the Liberation.

SOE agents were sent to France by every possible means of transport, although this was always begrudged by the British service chiefs who had little enough equipment and men to meet their own needs.

Flying was the most practical method, but the RAF needed all the pilots it had to keep the Luftwaffe from bombing British towns and cities and, in places like Coventry, totally destroying them. Thanks to their courage, the RAF would eventually win the Battle of Britain.

In most cases SOE's men made parachute drops or were landed by Lysander planes. The Lysander was a small, 870hp single-engine aircraft, and very easy to handle, but it could barely carry three passengers. Pilots were specially trained to land Lysanders by night and on uncertain terrain, often in a field or a forest clearing. Very few were shot down by the Germans. Towards the end of the war, bigger aircraft were used such as the Halifax, Hudson and Lockheed.

The agents were welcomed onto French soil by the so-called reception committee, a group of resistance workers who arranged to hide them with the aid of local country people; they also provided the agents with news of the local political situation and current circumstances and generally familiarized them with the area, thus doing their utmost to support the agents in their work.

If the SOE men were to arrive by sea, they used either fishing boats or naval vessels, fast patrol boats which could land them on the Channel coast. For landings on the Atlantic and Mediterranean coasts they used submarines based at Gibraltar, which would cruise along the coastline at night; the men would then transfer to small inflatable dinghies in order to get ashore, or sometimes they were picked up by French fishing boats at a prearranged rendezvous following a message broadcast by the BBC.

Entering France by land was often much more difficult. An SOE agent coming from Spain not only had to watch out for Germans but for the Spanish Guardia Civil as well; the latter were always on the alert for spies, whom they often caught and jailed at the notorious prison camp of Miranda de Ebro. It was generally better for an agent to entrust himself to smugglers who knew the mountain crossings over the Jura or Pyrenees – even though the smugglers sometimes abandoned them at the top, just where the going was hardest and the Nazi frontier guards most vigilant. Obviously the safest way of crossing the frontier was to use one of the resistance smuggling lines, but there weren't many of these in existence in 1941. It was only later on that SOE managed to organize really reliable line-crossing groups, so that a man could travel all the way from Spain to Belgium, or vice versa, in complete safety. By contrast with the numbers of people who entered France from Spain, there were very many more who travelled in the opposite direction: as Colonel Buckmaster has said, 'That was the usual way out.' Agents and couriers for both SOE and the BCRA, not forgetting RAF aircrew shot down over the Continent, and prisoners of war who had escaped – they all used this route.

So agents continued to land in France, despite the initial shortage of transport. From 1944 the sea crossings and especially the flights became ever more frequent and more acceptable to the Allied High Command. Now the SOE agents were ready to start work.

The first step, even before starting to find new recruits for the group, was to establish a radio link with London. This was of course the radio operator's job, for which he had been specially trained. He would land with a suitcase containing the wireless set, and immediately notify 'home station' at his British HQ of his safe arrival. One such station was in Oxfordshire, another in Bedfordshire; others were set up later when the Normandy landings were being planned. Each operator had his own code and his own wavelength, so he could tap out his

Morse-coded message to England at any time of day or night.

All signals from France were received at the home station, then delivered to Baker Street by special motorcycle teams, always at the ready for a record-breaking dash into London.

SOE's radio operators ran the greatest danger of all, for it was easy to trace a transmitter while it was operating. They had to find a safe hiding place for the precious suitcase with people they completely trusted. Then they had to find as many locations as possible where they could use the set, so that they could switch from one place to another all the time, trying to avoid the Germans and their numerous radio-detector vans. These were sometimes ordinary-looking trucks with the special apparatus hidden under a tarpaulin; but sometimes, as in Lyons, they were specially converted vans that were in effect mobile laboratories. The equipment could listen in to a transmission and work out where it was coming from; then the van would pull up in front of the block of flats or the house where the signal was strongest. Just before raiding the place, the Germans would often cut the electricity supply for a few seconds, to put the suspect out of action. Then, when the signal stopped, the van would enter the area and wait for the electricity to go on again, to check that the signal had resumed in the same place.[1] Many operators and their assistants were caught in this way, in the middle of transmissions, like Peter Le Chêne ('Grégoire') in Lyons.

Although it was not part of SOE's job to collect military intelligence – Colonel Buckmaster makes this very clear – it was nevertheless supplied on more than one occasion in response to requests from Allied Intelligence HQ. Moreover, some SOE agents concentrated on collecting information about French industrial plants, especially factories that were producing all sorts of war materials for the Nazis; later these places would become the target for sabotage or air raids.

We have already seen some of the first operations organzied by SOE agents in France, such as those involving the de Vomécourt brothers. Sabotage could take many different forms and with mixed results, but every contribution helped to bring about the downfall of the Germans' economic and military strength.[2]

It must also be remembered that SOE agents had a duty to arm and train the resistance and maquis; Jean-Bernard Badaire is a case in point, in that he devoted an ever-increasing proportion of his efforts to this task, right up to the Liberation.

SOE had decided to set up a large network based in Lyons, the largest town in the Unoccupied Zone. But this could be awkward if members were not to

---

1. See below pages 86–88 for a fuller description of the radio operator's work and the risks that he ran.
2. The sort of operation undertaken by SOE is described in Part II, chapter 3, and the main operations in Part III, chapter 1.

know each other – isolation being the first rule for preserving security. The answer was to install a 'resident', one agent who was there permanently. This key figure would become the fulcrum of the group; he would find safe accommodation for local agents or those passing through, receive and transmit messages, take delivery of parachute drops of transmitter sets or weapons and hide and distribute them, provide shelter for men on the run, and much else besides. Exposed to constant danger he would need to be cool, level-headed and sufficiently imaginative to disguise his clandestine activity.

Jacques de Guélis went to Lyons in person, despite the risks this entailed for such a senior officer of SOE, to install the first resident – the first woman, in fact, to be entrusted with such a task – the famous Virginia Hall.

Miss Hall was thirty-five years old, an American journalist, the *New York Post*'s official correspondent in unoccupied France. She was an unmistakable figure – something of a disadvantage for a secret agent. As M. R. D. Foot has written, 'She stood out in a crowd, with her flaming red hair, pronounced American accent, artificial leg and fiery temper.' As soon as she arrived in Lyons she had to register at the police station; but she took advantage of this opportunity to win the gendarmes' confidence, which later proved very useful.

Arriving from Madrid in August, 1941, she adopted the codename 'Marie' – or 'Marie de Lyon' as some affectionately called her. To others she was known as 'Germaine'. Having worked for SIS since the outbreak of war, she was already well accustomed to the clandestine life. Possessed of great intelligence and untiring energy, she was not in the least handicapped by her artificial leg, which she jokingly called 'Cuthbert'.

It was Miss Hall who introduced Langelaan to Édouard Herriot, who refused to go to England. She was in regular contact with Philippe de Vomécourt, Benjamin Cowburn (who was parachuted into France that September) and the South of France agents Robert Lyon and Philippe Liewer. For more than a year she met new SOE agents when they arrived, helped them find their feet, and hid them in the Lyons flat that de Guélis found for her. She gave them money, supplied them with transmitters, showed them escape routes and so on. In short, she offered a safe refuge for SOE agents in France and a permanent contact between them and Baker Street.

She knew all the SOE agents in Lyons itself, both those who were based there like Dr Rousset and those who were merely passing through. In January, 1941, she met Peter Churchill,[1] who described the encounter thus:[2]

> All I knew of her was that she was a tall American woman, about thirty-three, who was working as a journalist. At the War Office

---

1. Peter Morland Churchill (despite the name he was no relation to the Prime Minister) was a British officer who had been recruited by SOE. He had two brothers: Walter, an RAF officer who was later killed in action; and Oliver, who worked for SOE's Italian section.
2. Peter Churchill, *Missions Secrètes en France* (Presses de lat Cité, Paris 1967).

they couldn't tell me whether she was dark or fair, but they did say she had an artificial foot, the result of a riding accident. But this was so cleverly disguised and affected her gait so little that it would be no use as a distinguishing feature. The only way to find out would have been to make her walk on tiptoe! I left a note at her home with the address and telephone number of my hotel, saying that I wanted to see her urgently.

I was lying on my bed when the telephone rang. It was 'Mademoiselle Germaine Le Contre'. I was delighted to hear her voice, especially when, after I announced that I had news of her 'sister Suzanne', she invited me to dinner with her. By now I was sure I was talking to the right person, for her accent was certainly not that of a native Frenchwoman. Shortly afterwards, back in the lobby of the Grand Nouvel Hotel, I was shaking hands with Germaine. She promptly took me off through the snow to a little restaurant run by a Greek. The owner gave her a welcoming hug and I had a feeling that all would be well, although it was past nine o'clock by then.

When our drinks had been brought, Germaine said: 'A courier told Charles last week that you were coming, and he warned me to expect you. I'll arrange for you to meet him tomorrow.'

After a splendid meal we left the restaurant about eleven thirty. Germaine showed me the café where Charles would meet me at eleven the next morning; then I escorted her back to her hotel and returned to mine. I slept extremely well, and woke up late.

At the café I settled down at the back with a bowl of soup made from meat substitute. I saw Germaine arrive. She came straight over to my table and we shook hands like old friends. I ordered another bowl of soup and five minutes later Charles joined us. He was a tall, thin young man, quietly dressed. I'd heard a lot of good about him in London. He lived in the Lyons suburbs and went about his work without fuss. Germaine found some polite excuse to leave us alone together.

Charles told me all about his district, the places he had arranged for parachute drops or landing strips, his contacts with railwaymen, seamen, police, magistrates and so on – all of which would be very useful. We spoke freely, only changing the subject when the waiter went past. Charles confirmed what Germaine had told me and promised to get me an authentic-looking ration card.

After lunch we took the tram back to his house. There I left him for a while to go and collect some money – he had asked for only 200,000 francs. Then I asked him a few questions of my own.

'They say I can count on you to get specimens of all the food ration cards currently in use in France, apart from the one you're getting me.'

'Certainly,' he said. 'I'm glad to say my contacts are working very well. When Germaine told me you were here, I arranged to get some false cards prepared. You will also get coupons for tobacco and clothing, valid for 1942.'

'Splendid. Now another thing: can you find us some suitable landing sites to the north of Lyons, near a river if possible so the pilots can find their way there by night?'

'How many sites do you need?'

'About half a dozen.'

'How big?'

'At least 1,600 by 800 metres for bombers. The essential thing is that the ground should be firm and as level as possible – though levelness is less important to the RAF than the lack of ditches or other holes in the ground! Nor should there be any telegraph poles or trees at the ends of the landing strip. It doesn't matter if there are small pools or streams, so long as they aren't in the middle of the strip. For the Lysanders, about 800 metres by 400 would be enough. Naturally they must be easy to find from the air. According to our maps there is plenty of flat ground in the area, but we can't tell if there are any irrigation ditches.'

'The maps are right,' said Charles. 'I've been up the Saône in a barge with some friends, so I've actually seen for myself – masses of flat countryside as far as you can see.'

'Good. That will please the RAF. But you'll have to visit these sites and check whether there are any side roads or tracks. You'll need vehicles to get people there and then get the deliveries away.'

'Who will be in charge of these operations?'

'You will, old chap!'

'Suits me . . .'

Peter Churchill's account gives us just a glimpse of the activities of Virginia Hall and the SOE groups in Lyons and the Rhône-Alpes area. The man he calls 'Charles' was none other than George Dubourdin, or 'Alain' as he was also known, leader of the large SOE circuit called Spruce; later on, this network would be taken over by 'Nicolas' (or 'Boiteux'), alias Robert Burdett.

Thanks to Virginia Hall, Lyons became the centre of SOE activities in southern France. Her tasks were 'quite as dangerous as actual sabotage, and much duller,' writes M. R. D. Foot, 'but without her indispensable work about half of F Section's early operations in France could never have been carried out.'[1]

1. M. R. D. Foot, op.cit.

# — 2 —

## ACTION

Pierre de Vomécourt's personal story is of particular value in showing how one man had managed to set up the first SOE circuits in France. Learning from experience, SOE now began to extend operations throughout France. To understand how these operations were planned, developed and carried out, we need only look at one example: the area around Lyons and the Rhône-Alpes region; and at one specific period, from 1 January to 11 November, 1942. But first a few general comments to help us follow the chronology of events.

Virginia Hall was kept constantly busy, for Lyons by now was a veritable nest of resistance workers. Moreover, it wasn't easy to disguise the work of secret agents in a town where the police were chasing all the underground movements such as Combat, Libération, Franc-Tireur, Le Coq Enchaîné, France-d'Abord, Témoignage Chrétien, L'Insurgé, etc.

On 1 January, 1942, Jean Moulin ('Max') was parachuted into Provence, near Eygalières. As de Gaulle's official emissary he had brought funds and instructions for a very specific mission: to combine the various units and resistance groupings under de Gaulle himself.

Shortly afterwards, Peter Churchill ('Michel') was landed by submarine just west of Cannes, and arranged to meet Virginia Hall (now variously known as 'Marie', 'Brigitte', 'Germaine Le Contre' or just 'Germaine'). He had been sent as a special envoy with a single brief errand – to deliver orders and supplies to certain SOE agents. Miss Hall duly put him in touch with them, notably with Georges Dubourdin ('Charles' or 'Alain'), head of the new Spruce circuit, and his deputy Marcel Fox ('Georges'). On his return to London Churchill met 'Benoit' (Benjamin Cowburn), another special envoy who'd been given a similar errand in Lyons.

Back in France in March, 1942, landing by sea again, Churchill returned to Lyons along with Edward Zeff ('Eugène', 'Mathieu' or 'Georges 53'). Zeff was a radio operator and his presence was urgently required because of the recent expansion of SOE networks in Lyons and the surrounding area. He made his transmissions either from Joseph Marchand's flat at 2 Quai Perrache (Marchand's codename was 'Ange') or from the home of Madame Serre ('Andrée') at 9 Rue Camille in Montchat.

Churchill naturally called on Virginia Hall while he was in Lyons, and also visited another of the group's central figures, Dr Jean Rousset ('Pep') at 7 Place Antonin-Poncet. Rousset's surgery was the ideal meeting place; agents could come and go in perfect safety, pretending to be his patients. Rousset also helped to hide transmitters, documents and visiting agents, whom he supplied with false papers if necessary, all excellent fakes – identity cards, coupons for food and tobacco etc. He was a shrewd recruitment officer for SOE, enlisting further agents and radio operators such as André Courvoisier. He also helped numerous Jews, Freemasons, Communists and wanted resistance workers to escape, thus increasing the dangers of 'blowing' his own cover. To some extent, his was the local safe-house, and his surgery was virtually the command post for the Heckler circuit.

Thanks to Miss Hall's and Dr Rousset's help in providing safe-houses and contacts, Pierre de Vomécourt, Peter Churchill and SOE successfully managed to set up several more groups in 1942, in and around Lyons. They were also helped by oustanding local supporters like Joseph Marchand and his wife; Jean Régnier; Dr Jean Wertheimer; Jean Terrisse, and many more. Altogether they set up five new groups besides the Heckler circuit, which provided all the necessary security and contacts for them, a kind of permanent local framework for SOE headed by Miss Hall and Dr Rousset. Among the new groups were the Spruce circuit, led by Georges Dubourdin ('Alain') and later visited by Benjamin Cowburn ('Benoit') when he was on a local operation; the Newsagent circuit, under Robert Burdett ('Nicôlas');[1] the Tiburce circuit, which Nicolas entrusted to Joseph Marchand and which was therefore part of the Newsagent circuit; the Prunus circuit in Toulouse, whose task was to equip certain trustworthy resistance fighters with weapons and tactical training and generally turn them into separate units (Prunus was set up by Maurice Pertschuk, or 'Eugène', and Victor Hazan, or 'Gervais', who had been dropped near Loches and been met by Philippe de Vomécourt, alias 'Gauthier'); and finally the Stationer network, set up in the Jura mountains and extending as far west as Lyons and as far east as the Swiss frontier. Stationer was led by Harry Reé, known as 'Henri Rehmann' or 'César', and would later expand still further.

By the end of 1942, therefore, SOE had established a firm base at Lyons,

1. Buckmaster had in fact appointed Nicolas as head of Spruce, Alain having been recalled to Britain. But Alain refused to leave either Spruce or his girlfriend in Lyons. So Nicolas formed his own group, Newsagent. After the war he was made a 'citizen of honour' in Lyons by the city's mayor, Louis Pradel, who had worked closely with him as well as with the Coq Enchaîné movement.

with specialist groups radiating out across the whole south-east and east of France.

But if these groups were to survive, they badly needed both money and equipment.

The first parachute drop intended specifically for these new groups was made on 28 March, 1942, at Blyes near Lagnieu in the province of Ain. It had been organized by Marcel Claeys and his friends at Coq Enchaîné, in co-operation with Dubourdin and the Spruce network. Many other drops were to follow that year: at Anse and Villenfranche to the north of Lyons, in June; Loyettes, to the east, in September; Uchyzy and Pont-de-Vaux, in Ain province again, in October; Mauziat and Tournus, near Mâcon (north of Lyons again) in November, and so on. Each dropping zone was given a code name – Eagle, Junot, Marguerite, Orion, Courgette, Chestnut, Spinach, Pear, Banana, etc. The following summary gives some idea of the Buckmaster networks' intense activity during this period, and shows what excellent communications the groups now had with London.

On 17 April, 1942, General Giraud escaped from the fortress at Koenig-stein where he'd been imprisoned and went into hiding at Saint-Didier-au-Mont-d'Or, a few miles north-west of Lyons. Helped by various SOE groups, he presently managed to reach North Africa.

But Giraud's successful escape from France had underlined the need for specialist networks to help other escapees. And so, on 20 April, 1942, Peter Churchill returned to France once more, again by submarine; this time he was accompanied by Victor Gerson ('Vic') and Marcel Clech ('Bastien'). Vic went to Lyons and there met Georges Liévin [1] and the Rachline brothers ('Socrate' and 'Lucien'), whom he promptly enlisted to help him set up an escape line. Very soon they had organized a remarkable escape route right across France, from north to south and thence across the Pyrenees into Spain; they would be kept constantly busy to the very end of the war.

Meanwhile, the SOE networks were continuing to spread. Marcel Clech went to see Virginia Hall to collect Georges Begué's transmitter – Begué had just been captured – and to meet Raymond Flower ('Gaspard'), who was to set up a new group, Monkeypuzzle, in Sologne.

At the end of April, 1942, Jean Menesson ('Henri' or 'Jean') had been landed near Barcarès by a Spanish fishing boat. With him were Maurice Pertschuk ('Eugène' or 'Martin'), from the Pimento network, and Paul Le Chêne ('Victor'), who were to set up another new group, Plane, at Clermont-Ferrand, west of Lyons. Menesson stayed at Dr Rousset's and there met August Bussière, owner of the Grand Bazar in Oullins, who agreed to let Menesson use the shop premises for storing provisions and arms. Menesson also set up a radio post in the shop, a safe place from which to transmit his secret signals to London. And, dressed as a Scout leader, he

---

1. It was Madame Gaby Pierre-Bloch in Villamblard who sent Liévin to Lucien Rachet, and Rachet then put him in touch with Vic Gerson.

managed to travel around the country looking for suitable dropping zones for future parachute operations.[1]

On 14 July, 1942, there was a mass demonstration by the people of Lyons in front of the Monument to the Republic in Place Carnot. Despite brutal police handling of the demonstrators, they had shown that a large proportion of Lyons' citizens were fundamentally on the side of the resistance.

The following day, 15 July, two SOE officers met Virginia Hall to collect a transmitter set; their names were Ernest Wilkinson ('Alexandre') and Denis Rake ('Justin') and their job was to set up a group in the Limoges area. But as soon as they reached Limoges they were caught.

Meanwhile Madame Pierre-Bloch had been helping to organize a mass escape from Mauzac prison camp, in the Dordogne, where her husband and several other SOE agents were being held. That same day, in fact, 15 July, she managed to bribe a prison guard – and the eventual result was a particularly successful break-out (see below, p.183–6).

In September 1942, the two Newton brothers were dropped near Loches, with Brian Stonehouse ('Célestin') as their radio operator. Henry Newton ('Hubert Norman') and his younger brother Alfred ('Arthur Norman') had a very personal reason for their passionate determination to fight the Germans. On 25 September, 1941, the ship carrying their father, both their wives and their children back to England had been torpedoed by a U-boat off the Portuguese coast; there were no survivors. Now the Newtons were about to set up a new group for SOE in Lyons itself – the Greenheart network, whose sphere of activity would extend as far as Saint-Étienne and Le Puy.

On 24 September three more SOE agents arrived in Lyons – Brian Rafferty ('Dominique'), Simon Hudson ('Charles') and John ('Isidore') – having been parachuted into the Puy-de-Dôme. Their task was to set up the Headmaster network; but they were soon caught, and Isidore was seriously wounded.

On 28 September, the *Funkabwehr* (German security police) paid a quiet visit to Lyons, with the connivance of Pierre Laval;[2] one of their duties was to detect clandestine radio transmissions. From now on, SOE's 'pianists' would have to double their security measures; indeed, the dangers increased still more when the Germans invaded the Occupied Zone a few weeks later, on 11 November, for in their wake came the formidable forces of the Gestapo. Besides, the Vichy government had introduced the death penalty several months earlier for anyone found in possession of a transmitter set.

Edward Zeff ('Mathieu' or 'George 53') had been kept desperately busy for the past six months, transmitting not only for the Spruce network in Lyons

1. On his second mission to France, Menesson was captured; his eventual fate was never discovered.
2. See M. Ruby, *Klaus Barbie de Montluc à Montluc* (L'Hermès, Lyons 1983).

but also for other SOE groups that had lost their 'pianists'. Exhausted by all his clandestine work, he asked to be relieved for a while. Permission was duly authorized in October 1942, and Colonel Buckmaster sent Pierre Le Chêne ('Grégoire') as his replacement. Zeff, accompanied by Sheppard, decided to make for Spain; but they ran into a German patrol. Both men were deported to Mauthausen prison camp, and Zeff later died there.

Grégoire, meanwhile, went into hiding at Dr Rousset's. He made some transmissions from Rousset's home, but also from Marchand's (2 Quai Perrache), Raymonde Pejot's (6 Rue Émile-Zola) and Andrée Serre's (9 Rue Camille, Montchat).

On 24 October, 1942, a Lysander landed near Pont-de-Vaux in Ain province. It had brought two more agents – J. Paimblanc ('Carp') and Auguste Floiras ('Albert') – and would return to England with Ben Cowburn, who had successfully completed his mission, and Georges Dubourdin ('Alain'). Robert Burdett had to force Dubourdin to go, knowing that these were Buckmaster's orders and must be obeyed; knowing, too, that Dubourdin's relationship with the girl in Lyons might cause complications. SOE agents had been warned to avoid such entanglements at all costs, for they might threaten not only themselves but also their colleagues. In fact, Dubourdin would return five months later on another mission, making a parachute jump near Compiègne on 24 March, 1943, along with Francis Cammaerts ('Roger'); their plane was then to pick up Peter Churchill and another SOE agent, Henri Frager ('Paul'). But Dubourdin would run out of luck on this mission; he was captured and deported to Buchenwald, where in April, 1945, he was executed.

On 7 November, 1942, the gallant Dr Rousset was arrested. He too was sent to Buchenwald. But 'Pep' refused to talk, even under torture. Yet he knew about virtually all SOE's plans in Lyons and the Rhône-Alpes province – and score upon score of names . . .

Two days later it was Pierre Chêne's turn. He was caught on 9 November in the middle of a transmission at 9 Rue Camille in Montchat. The man who was meant to be his look-out had fled when he saw the Germans arriving in force. Le Chêne was sent to Mauthausen, where he stayed until May, 1945, when the Allies liberated the camp; but his health had suffered terribly and he died a few years later.

On 8 November the Allied landings in North Africa gave new heart to the clandestine fighters in France. Victory was at least a glimmer on the horizon now. But on 11 November the Germans invaded the southern zone too. Virginia Hall managed to reach safety just in time, thanks to the escape line Vic.

General de Lattre de Tassigny, refusing to surrender to the Germans, was arrested and held in Lyons' Saint-Paul prison. There he was joined by Philippe de Vomécourt ('Gauthier'), who helped him escape to England via the same route as Miss Hall.

In November, 1942, Robert Burdett twice had a narrow escape (Klaus Barbie was offering six million francs for his capture!) and, now that his cover in Lyons was blown, he was ordered back to Britain.

This brief chronological survey of SOE's activities in one region is obviously very incomplete. It does, however, help us to follow what Buckmaster's agents were doing during this period. First they set up safe-houses, through Miss Hall and Dr Rousset, to provide a central base. Then, working from this secure grounding, other agents began to set up new groups in carefully selected areas, spreading across much of the country from the Puy-de-Dôme to the Swiss frontier, from the Jura mountains to the rivers Isère and Loire. SOE staff officers were sent to supervise the organization of these groups, to inspect their progress and deliver instructions and money. Meanwhile the new circuits maintained regular radio communication with SOE headquarters in London. From time to time they were sent, either by submarine or (more often) by parachute delivery, more agents to reinforce the existing groups or to start new ones, and of course more supplies of arms and money. Thus the circuits were able to recruit, train and equip even more French citizens.

Gradually the networks began to expand, covering more and more of France. Lysander aircraft delivered men and equipment, and returned to Britain with agents who were worn out or 'blown', or those who had accomplished their mission and now needed fresh instructions from London.

Daring and effective, the SOE networks were now in place and functioning well – though not without the occasional crisis, for arrests and losses were frequent. What is remarkable, however, is just how much a handful of very determined men and women could achieve if they were well enough armed and trained.

As a final note to this brief outline of SOE in action, there is one particular mission entrusted to Buckmaster's agents that deserves mentioning: the attempt to persuade certain high-ranking political figures to leave France and go to London. As we have seen, George Langelaan was parachuted into France on 6 September, 1941, and landed near Argenton-sur-Creuse. This former journalist with the *New York Times* was now an SOE officer, and with him he had brought a personal letter from Winston Churchill, with orders to get in touch with Édouard Herriot, the President of France, and urge him to join the Allies. But Langelaan's mission ended in failure, and he himself was arrested in Châteauroux. Another attempt was made by Georges Dubourdin, with the same result. On 31 August, 1942, France Antelme ('Antoine') made a parachute jump near Poitiers, again on the same errand but this time with a message from Roosevelt. This was Édouard Herriot's reply to the American president: 'You have asked me to join you . . . If I hesitate it is because of the unfortunate people of France; suffering and confused as they are, they need their few remaining leaders to stay with them. If I were to leave now without being able to explain the reason for my departure . . . I fear they would suspect me of trying to escape the danger, of fleeing the hardships which face us all.'

Antoine, meanwhile, was arrested by the Gestapo, deported and finally executed.[1]

And so, by the end of 1942, following the Nazi occupation of the whole of France, the SOE networks were firmly established across the whole country, gradually making progress on many different fronts. But one can well imagine what their life was like, these undercover agents, outlaws, 'terrorists' . . .

---

1. See M. Ruby, *La Résistance à Lyons* (L'Hermès, Lyons 1979).

# — 3 —

## UNDERCOVER AGENTS

Before we examine in detail the clandestine life that SOE's agents had to lead, we should first take a look at the parachute operations, covert deliveries, sabotage action and routine hardships that they faced in their everyday lives.

The burden of most airborne operations fell on the tiny but easily handled Lysander aircraft and their ever-cautious, ever-capable pilots.

On 1 June, 1942, there was one drop which is still remembered in Lyons today. It was described in the 28 November, 1944, issue of *Le Démocrat* (a weekly publication issued by the Rhône Radical-Socialist Party) by Lucien Degoutte, a member of the resistance group Le Coq Enchaîné, who became the MP for Rhône after the war:

> In the middle of the market place [at Villefranche-sur-Saône] Piniot, Collier and Calmels were waiting for me. Longtime members of the Radical Party and staunch patriots that they were, they had decided not to involve anyone else. Piniot began by assuring me that they had worked it all out logically. Collier had all the details, for he lived near the dropping zone. Calmels added that they'd found a massive conduit in which to hide everything. In the meantime, Marcel [Marcel Claeys] had spoken to the owner of a café beside the Saône, who had happily agreed to help the men from Lyons.
>
> All was now ready for the famous Anse drop. On 30 May, 1942, the BBC broadcast the prearranged message to let us know the operation was on. At ten o'clock the following night, everyone was in position: ten men, with Alain as leader, all waiting for two British officers and no one knew how many containers of goods.
>
> Two o'clock came, and with it a distant throbbing in the sky.

The Polish pilot, a last-minute stand-in for the normal one, had flown over without seeing the landing lights. He began to reduce height – he was going to alert the anti-aircraft batteries . . . Then he realized his mistake. He came back, released four parachutes 1,200 metres too far to the south, and promptly flew off again. The northerly wind, which he hadn't allowed for, made matters even worse. Two of the parachutes – each carrying three 50-kilo boxes of arms packed into a single container – floated down on top of some poplar trees, right beside the Azergues. Meanwhile, the two men had landed in the village of Anse itself.

'Patrice' [Robert Sheppard] found himself on Madame Charpy's roof, just a few yards from the police station.[1] It was a real disaster. The police could hardly fail to notice all the shouts of alarm from the neighbours. By sheer coincidence the police sergeant was Captain Doussot; he guessed what had happened and did his best to delay things – but to no avail.

The second parachutist, 'Nicolas' [Robert Boiteux], was luckier. He hid in a ditch till morning, then started walking down the road, and eventually caught a bus into Lyons. That was where we found him – incredulous but delighted that he was safe.

For it had been a night of misfortune all around. The reception committee spent three hours searching the countryside in vain. By then it was nearly dawn. The three local men went off home. The others returned to Marcel Claeys's car – and found they had run into a trap. Marcel, Alain, Berthier and Georges Pezant were all arrested. All four of them, plus Patrice, were taken to Lyons by Captain Doussot. The local commissioner, however, reduced their sentences to the absolute minimum and actually let Alain escape, so the network itself was not compromised.

The commissioner's conduct landed him in trouble with the authorities for more than two years after that, but his gesture was all the more appreciated for coming at a time when collaboration was the rule. In fact Commissioner Triffe was a leading figure in the Lyons resistance, and he had allowed Alain to escape when his friend Marcel Claeys told him during preliminary questioning that Alain was a British officer on a special mission.

Many years later, on 17 April, 1978, Robert Sheppard gave the French radio station 'Europe No 1' his own account of this unforgettable incident.

He was just twenty years old when he volunteered for SOE, he said, and he remembered that it was exactly ten o'clock on the morning of 1 June, 1942,

1. Marcel Claeys, who witnessed the incident, says that Sheppard landed on a building right next door to the police station. Sheppard himself confirms this.

when he finally entered the office that served as Bodington's and Buckmaster's headquarters. As an SOE recruit Sheppard had by then undergone a lengthy and very thorough training, both physical and psychological, which turned him into a secret agent – or, to use his own words, 'a villain'.

Buckmaster and Bodington showed him a map of France, and indicated the little Beaujolais village of Anse where he would have to make his jump that night. They gave him a silk belt containing 500,000 francs, a considerable sum for those days, to hand over to the French resistance.

Sheppard left the office about midday, when he received confirmation that the BBC had already broadcast the message that he would be arriving that night: 'Body fills a hole in the Isère.' The message would be broadcast again a few hours later to signify that the operation was going ahead.

At five o'clock Sheppard received his last-minute instructions from Bodington, who made him go through all the details of his new identity. His codename would be 'Patrice' and while in France he would become the son of an officer in the Foreign Legion who had died in North Africa and whom he had hardly known. Then he was driven to a little-known airfield, used only by the secret services. After an excellent meal he changed into his flying suit and put on the rubber helmet. Someone gave him some food rations, enough to last a day or two, and a 7.65mm automatic. At the same time the officer casually handed him a small box of pills – 'to give you energy' – and a tiny cyanide tablet 'in case you run into any bother'.

When it was time for Sheppard to board the aircraft, Buckmaster shook his hand, wished him luck and told him: 'Don't worry, you'll land on a bed of roses.' It seems that Colonel Buckmaster was no prophet!

The flight went smoothly. At two in the morning Patrice was just about to jump. His mind whirling, he found his thoughts turning first to his boyhood, then to the war in France where he had already served in the army, before managing to escape via Spain and thence back to the battle. He also thought about the men down there in the darkness, strangers, waiting for him, resistance workers who'd formed a reception committee to meet him . . . Then it was time; he was given the order to jump.

The multicoloured canopy blossomed open above him. All was well. But in the darkness Patrice landed on the roof of a house. He could hear the noise of falling tiles. His parachute, meanwhile, was caught up on some telephone wires. Lights went on in the house. Two dark figures appeared in the courtyard and shone their flashlights up at him; he noticed they were wearing pyjamas.

'French police!' they shouted. 'Who's there? Answer!'

Patrice hesitated, then pulled out his pistol. But he had come to help the French in their fight for freedom, he couldn't shoot at them. He edged forwards into a patch of light.

'Get me down, then,' he called.

The two gendarmes showed him how to get down through a little skylight and led him into their private quarters, where they and their families lived. Women and children milled around anxiously; Patrice gave them some bars of chocolate. The two gendarmes helped him out of his flying suit and seemed to have trouble believing he had really come from London.

But they were good Frenchmen. 'We don't want a fuss,' they told him. 'But there are other police here who don't see things the way we do. Go on, run. Cross the little square, and just keep going. We'll say we chased you but lost your trail.'

Unfortunately the plan didn't work. A frightened neighbour had telephoned the police station and the other police were waiting downstairs, curious to see this man who had fallen out of the sky. So, much to his disgust, Patrice was arrested.

Here Robert Sheppard's account merges with Lucien Degoutte's. Freed by the courageous Commissioner Triffe, Patrice went back into action, training saboteurs and helping to step up operations. Finally he was recaptured and sent to a concentration camp. He is still something of a local hero to the old resistance men in Lyons, who greet him with enormous warmth whenever he returns and always remember his adventures that night at Anse.

The problems involved in an arms drop are illustrated by one operation that took place in September, 1942. It was arranged by Jean-Marie Régnier and Nicolas (Robert Burdett), and the object was to take delivery of an arms supply destined for one particular resistance unit. This is Régnier's own account of the operation:

> Most parachute drops were made at the time of the full moon. London never used to warn the group's leader exactly when the drop would be made, but would tell him to listen in for a particular message on the BBC, to be broadcast on one of three consecutive days at seven in the evening and again at nine. The seven o'clock message would warn us to start preparing the reception committee, and the nine o'clock one indicated which of the dropping zones would be used, according to prior arrangements. Constant jamming by the Germans made it very hard for us to hear the broadcasts; we had to have several wireless sets in several different places in order to stand any chance of catching the messages and thus knowing where the drop would take place and where we should have to go. . . .
>
> On this particular occasion we met up at Joseph Marchand's place. Nicolas and Marcel Roux left first; René Douris, Marius (an employee of Douris's) and I followed shortly afterwards, all making for Raoul Léger's house. Waiting for us there were Henri Dufournel and a young engineer from the Lyons gas board, as

well as a former technical officer with the 35th air division who came from Bron.

About half past ten, after the usual drink and toasts to friendship and good fortune, some of us left for Messimy: the young engineer, Dufournel, Douris, Marius and I.

Nicolas had told Douris, as a precaution, to muffle his van's exhaust pipe and to keep several different number plates handy so that we could switch them quickly if the need arose. But Douris had not followed this advice. As we went down Rue Puits-Gaillot, I remember the noise was appalling.

All went well as far as Neuville-sur-Saône. We had gone through Neuville and were out on the open road again when we saw flashlights up ahead, indicating that we should stop. I told Douris, 'Switch off your lights at the last moment, and keep your speed up – don't stop.' The moonlight, after all, was bright enough to see by. But I suppose Douris thought it wiser to stop; he pulled up just where the two gendarmes were standing. The older of the two looked into the cab.

'Where are you going?' he asked Douris.

'Ask the boss,' said Douris, pointing at me.

I was still young then, and my reflexes were fast. 'We're going to a place near Montmerle,' I told the gendarme quickly, 'to collect some cabbages to make *choucroute*. The van's always used in the day so we're taking advantage of the moonlight tonight.'

'Oh, good,' said the gendarme. 'Then you can drop us off in Trévoux. We've been on the road all day, after taking some prisoners to Rivesaltes yesterday. We caught the last train back to Neuville but missed the bus to Trévoux.'

Douris immediately invited him into the cab and told the other man to join our three friends on the back. He asked Marius to pass us the bottle from his knapsack. And so we drove on, all taking swigs from the litre bottle of red wine, including the two gendarmes. When we got to Trévoux, they told us to stop near a road which went off to the right, leading uphill. I noticed that the younger of the two gendarmes, the one who'd been in the back, got out on the offside instead of the nearside, and walked around the van taking a good look at our number plates. Nevertheless, we parted on a very cordial note.

About fifteen or twenty minutes later we reached the dropping zone. Douris parked the van some distance away, fearful that a container would land on the *gazogène* tanks on the back.

The dropping zone was a field which I'd been to look at a few days earlier. But the corn had since been cut and the field was newly ploughed – and re-sown too, I thought – which didn't make our job any easier. The van could not now be driven across the field to collect the containers wherever they landed. It was also much harder to tramp around on the newly sown earth. But we just had to put up with it.

We went to the middle of the field with the knapsack and waited for the plane. It was hardly late at all; we soon heard the by now familiar drone of engines overhead.

Nicolas immediately ordered us into position, all holding out the red-beamed landing lights. These were just ordinary pocket torches, only we covered the beam with red transparent paper coloured with toothpaste. The lights had to be held up at arm's length to form a triangle a hundred metres long on each side. Nicolas used a white torch to give the pilot the prearranged signal in Morse. He would stand near one of the points of the triangle to indicate which direction the wind was blowing. The wind being in the north, he stood beside me; I was marking the southerly point of the triangle. I confess I was quite impressed by these simple arrangements, and being totally ignorant of all aviation matters I could hardly believe that an aircraft could come all the way from England and find this tiny triangle of three red lights, just a hundred metres apart.

The aircraft made a wide turn to lose height, flew over us again – and disappeared. Our signal was not the one he was looking for; he was heading for Loyettes. A few minutes passed, then we were alerted by the sound of another plane.

We switched the torches on again. The plane circled as before to lose altitude and this time responded correctly to the signal we flashed. Flying over us a second time, at a height of about 500 metres, it dropped four containers. They landed rather far apart, which meant that we took longer than usual to collect them. We opened the containers and took out three Colt revolvers, two Sten guns and several boxes of ammunition. This was for our own defence, in case the police caught us at the dropping zone or on the way back to Sathonay, the village where we had arranged to store everything. We never took arms with us on the way to meet a drop. As long as our identity cards and travel passes were in order, we could normally expect to avoid any trouble at police roadblocks. On the other hand, our orders were very clear. As soon as a container was dropped we were supposed to extract one weapon for every member of the team, so that we could defend ourselves properly if the police somehow caught us. The weapons we received were vital for our cause, and must at all costs reach whatever destination the group leader had settled on.

Because the containers were so widely scattered over the

ground, finding and loading them into Douris's van was a slow, tiring business. As soon as we'd finished we started changing back into our town clothes, which would look more normal than the sort of thing we wore for these operations. Suddenly two of us noticed the dark figure of a man at the far side of the field, the Messimy side, silhouetted by the moonlight . . . We all sprang into action, running across the field, but he had vanished. We spent several fruitless minutes searching among the hedgerows and bushes. Afterwards we learned that it had been the Messimy forestry warden.

We next had to hide the goods at a poultry farm just outside Sathonay, owned by a man named Cholet. A few days previously Nicolas had taken me there to introduce us and to let me see round the place. I had decided that we ought to avoid Trévoux on the return journey. But this didn't suit René Douris and led to a bit of an argument; in the end I reluctantly had to overrule him at the crossroads just before Trévoux, to make him turn left towards Villard-les-Dombes. Halfway along the road I told him to turn right, up a narrow lane which I was convinced would take us in the right direction. Unfortunately, I didn't know my way around this area very well. We ended up, at about three in the morning, actually in the village of Sathonay and had to do an about-turn to find Cholet's house. We probably woke most of the villagers with the van's noisy exhaust.

The lane leading to the farm where we were going to hide the new supplies was a dead end. We had agreed that Cholet would wait for us beside the gate into the farmyard and open it to let us through. And as arranged, Cholet was there. He opened the gate and closed it again behind us, then gave us a very hearty welcome; he'd been starting to worry as we were supposed to have turned up about two o'clock. He was also worried about the noise he'd heard us making when we turned the van round in the village.

The van was soon unloaded and the various packages hidden all over the place – in the roof, in the cellars, in all sorts of nooks and crannies. Then Cholet invited us in for a meal of ham, sausage, omelette and cheese, all washed down with red wine. I'll never forget it, that midnight feast he laid on – a rare treat in those days, especially after all our physical exertions that night.

When we were leaving I told Cholet that Nicolas would be arriving later in the day, to make a list of everything we had hidden. Cholet said he'd be out all day, as he had arranged to go shooting; but the following day, a Saturday, he would be happy to see Nicolas anytime he wanted.

We got back to Lyons at six that morning, after an uneventful drive with no problems at all.

I heard later that I'd been wise to avoid Trévoux on the way back. The police had set up a roadblock to catch us. The obvious conclusion is that the two gendarmes we had given a lift to between Neuville and Trévoux had been suspicious of our story about making a late-night journey to find cabbages for *choucroute* . . . And I also discovered later (though not until 1944) that the two British aircraft had been spotted by German radar as they crossed the Demarcation Line, so the police had been alerted throughout the whole of southern France.

Back in Lyons that morning, between six and seven o'clock, everyone who'd been on the reception team went home for a well-earned rest.

At eleven thirty I went round to the Récamia laboratories at 107 Rue Pierre-Corneille, to see Joseph Marchand. Nicolas and René Douris were already there, which gave me a chance to remove the shoes I'd worn that night from Douris's van.

Nicolas was well satisfied with the way things had turned out. I told him Cholet could not see him that day, but would be free the following day to help him check out all the equipment.

Late the next morning, Saturday, I wanted to see Marchand again and went back to Rue Pierre-Corneille; but the perfumery's manageress told me that her boss had already gone home for lunch.

On my way to Marchand's flat in Quai Perrache, I decided to call in at Place Raspail, to see if René Douris or his employee Marius happened to be at the shop-cum-agency that was run by Marius's parents. But Marius's father stopped me before I could even say hello.

'Go away, go away!' he said, looking very agitated. 'It's too dangerous here. The police came and arrested my daughter-in-law this morning, they left us to look after her baby. They said they've got René and Marius in prison at Mâcon – they're accused of taking part in an arms drop and then hiding the arms somewhere in Sathonay.' He added that the owners of the land where the drop was made had been caught too, and had been in prison since the night before.

I rushed off to Quai Perrache to warn Marchand. He and his wife were expecting me to lunch, and were horrified to hear the terrible news – especially as Nicolas and Jean Calmin (who worked for Nicolas) had left the Marchands' house only three-quarters of an hour earlier, going to see Cholet as arranged. They had intended to take the tram from Lyons, then go the rest of the way on foot. We realized that even a champion cyclist would never catch up with them in time. It was almost certain they would be captured. So we concluded that our best bet was to rearrange our plans and carry on as far as possible without them.

An operation had been planned for that Saturday night, when a Lysander would land to pick up Alain and fly him back to England. Marchand and I were not part of this operation; in fact, I was due to leave for Toulouse the same evening to deliver a transmitter set to Martin, head of the group's south-western branch. But as Marchand told me: 'You'll just have to find someone else, some friend who can take the transmitter to Toulouse in your place. If the BBC announces that the Lysander operation is on, I'm afraid you and I will simply have to go to Pontaneveaux instead of Nicolas and Calmin.'

Realizing Marchand was right, I hurried off to catch my friend Claude Crost at lunch-time, at his home in Place Morel, Lyons. I explained what I wanted him to do and to my delight he seemed very eager to take on this errand. I arranged to meet him at Perrache station ten minutes before the train left, to give him his ticket for the journey and the suitcase containing the transmitter.

At about five that afternoon I went back to Marchand's house, and was overjoyed to find that Nicolas and Jean Calmin had not fallen into the police trap as we had thought.

When Nicolas had reached Cholet's farm and rung the bell at the gate, a woman had appeared and told him that the Cholets had been arrested the evening before, after a police search; she was just a neighbour, looking after the animals for them. Needless to say, Nicolas and Calmin beat a very hasty retreat to Lyons.

The original plan was thus unaffected, and I was able to leave for Toulouse to carry out the errand myself. . . .

Each in its own way, these two accounts by Lucien Degoutte and Jean-Marie Régnier provide a fairly typical picture of SOE parachute operations in France.

Now let us follow Jean-Marie Régnier, the SOE agent in Lyons, as he goes on his new mission to Toulouse:

My train journey from Lyons to Toulouse with the transmitter was normal enough. At Toulouse station, there was only one way for passengers to get out and this involved passing between two lines of police, customs men and officials checking our cards. They picked people out at random to look at their identity cards or examine the contents of their luggage. My suitcase containing the transmitter weighed 18kg, which obviously made me walk rather heavily; there was a good chance that I might attract unwanted attention.

Suddenly an idea came to me. Crowds of passengers were starting to file through the two lines of officials, and on my immediate left stood a very smart-looking captain in the Armistice army. Just as we reached this human funnel I knocked my suitcase quite hard against the captain's right leg. He staggered and gave me a thunderous look. I apologized profusely and went on talking to him, all about the problems of making a journey nowadays and how exhausting it was – and I continued talking all the way down the inspection line. Admittedly I got no response whatever from the captain, and he must have thought me a terrible windbag. But the police and other officials, seeing me talking to this army officer, did not dare pull me out for a spot check.

Outside the station I was meant to be meeting Eugène, a radio operator, and Martin, who ran a group in the Toulouse area. Unfortunately they weren't there, which was going to cause complications. I went to the Hotel Terminus, opposite the station, and sat down at a table in the coffee lounge where I could watch out for them in case they were just late in arriving.

I spun out the time by drinking ersatz coffee and eating some revolting biscuits for about an hour, expecting them to arrive at any moment. But in vain. Fortunately, Nicolas had told me that if necessary I could contact someone else: a girl who was secretary to a students association, whom I could find at a big brasserie in the Place du Capitole.

When I was paying my bill, I asked the waiter if I could leave my suitcase with him for an hour or so. He took the case and the transmitter it contained, and left it in the cashier's little cubicle at one end of the bar.

I caught the tram to the Place du Capitole and found the brasserie that Nicolas had mentioned. But the cashier told me that the students association secretary never came to the brasserie on Sundays and I wouldn't be able to see her before the following evening, Monday evening in fact. The cashier added that she didn't know where the girl lived. This was obviously a sensible security precaution, but I now found myself stuck in Toulouse until the following evening, although I had meant to go back to Lyons the same night.

I booked into a hotel just off the Place du Capitole; then, again as a security measure, returned to the Hotel Terminus to fetch the transmitter. In the coffee lounge I noticed that the cashier had gone and her place had been taken by the manager. I sat down at the end of the bar near the cashier's cubicle and asked for a drink, which gave me a chance to talk to the manager. I noticed that in his buttonhole he wore the *Francisque*, the badge of a former member of the Foreign Legion, which meant that he was probably a Pétainist. I asked him to give me my suitcase.

'Oh, so it's yours, is it?' he said, glaring at me. 'Then you must be one of those black-marketeers, letting other Frenchmen starve!'

I replied that my case was only heavy because it contained potatoes, which I was taking to relations who had not been able to get any . . . Then I made a hasty exit, for if I stayed there I might jeopardize my mission.

In a nearby street I had spotted a shop with a sign outside saying 'Storage Depot – Parcels may be deposited here.' So I went in and left my suitcase, having first checked the place was open twenty-four hours a day, including Sundays and holidays. Then I had lunch in a restaurant in the Place du Capitole. After lunch I was just walking through the square when I noticed an underground lavatory which had left-luggage facilities in the attendant's office. I decided to go and fetch my suitcase there and then, and leave it in this unlikely place instead. Then, not knowing what else to do with myself, I went to the cinema.

When I came out of the cinema I returned to the public lavatory to check that the suitcase had not been moved, and found it was still safe. Just as I was going back up the steps, intending to mingle with the throngs of people out for their usual stroll at six thirty on a Sunday evening, I was astonished to find myself face to face with Eugène and Martin. Like all the other good citizens of Toulouse, they were taking the traditional late afternoon stroll around this famous square.

We immediately repaired to a nearby brasserie and sat down at a table outside. Eugène and Martin quickly began to explain. The previous night they had been involved in a parachute operation a long way out of Toulouse, and it had been physically impossible for them to return in time to meet me outside the station as we had arranged.

I fetched the suitcase and handed it over to Martin, who went off with it and returned later to join us at the restaurant for dinner.

The following morning I caught the first train back to Lyons. The return trip was quite uneventful. . . .

A few days after my visit to Toulouse, towards the end of October, 1942, Nicolas asked me to deliver another transmitter, this time to Marseilles. As far as I was concerned, there was no question of my refusing. I went on a Sunday morning, on the first train. As usual, I had told the Franc-Tireur leaders where I was going, and they gave me another suitcase containing underground papers which had to be taken to Marseilles. I was to give the case to a young lawyer who lived in Boulevard Liautaud and he in turn would deliver it to one of his student friends, an activist in the Franc-Tireur movement. I would thus be able to kill two birds with one stone.

The transmitter had to be handed over to some people staying in a hotel in Cours Belzunce. The man was English and his companion was a very young American girl; officially they were father and daughter, on a business trip.

When I arrived at Marseilles' Saint-Charles station, I bought myself a town plan, for I'd only been there once before and that was when I drove through on a motorbike back in 1938! First I made for the hotel in Cours Belzunce. At the reception desk I was told that Monsieur and Mademoiselle X had gone out for a walk and wouldn't be back until late afternoon. This was a bit of a setback. I asked if I could leave the suitcase there, and when they agreed I told them I would return at six thirty that evening. Meantime I went off on the other errand.

At the young lawyer's home I saw his father, who told me he had gone to church but would certainly be back at midday; this left me with the choice of either telephoning him or coming back later. He also questioned me about the case which I had told him I wanted to leave, and I explained that it contained books that a friend of his son's wanted him to have. We arranged that I should return about twelve fifteen.

I duly went back to the house at twelve fifteen – and I'll never forget the welcome I received from that young Marseilles lawyer. When I rang the bell of his flat and he opened the door, I saw he was holding the case full of clandestine newspapers.

'Take this stuff away!' he shouted furiously. (I should explain that the case wasn't locked and he must have opened it.) 'And tell whoever it was who sent you that I have no sympathy at all with this sort of thing – and a lot of people are going to be in big trouble with the police. I know what I'm talking about and I have no intention whatsoever of risking my job by taking part in such activities!'

I remember telling him: 'If you want to save your job, you'll have to rely on other people risking theirs!'

As for the transmitter set, that was eventually delivered without any problems . . .

These lively incidents related by Jean-Marie Régnier are just a sample of what was going on. But they very clearly convey the sort of atmosphere in which SOE agents and resistance workers in general were working then.

To collect arms drops, carry them around and hide them, to deliver clandestine newspapers or transmitter sets or just pass on messages may all seem fairly trivial activities. But in reality, the people entrusted with such missions were literally risking their lives every time they went out.

We have already seen what a vital role the radio operator played, and also something of the dangers he faced. Security was always a major consideration.[1] If the authorities detected his transmissions, there were four possible consequences.

Firstly, the set alone could be seized, while the operator and his codes remained safe. Secondly, both the set and the codes could be seized, but not the operator. Thirdly, the operator and set might be found but the codes remained safe. And finally, the enemy might seize all three – operator, set and codes.

In the first case, the danger was slight. The operator would arrange for the codes to be destroyed, then try to join the nearest group with a transmitter of its own. If this was not possible he would nevertheless work for the group in whatever way he could.

In the second case, there still wasn't much danger. Enemy operators who tried to use the captured set and codes to infiltrate the organization would give themselves away by their different handling of the set and inevitable mistakes.

If the Germans caught the operator as well as his transmitter, they would usually try to make him work for them. But the operators were trained for just such an eventuality; they were told to choose a slightly different wavelength, so that the group would hear the signal, but not so close that the enemy would know the real wavelength. And then the idea was to transmit meaningless nonsense.

In the final scenario, however, there was no obvious way out. The captured operator was advised to obey the Germans' orders – but to make the same mistake in his signal three or four times running; if the enemy noticed, he should excuse his clumsiness on the ground of nervousness.

In fact the German radio-detection system was extremely efficient and very active. We have already seen the basic principle on which it operated. To examine it in greater depth, we can return to Lyons for an example.

The German detector teams arrived in the Unoccupied Zone in September, 1942, using the French police to camouflage their presence. The first team to start surveillance in the Lyons area set up their base at Charbonnières, a little spa town just a few kilometres from Lyons. They installed their permanent detection apparatus on the first floor of the Casino, which was surrounded by uniformed German guards.

All this, it must be admitted, was the result of one French inventor's work,

---

1. See M. Ruby, *La Résistance à Lyon*.

which he had incautiously allowed to fall into German hands during the war. In principle the system worked like this. The waveband that was being watched would appear on a dark cathode-ray screen as a luminous horizontal line, a few tenths of a millimetre wide. The screen looked a bit like the face of a clock, the waveband could be varied in depth according to the target of the surveillance. At Charbonnières they had several such devices, each watching over a particular section of the shortwave frequency. . . . In fact, the Germans maintained continuous surveillance of the shortwave frequencies from the first floor of the Casino in Charbonnières, working in liaison with their cypher office.

A suspect transmission was first traced on the Charbonnières equipment. Then, assuming that the clandestine radio operator would sooner or later return to the same wavelength, there was nothing to do but wait. After several such interceptions it was often possible to work out when the operator would start up his next transmission, and just before he did so, a fleet of three detector vans would set off roughly in the appropriate direction.

Private citizens were always kept well away from these vans, but they were known to contain a receiver, a direction finder and a compass. The receiver would be sent radio messages by the Charbonnières base, always on the same wavelength. In any case, the vans were easy to spot: firstly because they were very wide, and secondly because they did not have a roof, which would have interfered with the signal. The door was just behind the driver's seat. From the outside they looked like large motor caravans. The receivers did not work while the engine was running, presumably because of the interference it would cause.

Each van had a driver and three operators. Moreover, every time a van went out it was always accompanied by a truck carrying a driver, a German officer in plain clothes, an interpreter and one or two others.

Before they reached the area where they suspected a clandestine transmission was in progress, the vans used to separate and circle the place from a distance of several kilometres. As soon as the transmitter started up again, the three surveillance vehicles would tune in and each take a bearing on the signal; the intersection between the three bearings would then indicate where to search.

In practice, however, the first result was only approximate, and it left a 100–300 metre margin of error. . . . The final stage involved a more precise instrument which could only measure the signal when it was very close. One of the German surveillance officers would walk through the streets with it, roughly in the direction of the transmission. Gradually, by turning this way and that, he would find the signal getting stronger and stronger. The hunt would close in inexorably as the police were gradually led to the very building in which the transmitter was working.

The only snag at this last stage was the problem of camouflaging the detection apparatus, which was rather cumbersome. The batteries, valves and so on would have to be distributed in the officer's pockets, as well as in a briefcase under his arm, and the aerial would be attached to his back. The earphone, a very small one such as a deaf person might use, would be stuck in his ear; to hide the connecting wire, some operators wrapped a bandage round their neck. Later on the Germans improved their technique considerably. This sort of radio-tracking was used in the Rhône from the end of 1943 onwards; up to then, the Germans had not perfected their methods and their results were generally poor.

It is well known that scores of radio operators were caught, sometimes actually while they were on the air, with their headphones on. Many of them were killed as they tried to defend themselves, or died in concentration camps. They should not be forgotten, these anonymous heroes. Without them, without their coolness and their constant bravery, communication was impossible and sabotage operations wasted.

The *passeurs*, too – the men and women who worked for the specialist escape groups – often remained anonymous, as Philippe de Vomécourt himself reports:[1]

> Thousands of people made a contribution to these groups, though their names may never figure in a book. The sole remaining evidence of what they did may be a framed certificate on their wall, or perhaps a photograph of a young man looking stiff and awkward in borrowed clothes. The escape groups all had the same objective: to help soldiers, airmen, refugees (particularly Jews) to cross the Demarcation Line and thence through southern France to the Spanish frontier. There they would be handed over to a guide, either French or Spanish, who would lead them across the Pyrenees and into Spain, where ultimately they hoped to reach Gibraltar. Some of the French guides would take only servicemen; others took anyone who could pay enough.
>
> Sometimes a man on the run would have to wait on the coast somewhere, until London agreed to send a fishing boat or a submarine to pick him up – or, less frequently, a ship that could take him to Gibraltar. Both operations meant weeks or even months of waiting around and moving from place to place. . . .
>
> The ordinary men and women who helped these groups tended to see their actions in a very different light from the authorities; in their eyes, they were simply helping a man on the run, not committing a 'criminal action' against the Germans and the Armistice agreement. For them it was a patriotic duty, a humane act, to help a combatant escape from the Nazis – yet for reasons of

1. Philippe de Vomécourt, *Les Artisans de la Liberté* (Editions PAC, Paris 1975).

religious or personal scruples they would never have agreed to take part in active sabotage. While disagreeing with their opinions we had to admit they were sincere, even when the individuals concerned happened to be leading figures in the Vichy government, opportunists, parasites, schemers or sycophants, who thought of nothing save their own personal interests.

The agents who specialized in the escape lines were of particular value to us, for we knew they would never be arrested for other clandestine activities; this reduced the risks not only for them but for us as well. It became one of the golden rules in the resistance movement that each group should keep its activities separate and secret. No group should have any idea of what other groups were doing elsewhere. This was by far the best way, for no one could reveal something he did not know, even under torture or pain of death.

We were advised to have as little to do with the escape groups as possible, but it was difficult to avoid any contact entirely. In fact we were often in touch and provided each other with mutual support.

Although SOE had its own ways of getting someone out of France and back to England, as well as vice versa, some agents were obliged to turn to groups they didn't know. This was what happened to Benjamin Cowburn, whose vivid account below describes one of his escapes from France via Spain.[1] Cowburn had missed a rendezvous with a boat on the Channel coast, so he went to Lyons to find the ever-helpful Virginia Hall:

In Lyons I went in search of someone that Gauthier had mentioned, and was delighted to meet this tall, blonde young American, very charming and obviously very capable, who answered to the code name 'Marie'. She told me how to get in touch with an escape line based in Marseilles. She also introduced me to a man called Joseph, a member of the same group, who very hospitably offered me the use of his flat; I was thus able to enjoy the luxury of a hot bath, pyjamas and a comfortable bed.

I went to Marseilles the following evening and found my way to a bar called Le Petit Poucet. I had a bit of trouble persuading the manager that he could trust me. But my story and the name of the person who had sent me finally convinced him, and he agreed to introduce me to a certain gentleman. The latter, too, was very wary at first; but he took me to his home and after a long conversation I managed to reassure him that I wasn't a police spy.

1. Cowburn, op.cit.

Fortunately, prior to the war I had often been in this area on business, and I was able to describe several mutual acquaintances, which removed his last remaining doubts. The attitude of this man and his wife, as well as all the precautions they took in their work, showed me that this organization really meant business. They offered to put me up for the night, and the following morning, along with several other 'clients', I caught the train for Toulouse – the first stage of our journey.

In Toulouse we were met by a Spanish guide, who took us by rail from Toulouse to Banyuls and thence to Perpignan, an uneventful trip. Night had fallen. After leaving Perpignan station we climbed back up the embankment onto the railway lines, intending to follow them out of the town. Our long cross-country hike was just beginning. At one stage the guide told us to climb down; the line passed over a bridge and he didn't want to risk our silhouettes being seen. Soon we reached the first small hills. We cut through a grove of cork trees and began to climb. . . .

Towards three in the morning our chaperone stopped and made us go into a very small hut with a roof so low one couldn't stand upright. In normal times it was used, he told us, as a shelter for the pigs when they were up on the mountain. It was bitterly cold but what we most suffered from was the lack of tobacco. While we huddled together and tried to sleep – it was quite an effort – a man came in, gasping for breath after the climb. He evidently knew our guide, whom he spoke to in Spanish. We gathered that he too was a mountain guide, and was supposed to be bringing two more clients to join our group and cross the frontier. The piggery had been the agreed rendezvous. Unfortunately, the trio had not been as lucky as us, having been fired at by frontier guides; and in the commotion he had lost his clients.

When the first glimmer of dawn pierced the night sky, we stretched our stiff legs, only too glad to be leaving that uncomfortable shelter. Over rocks and through bushes we scaled the slopes until midday. The sky was overcast and the cold just as penetrating. We began to get tired. In a wild, magnificent spot we paused for lunch. Then we went on climbing.

Once we were over the last peak and were on the Spanish side, the going became easier. We came in sight of a village and had to hide until night. But the difficult part was over. By eleven o'clock that night we had reached Vilajuiga, the end of this stage of our journey. The following morning we caught the train and, thanks to the excellent organization of the escape circuit, arrived in Barcelona without once being challenged on the way.

One detail, which doesn't seem so much today, struck me very forcibly. When we left the station, a guide took us into a café where they served us milk: I hadn't even seen milk for several weeks! Then, trying not to seem in too much of a hurry, we went for a little walk. As though by chance our route took us past the British Consulate. At a given signal, we all dashed into the building. From then on we were relieved of any worry about possible Falangist attentions.

I was immediately taken in to to meet the Consul. He had literally just received word that I was coming, and arranged for a car to take me to the Portuguese frontier, via Madrid. Eventually, after an exhausting muddy walk, I crossed the frontier between Badajoz and Elvas, reached Lisbon and a few days later found myself on board an aircraft taking off from Cintra airport.

While not forgetting the biggest and most efficient escape route of the whole war, the one set up by 'Vic' for SOE, the gallant Benjamin Cowburn's story nevertheless demonstrates that SOE agents sometimes had to use the routes organized by other escape groups; and that in the field they were able to co-operate with other resistance groups when the need arose.

The same was true of sabotage operations, which also had to call on the services of other resistance workers outside the SOE networks.

The object of SOE sabotage operations was very simple: namely to destroy a part of the German war machine, no matter how small. For in the long run, thousands of such operations would clearly wear the enemy down. Attacks were therefore made on factories that were working for Germany, on the raw materials they used, their warehouses etc, in order to limit production for the enemy. As well as industrial sabotage there were raids on transport – railways and trains, dockyards, canals, etc – and communications, notably cutting electricity lines, high-tension cables, underground telephone cables and the destruction of transformers. Finally, when the time came, the saboteurs launched attacks on the enemy forces themselves – derailing trains that were carrying troops, whether they were heading for action or going on leave, as well as munitions etc – and generally inflicting increasingly heavy losses on the Wehrmacht.

The saboteurs had the extra responsibility of working out the precise consequences of any action they took. They had to do all they could to avoid harming civilians; attacks on the railway lines, for example, always had to be carried out well away from inhabited areas. They also had to avoid causing irreparable damage to certain installations of national importance. Thus it was preferable in a smelting works to wreck some small vulnerable machine parts rather than dynamite the whole foundry.

The damage wrought by sabotage was infinitely less dangerous to people and property than Allied air raids, which all too often caused losses to human life that were totally out of proportion to the material results. Sabotage was much more effective in reaching the desired objective and caused practically no casualties among local inhabitants.

But the saboteurs had further, subsidiary objectives too. They wanted to disperse the German forces as widely as possible, by obliging them to install guards and patrols on thousands of sensitive areas – bridges, works of art, railway stations and sidings, factories, warehouses and such like. They also wanted to sap German morale. Harassed at every turn, the enemy had to stay constantly on the alert, which was wearing on the nerves and ultimately weakened the resolve. Little by little, the German soldier would find himself in a perpetual state of insecurity, besieged by a hostile population which sheltered and protected those who attacked him from the shadows.

As we have already seen, the saboteurs made use of a new weapon – plastic explosives, or just 'plastic' as they called it, the guerrilla fighter's delight. This undoubtedly produced a revolution in sabotage techniques. A single individual with 200 grams of this miraculous substance and a detonator in his bag, was possessed of a very considerable destructive potential.

This is how Benjamin Cowburn, himself an expert on sabotage, describes the perfect saboteur:[1]

> The saboteur's first consideration was to determine precisely what was the most important piece of machinery. Then he had to get into the factory and put that machine out of action by destroying some component that he knew could not be repaired or replaced for a while. He had to use a few hundred grams of explosive, making sure that it was in contact with the metal. A small amount like this produces a relatively minor blast, which hardly affects the rest of the machine. Contact with the metal was essential to produce the required shockwave, like a tremendous hammer blow, which was transmitted through the metal and caused it to fracture. The effect would be nullified if there was even the tiniest gap between explosive charge and metal, or if some shock-absorbing material came between them. You can therefore understand that the saboteur really needed to know precisely where and how to place the charge, which meant that he first had to have reliable information. He needed above all to succeed at the first attempt. Otherwise he ran the risk of never getting a second chance; if the first explosion failed, attracting enemy attention, it would lead them to reinforce the factory's security arrangements, and perhaps to discover and deal with certain laxness, accomplices or mistakes that had been turned to the saboteur's advantage.

1. Cowburn, op.cit.

Whatever the target was, success was always completely dependent on advance research. Take a familiar example, the steam locomotive. These had become primary targets because they were used for transporting heavy goods. Put a small bomb on the side of the engine's boiler, and it will be undamaged. Put the bomb on a wheel or axle and it will have virtually no effect on their heavy steel construction. Hide the bomb in the coal to be shovelled into the furnace, and any damage will probably be easy enough to repair in the workshops. But put the bomb against the blocks supporting the steam cylinder and the locomotive might be out of action for months. These cylinder blocks are made of cast iron and so are easily cracked. Moreover, these are parts that don't normally wear out and the workshops tend not to keep many in stock. It takes quite a while to manufacture new ones.

There were also various forms of sabotage that did not require explosives: these demanded a certain element of skill if they were to be really effective.

The training that agents were given in England included instruction in all these methods, so that they in turn could instruct new recruits. It was very important to teach the resistance workers properly, for it was a question not only of achieving satisfactory results but of preventing brave men from risking their lives in vain. . . .

[*But as we know, the basic method was to use plastic explosive. Cowburn goes on to describe one typical incident in which he took part:*]

From time to time, after there had been a parachute drop and all the goods had been transferred to our munitions depot, I would have to perform a small task: the construction of a few bombs. This involved slicing the explosive into cubes about seven or eight centimetres square. Inside each cube one had to bury a small cylinder with a hole in it, made of solid explosive; this was called the 'primer', and it contained a length of detonator wire, both ends of which had to come out through one side of the cube. (When the time came, these wires would be attached to the detonator and the device would be armed.) The bomb was then wrapped in a black cloth tied on with a few bits of insulating tape.

The smell of almonds given off by the plastic explosive used to fill the house; and when I was working, sitting at the table in my shirt sleeves and surrounded by piles of grenades, incendiary devices and row upon row of machine guns and pistols, it suddenly dawned on me that I must look just like the villain in a melodrama, preparing to blow up some Grand Duke. I lacked only the long moustache and whiskers.

Philippe de Vomécourt, too, has written about some of the operations he took part in – notably 'the art of blowing up bridges'. Here are three of the incidents he describes:[1]

There was one bridge that particularly interested us. The Germans had forbidden civilians to use it and had posted sentries all around, which complicated our usual routine. After giving the matter some thought, Alex came up with an idea.

We began by buying a pony and trap, a very elegant-looking affair, and Alex bought himself the sort of clothes a well-to-do country gentleman might wear. Alex was very keen on horses, and he took great pleasure in driving around the countryside for the next few days. Soon everyone had got used to seeing him around, and he felt ready to risk visiting the bridge. The sentry saw him but said nothing. Alex slowed down – a horse should never be allowed to trot across a bridge – and took full advantage of this chance to see where a bomb could be put to best effect. Mentally working out how much explosive he would need, he raised his cap politely to the soldiers and calmly crossed the bridge. He spent a few hours trotting around, regretting that he couldn't always work under these conditions. Finally he returned across the bridge, and the sentry, staring admiringly at this fine-looking turn-out, made no attempt to stop him.

One night about two weeks later, Alex blew up the bridge, rendering it quite unusable. No one saw the pony and trap again till after the war. Resistance fighters had one great advantage over regular soldiers in that we could choose when and how to act; and the regular army would never have agreed to finance the purchase of a thoroughbred pony and trap for such an indirect operation . . .

There was another bridge that gave us a bit of a headache. It was not very big but it carried a main road over the canal, and it too was guarded. Alex knew exactly how much explosive he would need, and the only problem was how to place the bomb under the bridge without the guards seeing. As local inhabitants were not prevented from using the bridge, however, the idea seemed perfectly feasible.

One of my men went for a stroll round the area and returned with encouraging news: 'There's a barge on the canal, barely ten metres from the bridge. If we could just get the barge underneath it . . .'

His plan worked very well. We just paid out the mooring rope a little bit more each day, and the barge inched towards the bridge,

1. From Philippe de Vomécourt, op.cit.

moving so gradually that no one noticed, until one day it was just underneath the first arch. Time to start work, we decided.

Alex and his team took up their positions. Three men were posted as look-outs, with orders to overpower the guards if the alarm was raised. Alex had prepared two charges of plastic explosive. He climbed down onto the barge with them, followed by another member of the team carrying a stepladder. A third man eased out the rope a bit further until the barge was directly under the bridge, then moored it securely. In the silence of the night, Alex climbed up the stepladder and set to work with characteristic, unhurried skill. He began by fixing the first charge, then his companion held up the second one for him to take; bigger than the first, this was the one that would do the real damage. But the bomb slipped from Alex's hand – though it didn't fall far. Alex could feel it on the rung beside his foot. Holding his breath, he bent down and managed to reach it without losing his balance. Quickly he set about fixing it in position on the bridge; but before he had finished, the timing mechanism snapped and set the delayed-action fuse going.

Alex skidded down the stepladder and dashed ashore. The member of the team who had moored the barge was waiting for him on the bank, but the man who had been on the barge with Alex was nowhere to be seen.

'Didn't he come ashore?' Alex whispered.

'No one else has come ashore since I got here.'

They waded into the water and found the man unconscious. Hoisting him up the bank, they carried him off to where their three companions were on guard. Alex had calculated that the bomb would go off within ten minutes – but twelve minutes had passed already, in perfect silence.

'Something must have gone wrong when it dropped,' Alex said. He decided to go and check.

'Hold on,' the others told him, 'you won't be back so quick if that thing goes off while you're looking at it.'

Alex was in no great hurry to reach heaven before his time. He let himself be persuaded.

Thirteen, fourteen minutes . . . Then 'that thing' exploded. A blinding flash, a glorious bang; the bridge had gone up in the air, and with it went two of the sentries, beating Alex to heaven.

When the unconscious man came to, he explained that when Alex had dropped the package containing the bomb, it had bounced off his head and then onto the rung by Alex's foot; and he considered the lump which now adorned his skull had been acquired in a very good cause . . .

During this period [*continues Philippe de Vomécourt*] a new kind of device appeared which the maquisards regarded as a total abomination: giant cranes, which the Germans had brought in to lift locomotives back onto the tracks when they'd been derailed by a mine.

One of these cranes, with a sixty-ton capacity, was kept on sidings on the south bank of the Loire. The Germans would move it around in a convoy consisting of two locomotives – one at each end – and several wagons on either side of the crane, equipped with machine guns and mortars. At any given time, therefore, the crane was ready to move in the required direction, well protected against possible attack, and in the event of a derailment only the front locomotive and leading wagons would be affected. Day after day we saw this crane repairing all trace of the havoc we had caused, and wondered how we could damage it sufficiently to keep it temporarily out of action (we didn't want to destroy it completely as it might be useful to us later on).

In the end we decided to use the Piat – a weapon that we used very seldom and usually without much success. It is a spring gun, very heavy, and it fires a sort of rocket. The technique for using it is rather like the technique for using a naval cannon. One must 'aim' at the target before it appears; in other words, in our case we would have to estimate the time that would elapse between the order to fire and the moment when the crane appeared directly in line with the rocket.

The day after we had made this decision, we spent several hours watching the convoy's movements, trying to estimate its speed by counting the number of seconds it took to cover a set distance and practising the order to fire. The operation was arranged for the following morning.

Alex and three other men from his team had found a spot with an excellent view of the railway line, and they arrived early. They manoeuvred the Piat into position, then lay down among bushes to wait. It was a glorious summer's morning, clear and warm, and the air was fresh and sweetly scented.

'There it is!' The locomotive was just appearing round the bend. Everyone immediately started counting off the seconds, then – 'Fire!' Alex pulled the trigger and the rocket flew off. It hit the front wheel of the wagon on which the crane was mounted, exactly as we had planned. Slowly the monstrous machine began to topple to one side; it looked like an ugly, ill-proportioned steamboat floundering. Then it crashed to the ground. The French railwaymen who were on the convoy tumbled out of their seats and came down to inspect the damage, shaking their heads in mock despair. The Germans rushed around, shooting in all directions; but Alex and his companions had already left the scene of their triumph with more haste than dignity.

In addition to bringing down the crane and destroying numerous canal locks, Alex had notched up scores of other successful hits. He had mined more than thirty roads, put over twenty telephone lines out of action, and demolished thirteen bridges in all. He always wanted to make it fourteen, but the opportunity never arose.

Before leaving this account of sabotage operations, it is worth mentioning one outstanding achievement in this field: the operation at the Peugeot plant in Sochaux. This is how Cookridge tells the story:[1]

The great motorcar works of Peugeot at Sochaux had been for a long time a priority target of the Ministry of Economic Warfare in London. Although Monsieur Robert Peugeot . . . secretly supported the resistance he was compelled to submit his factories to German control. The Sochaux works manufactured tank turrets and vehicles for the German Wehrmacht.

The RAF had carried out several bombing raids on the works, but the damage was slight and production was stepped up after the Germans had brought, in the summer of 1943, their own technicians to Sochaux. The workers, constantly threatened with deportation or imprisonment, had to do their jobs. The problem of the Peugeot works was discussed by Ministry of Economic Warfare officials with the Chiefs of Staff and officers of Bomber Command. Eventually it was suggested that the French Section of SOE should be brought in. Colonel Buckmaster asked Harry Rée to destroy the works by sabotage action.

This was a tall order, but Henri [Harry Rée] was determined to carry it out. The motor works were heavily guarded by day and night by strong units of German Field Police. A complicated system of passes had been introduced and every worker, clerk and visitor was searched on entering and leaving the factory area. Through his host at Valentigney, Henri had met Monsieur Sire, the personnel manager of the Sochaux works. Sire secretly supported the resistance, provided passes, and arranged that Henri should see Robert Peugeot.

'Monsieur Peugeot, I'm a British officer,' Henri said. 'Your factories are producing gun-carriers and tank turrets for German panzers. I know you don't like it, but you have to do it. We must put a stop to this business. We must blow up your works.'

1. Cookridge, op.cit.

Peugeot looked at him quietly. Then he said with a smile: 'I shall be delighted. But as the head of my family concern I find your suggestion a little . . . well . . . a little upsetting.'

'I quite understand that, and I'm sorry,' Harry Rée replied. 'But the Sochaux works is a major war objective. Air raids failed to destroy the factory. If sabotage fails, we must expect more bombing. It will probably cause a lot of casualties among the workers and civilian population. None of us wants this to happen. In a direct sabotage action we could pinpoint the target, let's say the transformer hall, the power supply, the assembly workshops. But this is only possible if I have your help.'

Robert Peugeot agreed. It was a brave decision for a man who had devoted his life to his factories to organize their destruction. Not only did he give the plans of the factory to Harry Rée and help to select the points for placing the explosives, but he also put him in touch with two trustworthy men who worked at his factory and who could carry out the actual operation. One was the foreman Schorp, an Alsatian who worked in the upholstery workshop, the other André van der Straaten, who became the contact between Schorp and Henri.

Preparations took several weeks. Harry Rée told me it was largely due to these two men that the explosion was confined to the factory area and that the town was spared. At ten minutes to midnight the party of five men whom Rée had selected entered the factory grounds. Schorp and van der Straaten had hidden themselves in clothes lockers on the office floor when the factory was closed in the evening. The plastic explosives had been smuggled into the Peugeot works during the day and hidden in small boxes in a cleaner's cupboard. Two members of the party who had passkeys freed the locked-in men and then left.

Schorp and van der Straaten placed the charges in the transformer hall, the assembly plant and the steel presses – machines which were extremely difficult to replace. Knowing every nook and corner of the factory, they succeeded in avoiding the sentries and let themselves out through the nightwatchman's room.

At ten minutes past midnight the Peugeot works were blasted by a series of heavy explosions. Fires started in a dozen places and within minutes large parts of the plant lay in ruins. The fire brigades, rushed from towns and villages in the vicinity, could do little but keep the conflagration from spreading. Within minutes SS and army units arrived and the whole area was cordoned off.

Next morning hundreds of workers employed at Peugeot's stood idly around while frantic Gestapo officials began their investigations. Nearly all the presses had been blown up, and there was no chance of restarting work for many weeks. The Germans arrested a few suspects, but Schorp, van der Straaten and their helpmates had escaped.

The German engineers were determined to restart production as quickly as possible. New presses for the tank turrets were sent from the Goering works at Fallersleben near Hanover. To get them to Sochaux the Germans had to use barges on the Rhine-Doubs canal. Rée and his friends had envisaged this possibility. As soon as the transport arrived – which took a few weeks – van der Straaten and his comrades decided to blow up the barges. The Canal du Doubs ran through a narrow artificial bed near Medière, behind some bombed factories and disused yards. There the saboteurs ambushed the first barge, opening fire from Sten guns. The French crew jumped ashore and ran for their lives; the German guards returned the fire, but were overpowered. Explosives were placed on the barge and it was blown up, blocking the narrow stretch of the canal.

This was a particularly gratifying success because the canal was used by the Germans for the transport of midget submarines from the east to the Mediterranean. Several weeks passed before the damage was repaired and another transport arrived, carrying two new steel presses, this time from a factory near Stuttgart. It was heavily guarded and SS men patrolled the shores. An ambush was impossible and Harry Rée's men decided to attack the transport when it reached Sochaux.

This was carried out in bright daylight as soon as the presses arrived on huge trucks in the factory yard. Hand grenades were showered at the trucks and several home-made bombs were lobbed from the roof of one of the buildings. Even after several months and much effort to replace the damaged machines, the production of tank turrets could not be resumed. The factory was not restored to its full capacity until the end of the war.

The Peugeot Works, earmarked by the Ministry of Economic Warfare as 'the third most important industrial target in France', which the Allied bomber raids failed to destroy, was thus successfully sabotaged by a handful of SOE men.

SOE agents, both British and French, were effectively outlaws and would never have managed to survive without the voluntary help and support of local French citizens. As Mao Tse-tung said of the Chinese partisans, clandestine activity stands no chance of real success unless the perpetrators can infiltrate the local population 'like fishes in water'.

To illustrate such partisan aid, let us follow two particular episodes. The first is taken from Ben Cowburn's book *No Cloak, No Dagger*. When

Cowburn found he had to travel from the Occupied to the Unoccupied Zone, he heard through a friend in the resistance that he could get help from some very willing railwaymen. At his friend's suggestion, he asked them for assistance and they readily agreed. This is how Cowburn himself described the events that followed:

As twilight fell, I put on the overalls and the three of us left the house together. We crossed the marshalling yards via a footbridge stretching right across the network of sidings. Passing the sentry's hut, we went down the steps towards the engine shops. All around us, goods trains were shunting noisily back and forth. French and German employees were busily coupling and uncoupling the links; armed soldiers were perched on some of the wagons. Other workers in overalls were, like us, moving around between the trains, and we managed to reach our locomotive without attracting attention. We stopped beside the tender; another engine standing on the track beside it hid us from the soldiers. The tender was enormous, much bigger than a British one. After glancing quickly around, my friends pushed me under the tender, between two wheels. Raising my head, I found that I was crouching under a black hole beneath the water tank. Everywhere else, the tender was supported lengthways by the chassis, but at this particular point there was a gap about two feet long and six feet wide, which you could only see from directly underneath as the tender's side walls were solid. (Incidentally, I never did discover the technical reason for this space below the tender; I can only suppose that some clairvoyant engineers dreamed it up especially to hide British spies!)

I hoisted myself onto the bogies and found I was in a cavity about two feet high. My friends then passed me some thick planks which I laid across the bogies underneath me, thus giving my hiding place a floor. Through the gaps between the planks I could see part of the axles and the wheels, as well as the rails and sleepers. I couldn't sit upright but was fairly comfortable when I stretched out, and there was no danger of my falling out onto the track.

A few minutes later I heard a grating noise and the wheels began to turn slowly backwards. I saw the sleepers passing under me, and several points, then felt the brakes being applied and we came to a standstill. There was a slight bump as we stopped and I realized we had shunted into a train which was about to be coupled up to us. Noises from all around the station reached me through gaps in the planking. There were a couple of whistle blasts, then the wheels started turning again – forwards this time.

The journey had begun. For a few minutes the constant rattling and grinding indicated that we were passing over dozens of points. Then they grew less; we must have reached the main line. Our speed increased, as did the noise, and as night fell the sleepers became just a dark blur, occasionally flash-lit by a burning cinder falling into the boiler's ash pan. Stretched out on my back, unable to see the outside world except by looking down, I was in fact in more or less the same position as on the aircraft that had brought me to France – although at a considerably lower altitude. I decided that, if all went well, I would travel the same way again whenever I had to cross from one zone to the other.

After half an hour or so, the brakes squealed and the train slowed down. We must have been at Langon, the last station inside the Occupied Zone, where we stayed for fifty minutes while the Germans searched the carriages. Several times I saw lights flashing on the rails and ground beneath me, as though torches were being shone under the tender. I heard a lot of comings and goings but felt completely safe in my little cubby-hole. At last the whistle gave a few blasts and the wheels started rolling. A few minutes later we stopped again. This time we were at La Réole, the first station inside the Unoccupied Zone. The beam of a flashlight was aimed on the ground below me, and through the planking I heard the engine driver say, 'You can come out now, and travel the rest of the way with us.' I squeezed to one side and piled the planks on top of each other so that I could remove them and give them to the driver. I dropped down onto the track and dodged between the wheels. Then, climbing the ladder, I found myself in the bright glow of the cab, between the array of levers, dials and other instruments covering the boiler and the coal chute of the tender.

I asked if a third man standing on the footplate would not seem a little unusual. My friends replied that there weren't any Boches here, and if anyone asked awkward questions we should say that I was an engineer making an inspection, and tell him to mind his own business . . .

Ben Cowburn would later use this same form of transport on many different occasions, for it proved a very safe way of crossing the Demarcation Line.

Sometimes the SOE people received help from unexpected quarters. The following extract is taken from Philippe de Vomécourt's book, *Les Artisans de la Liberté*:

There was no safer hiding place than in a brothel reserved for the Germans. A man on the run could be sure there was nothing to fear in such a place, with its rooms occupied by soldiers and its staircase echoing to the noise of their boots. No one ever searched a brothel; what could the Germans find there except other Germans?

Many brothels kept at least two rooms 'free' and put them at the disposal of the resistance, for the use of agents who had been sent to France and were now waiting to return to Britain. Other brothels, too, would never turn away an Allied airman. But things did not always go according to plan.

One British pilot, who was waiting for an escape circuit to make arrangements for his crossing into Spain, ended up staying in a brothel for over a month. He was well looked after and every need supplied. But one day, as he was going into his room the pilot was seen by a German officer. This officer had taken a fancy to one of the brothel girls whose room was next to the pilot's, and the German thought he had seen the man in civilian clothes entering her room.

'Who is this? What's he doing here? How did he get in?'

Madame had to come and calm the German down. She explained that this was an old friend of the girl's, who called in from time to time to say hello. But the German officer took a lot of convincing.

'Tell him to leave! Throw him out!' he kept shouting. 'Get him out at once – he's got no right to be here!'

The British pilot had to be hurried out of the house, pursued into the street by the German's yells of rage. It had been a close shave, and he was losing his excellent place of refuge; but happily the trouble ended there and he eventually managed to escape from France without further complications.

French brothels are undoubtedly seen as more romantic than those of other countries. The madame is ever alert to her clients' individual tastes. Her girls are always prettier and kinder than anywhere else in the world. For my part, I have always appreciated the help they gave us in the resistance.

One of the girls in Lyons had a permit to use a car. The Germans all knew her and trusted her implicitly. This was very useful to us, since we could use her car to transport agents, escapees and radio operators – always a very risky business. She used to go shopping for the Germans, but always kept some of the food she bought them to give to resistance workers and anyone sheltering clandestine guests. She worked for us from 1940 right through to the end of the war.

Many of the prostitutes served us very well. For instance, they took advantage of every opportunity – admittedly these opportunities were somewhat exceptional – to remove certain documents, have them photographed and then replace them before the client wanted to get dressed again.

Following a conversation that I overheard on a train one day, about British pilots eating carrots to improve their vision, I heard from a Paris optician that heroin produced the opposite effect. I asked SOE to get me a supply.

'What for?' they asked.

'I'll tell you later – when I know if it works . . .'

I duly received one kilogram of heroin, which must have been the subject of much debate in London. It arrived in the American diplomatic bag, and was handed over to the military attaché of a neutral country.

But I still had to find a way of feeding the drug to the Luftwaffe pilots. Where could I find the sort of people who were close enough to the German aircrews, and on a regular basis, to give them the drug without their noticing? The problem seemed insoluble.

There was a heavy concentration of Luftwaffe forces in the Tours area. I called on several brothel-keepers in the town and told them what I was planning. They agreed to help by recruiting girls who supported the resistance cause.

Some of the Germans were already taking heroin, and all we had to do was sell it to them. Others turned up at the brothels pretty drunk, and were easily persuaded to try 'just a little pinch, to see what it's like . . .'; the consequent feeling of well-being would then encourage them to try it again. For those who refused, the 'little pinch' would be hidden in a cigarette which, all unsuspecting, they would smoke.

The result was that a considerable number of Luftwaffe fighter pilots began to have trouble with their vision; each month their regular medical check-up would show that their sight was getting worse.

Inevitably, an inquiry was launched. The doctors questioned them endlessly about their habits, their hobbies, what they ate, what they drank, what they smoked. And by comparing the pilots' answers, the doctors discovered that all the men whose sight was affected had one thing in common: they all went to the local brothels. Moreover, some of them were very obviously drug addicts. The inquiry went on for several months, and fresh questioning revealed to the military authorities which of the local brothels were involved. As a result, the Germans arrested two prostitutes and both of them were shot. Brave women that they were, they had never underestimated the risks they ran.

Many similar instances of patriotism and covert but effective action, of enormous value to the resistance, can be found among the experiences of men like Philippe de Vomécourt, Benjamin Cowburn and their comrades in battle.

The civilians who worked for SOE or any of the resistance organizations had invariably made a personal choice, a decision to join the battle. But as we have seen, their decision was almost always the result of a random combination of circumstances. A man who volunteered to help SOE was taking a heavy burden of responsibility on himself, especially if he was still living on French soil – and even more especially if he happened to have a family.

At first the civilian volunteer did not always understand what the undercover fight would entail. He would henceforth have to live as an outlaw, never trusting anybody – not only for his own safety but also because he was responsible for his comrades' safety too. The deciding factor might initially have been a personal taste for danger; but later on, this was never enough, when his prime consideration became an absolute respect for orders and the self-discipline imposed by this new world he had entered.

This meant, above all, that he would have to lie to everyone around him, even – perhaps especially – to his nearest and dearest; his wife and children should never know anything about the head of the family's clandestine activity. If a wife did know about her husband's decision, he had to insist on her total discretion. Most difficult of all, he could never tell her what he was doing, even details that might have seemed very trivial (such as the name of that little restaurant where one could still find such marvellous food – and where he met other clandestine workers). It was also very hard for some agents to fit in with ordinary family life when they were asked to move somewhere, or to travel round the country, either without any explanation to the family or else with explanations that were false.

It also meant that he had to set aside all political opinions, personal ethics, views on religion, etc: the only thing that mattered now was the battle in hand, regardless of the individual's private ideas.

And finally it also meant that he had to learn the need for dissimulation. For example, if someone he met expressed disapproval of sabotage and complained that it was destroying the nation's livelihood, or that it wasn't really hurting the German war potential, he simply had to agree. The point was that the resistance must achieve its objectives; and to this end, the volunteer should never be suspected of sympathizing with those objectives, even if it made him look like a coward – and that, in wartime, is a very unpleasant position indeed.

Furthermore, the civilian who wanted to help SOE could never indulge in political discussions with friends, neighbours, colleagues at work, etc. He had, in effect, to make sure he was never noticed.

Once he had joined the fight, his decision was irrevocable. He soon knew too much about underground activities to be able to leave without endangering his companions in arms. Besides, senior SOE officers would do all in their power to 'put him out to grass'; or if the man had totally 'blown it' they would send him to Britain for an indefinite period – sometimes until the end of the war – which meant that he was totally cut off from his family.

Volunteering to help SOE demanded not just courage (for as General de Gaulle said, to join the fight was 'to hope against hope') but also a certain altruism. The fight must never be contaminated by selfish considerations, whether personal or collective – for example, hoping the victory would bring oneself financial gain, medals or status; or on the other hand hoping that one's Party would come out of the conflict as a stronger organization, better able to play a major role in post-war politics.

In short, clandestine warfare was synonymous with total dedication and blind obedience to orders.

It cannot be stressed too strongly that the overwhelming need was to protect the SOE agents' security, for they were exposed by the very nature of their undercover work to all the prohibitions imposed by the masters of the moment, the Germans and the Vichy régime.

It was vital that a secret agent should choose carefully when deciding where to live. He had to find somewhere that was not too close to the places where he met his contacts, or he might be tempted to go straight home afterwards. In fact, no matter where the meeting was, he should never go back the same way he had come, but make a wide detour on the homeward journey. And he should never enter his house until he was sure it was not being watched. It was also advisable that SOE agents should look for one or more alternative hide-outs – *planques* or safe-houses as they called them. Ideally they would find a single room, preferably self-contained and if possible with more than one exit. An agent generally visited his *planque* as little as possible, and went there only when he was in real danger; otherwise, if he were under surveillance, the house would become known to his pursuers and it would no longer be safe.

Some clandestine operations forced SOE agents to work together. For this sort of eventuality they set up all manner of innocent-seeming insurance agencies and businesses.

The greatest risk arose when two or more agents had to meet. (For security reasons, no one knew the names of more then a few of his fellow agents.) The venue had to be chosen very carefully: a doctor's waiting room, for example, where strangers could come and go without attracting attention. It had to have an emergency exit and the whole premises had to be thoroughly checked out in advance. Finally there should be one or more look-outs, to raise the alarm if necessary.

The SOE agent also had to find one or more hiding places in his flat, office or safe-house. The items he might have to hide would vary a great deal in size, and depended on what sort of activity he was involved in; they ranged from coded messaged written on cigarette papers to Sten guns or cases of explosives. Some of the commonest hiding places included the cupboard with a false base, the narrow gap behind the electricity fuse box, the partition between rooms where heating pipes might run, and so on. Further examples are given by E. Reval:[1]

> Take the bathroom, for instance. Suppose there is a built-in cupboard around the bidet, as there so often is, with a lid on top and a container for dirty linen underneath. If we lift not just the lid but the whole frame, we'll find the first hiding place below it. We'll call this the 'trick' hiding place, since it contains nothing of any value. To find the real hiding place, we have to remove the board which separates the bottom of the laundry box from the cavity below, then lift up the laundry box and look inside the base. As can be imagined, even if an informer tells the police, they will usually be content with whatever is revealed in the first cavity, and it won't even occur to them to search any further.
>
> In another cupboard the hiding place might be concealed behind a decorative metal grid. The grid has a hinge which snaps shut automatically, but it can be opened by inserting a blade into one particular slit at the top. This might conceal a space as large as the whole floor area of a room, capable of hiding two tons of weapons.
>
> I once saw a piece of office furniture that comprised a block of three filing cabinets fixed on one base. Remove the bottom drawer from one of the cabinets, undo two large screws and pull the whole lot towards you in a certain way. It then pivots on the base, revealing a recess about two metres long. Resistance workers used this recess to hide plans of railway stations, air bases, munitions factories, military installations and fuel stores. Some of these plans were more than six metres wide when fully opened out, and any one of them could have resulted in death for dozens of men. But despite frequent searches of the office in question, the Gestapo never did discover this precious hiding place.

The SOE agent also had to take enormous care over contacting someone. He could never rely on ordinary methods of communication like letters or the telephone. He had only two possible alternatives: using the 'letter-box' or meeting the contact in person. The letter-box was usually a mail box in the hall of a block of flats, preferably an open hall and a house which was

1. Quoted in M. Ruby, op.cit.

either empty – where the occupants were absent, perhaps as prisoners of war – or which sympathetic tenants or owners had made available to the resistance.

There were numerous precautions to be observed. A note could never be left in the box while there was anyone else in the hall, even a child. If the concierge could see into the hall, the agent had to check that she was not around before he made the drop. If the mail boxes were outside individual flats, the agent had to climb the stairs to the very top of the building, to confuse any pursuers, and only make the drop on his way down. There were also certain ways of alerting the agent; for example, the way the name plates were displayed could indicate whether the coast was clear or not, whether there was anything to collect or not, and so on. Obviously, once a box was 'blown', the agent immediately had to warn everyone else, to prevent notes being left there which might compromise the tenant or put themselves in danger, or even threaten the whole group; and also to prevent other couriers from walking into a trap when they tried to deliver something.

The other method of communication was to arrange a meeting in person. This was no casual encounter; it was a very serious business. Punctuality was of paramount importance. A fifteen-minute margin was generally considered safe but a man who kept hanging around for much longer than that would certainly get himself noticed. The venue itself had to be selected with care, as the agent had to avoid the sort of place that was more or less permanently under surveillance, such as bus stations, factory gates, large cafés, railway stations and their waiting rooms, etc. Timing had to be considered, too, so that the meeting place was not totally deserted; the best times were between eleven and two o'clock and from five to seven in the evening.

An agent who had arranged to meet someone would have to make his way there very cautiously, above all to make certain that he was not followed. There were numerous techniques he could use. Obviously he couldn't keep turning round, but he could stop in front of a shop window and watch the reflections of those who happened to be nearby, and just glance round. Or he could suddenly turn left or right down a side street, quickly noting who was following him and who was just ahead, then continue walking down the side street for a few yards before turning and retracing his steps; this was the best way to spot anyone that might be tailing him, because the follower would have to do the same, while someone watching him from ahead would have to turn round very quickly and thus give himself away.

If danger threatened, the meeting could be arranged in two stages. First, the person who had called for the meeting would apparently come out of, say, the first house in a particular street, while his companion simultaneously appeared from a house at the other end of the street and on the opposite side; they would walk towards each other and as they passed they would give some imperceptible sign of acknowledgement. Then the first person would continue straight on while his contact casually turned round and followed him, finally catching up with him much further on.

Meetings were always arranged at least an hour apart. The agent was also well advised to avoid going to two meetings in a row, because this could lead to several of his contacts being captured one after another if he himself was being tailed.

Naturally the SOE agent had to stay constantly alert. He could never read a newspaper or a magazine while travelling, even on public transport, in case he dropped his guard. He had to be suspicious of everyone, for his pursuers might be disguised as respectable old gentlemen, middle-class businessmen or even beggars. He had to abstain from amorous entanglements in case that charming young girl who started chatting to him so casually and who seemed so ingenuous might be working for the enemy.

The agent also had to avoid any rash moves, for the least slip might cost him his liberty or his life, or put his colleagues at risk. He should never mention his activities in ordinary conversation. He should never try to discover the real names or homes of any contacts outside his immediate circle. When he went out he should never take his lists of names or addresses of letter-boxes or safe-houses. He was expressly forbidden to keep a notebook to remind himself of appointments. He had to make sure that all his contacts learned by heart the addresses they would have to use. He and his colleagues should call each other only by their code names, and these could often change.

Needless to say, the agent also had to be able to hold his tongue, and never let himself drink too much. He also had to be wary of using both his telephone and his typewriter. Contrary to widespread belief, a 'bugged' line is not always detectable by clicking noises or crackling; even in those days, tapping techniques were silent and imperceptible. The Vichy authorities and the Germans both made extensive use of wire taps. The new recruit was therefore advised to avoid the telephone for anything to do with resistance matters. The typewriter too, however indispensable, was far from anonymous. Each machine could betray itself with tiny defects and irregularities, which would be reproduced in every letter; the police could easily tell whether a given document had been produced on a particular machine. If possible, it was better to use only new typewriters, which would have fewer defects, or ones that had been recently serviced. It was also necessary to find a hiding place for the machine when it wasn't in use. Finally, all carbon papers had to be destroyed; it would have been all too easy to look through them and see a good part of what had been typed.

But, despite all their precautions, some of SOE's agents did not manage to escape falling into enemy hands.

Capture might result from a slip-up, but was more often due to an informer or a traitor. Either way, the agent was never very surprised, for this was a natural hazard in the clandestine, illegal life that he led.

The only way to react was to deny everything and never budge from that position. This required exceptional determination, however, for the enemy usually resorted to torture in his efforts to make the prisoner talk. But there were also attempts to bribe some prisoners with offers of money or immunity from prosecution. No doubt many of those who were tortured did eventually talk, but they were never reproached for breaking under such circumstances. The essential thing was to say as little as possible, and to mix fact with fiction. And, if possible, warn everyone else so that they could take the necessary precautions themselves.

On the subject of money, we must not ignore the fact that financial inducements did play a certain part in proceedings. There were many traitors who sold their colleagues for money. The Germans offered considerable sums to those who could help them catch secret agents. But the very thorough selection and training processes helped to make SOE's agents much less vulnerable here than other resistance workers.

The captured SOE agent was on his own, even if he shared a cell with other prisoners. At all costs he had to avoid confiding in his fellow unfortunates – one of whom was often a 'stool-pigeon'. He could not even confide in his lawyer, if he was allowed one; he had to be content with asking the lawyer to defend him solely on points of law, never on the real facts of the case. And he had to preserve his morale and dignity in the presence of all, whether guards or fellow prisoners.

Undercover work, by uniting SOE agents and other resistance fighters in the dangerous world of illegal operations, turned them into new men. By forcing them continually to surpass themselves, it built up an élite force. But it also caused suffering and death.

# — PART III —

## SOE IN FRANCE

# — 1 —

# THE RECKONING

SOE's first operations on French soil have been mentioned at the beginning of this book – notably Savannah (15 March to 5 April, 1941), Fidelity (25 April, 1941) and Josephine B (11 May to 6 June, 1941). But that was just the start, for their activities continued right up to the end of the war. It would be impossible to examine them all in detail, but the following chronological account provides a general outline.

The first agents that SOE's F Section sent to France had arrived during the full moon of May, 1941. The very first was the legendary Georges Begué, who jumped blind – in other words, without a reception committee to meet him – on the night of 5/6 May; he landed near Châteauroux, between Valançay and Vatan. On the 11th it was the turn of Pierre de Vomécourt ('Lucas'), who also landed near Châteauroux, and on the 13th Roger Cottin (Albert') landed in Britanny. They had all been given the same orders: start creating a network of underground groups.

We have already seen something of the admirable work that Pierre de Vomécourt did. Cottin was less fortunate; he ran into various difficulties and had to join Pierre as deputy head of the Autogiro network which Lucas had set up. Georges Begué ('George Noble') had to make an exhausting trek by night, carrying his transmitter set, to the home of retired politician Maxime Hymans, a friend of Thomas Cadett who was running SOE's F Section at the time. Hymans ('Max') immediately put Begué in touch with several reliable men, including Renan the chemist and Fleuret ('Espadon') the garage owner, both in Châteauroux. Begué radioed London on 9 May to tell them Renan's address, which thus became SOE's first letter-box in France.

On 13 June, Philippe de Vomécourt, recruited by his brother, received the first arms drop intended for SOE operations; it landed on his own estate, Bas-Soleil, twenty kilometres from Limoges.

Also in June, a Chilean-born actress by the name of Giliana Balmaceda, now an SOE agent, arrived in France to spend three weeks in Lyons and Vichy, ostensibly on holiday, for her papers were completely above board. She was to return to Britain with a vast mass of information about conditions in France, which proved enormously valuable to SOE agents on later missions. Giliana's husband was an Englishman, Victor Gerson ('Vic'), who later became head of SOE's most important escape line. Two other special agents were also setting up escape lines at this time: Daniel Deligant ('Defoe'), a Frenchman who lived in Lisbon and whose escape route led to Spain; and René Bertholet ('Robert'), a Swiss socialist whose route ended in Switzerland.

On the night of 9 July, Burdeyron ('Gaston') was parachuted back into his native France, making a blind landing near Avranches with his radio operator ('Xavier'). But Xavier was caught the following day; he was arrested for his part in some previous criminal activities. Burdeyron had been supposed to start up a group in west Normandy; but, deprived of his only means of communicating with London, he sought refuge at his wife's home in Deauville. He did not remain idle, however, and completed the reconnaissance work at Carpiquet air base that Henri Labit had been unable to finish. Quite by chance, in Caen one day he bumped into Pierre de Vomécourt – the two men had met during training in Britain – and thanks to Pierre, the information that Burdeyron had collected was passed on to Lyons; and Burdeyron then joined Pierre's network.

Burdeyron's intended mission had been planned by SOE's F Section, but Operation Torture was set up by RF Section, which worked with the Gaullists. The Torture team were flown to France on the night of 8/9 July, landing near Caen; it comprised two young men from the Free French army, Henri Labit and Cartigny, his radio operator. Colonel Passy asserted that Torture's objective was 'to establish contact with a regional organization'; M. R. D. Foot, on the other hand, indicates that the plan had been 'to investigate the chances of sabotage at the large German air base of Carpiquet by Caen'. Whatever the reason for their mission, the villager who was supposed to be sheltering the two men denounced them to the Germans. Labit managed to escape and found his way to another group in Toulouse, but Cartigny was caught and shot.

Another mission arranged by F Section was Operation Tilleul. On the night of 6 August, two F Section agents were dropped near Saint-Désiré in the Allier: Jacques Vaillant de Guélis, the leader, and Georges Turck, his radio operator.

Turck ('Christophe' or 'Christa'), who injured himself when he landed, was caught the following morning, but had an amazing escape thanks to the intervention of Colonel Rivet, a Sûreté officer and member of the Vichy High Command. In fact, Rivet told the local authorities that he himself had sent Lieutenant Turck to England on a special mission to infiltrate British

Intelligence, and that they had sent Turck back because they thought he was going to collaborate with them!

Turck duly reached the south of France and was soon setting up communications both with London and with SOE's agents in Marseilles.

Meanwhile, Jacques de Guélis took less than a month to accomplish his mission. He began by collecting all the latest information on conditions in France, and every possible document that would help future SOE agents: ration cards, demob papers, official stamps, etc. Above all he started recruiting local volunteers for SOE, some of whom were to prove invaluable – such as Jean Pierre-Bloch, Dr Lévy from Antibes, Robert Lyon, Francois Garel and Philippe Liewer among others. He also paved the way for the first woman to be given the role of field officer for SOE – Virginia Hall. She reached Lyons from Spain at the end of August, and as we have already seen she was to play a major part in future operations.

In September, sixteen new agents were dropped in France, ten of them from F Section and five from RF Section (with Passy's agreement). The sixteenth was a Polish army officer, Count Dziergowski; his mission, codenamed Adjudicate, was to create a network of saboteurs recruited from among the 4,000 demobbed Poles who were now in unoccupied France. And, despite numerous difficulties, he eventually managed to recruit eighty-seven Polish soldiers.

Before Major de Guélis left France, he met Jean Pierre-Bloch in the Châteauroux area. Pierre-Bloch, with the de Vomécourt brothers and Georges Begué, had by this time established the strongest SOE base in France. Now de Guélis asked him, as a former socialist politician, to contact certain members of the party who had gone underground – Félix Gouin and Daniel Mayer in particular – and set up a radio link between them and London.

On 4 September the first Lysander landed in France, not far from the little village of La Champenoise, some fifteen kilometres from Châteauroux. Piloted by Nesbitt-Dufort, commander of the newly formed 138 Squadron, it had brought one passenger, Gerry Morel, and would return with Jacques de Guélis. Morel, one of the sixteen who arrived this month, had orders to organize a group of saboteurs.

Two days later, on 6 September, six more agents were dropped in a single operation. They were met by a reception committee laid on and led by Begué. The six were André Bloch ('Draftsman'); Ben Cowburn ('Benoit'); Victor Gerson ('Vic'); George Langelaan ('Langdon'), a former correspondent for the *New York Times* in Paris; the Comte du Puy; and Michael Trotobas ('Sylvestre'). Bloch was the only radio operator in the group; he crossed into the Occupied Zone to join Autogiro and set up several radio posts in the Paris region, and later in Le Mans. Ben Cowburn's task was to pinpoint vulnerable areas of the French oil industry with a view to future sabotage. The Comte du Puy also entered the Occupied Zone to go and join de Vomécourt.

The same night, 6 September, there was another drop near Paris. The two men involved in this operation, codenamed Dastard, were both from SOE RF Section and hence were in contact with Colonel Passy: Laverdet ('Red') and the radio operator Allainmat ('Red X'). Their job was to contact left-wing Gaullist supporters in the Paris area.

On the night of 10 September two more agents were dropped in Operation Fabulous: Henri Labit (this time using the codenames 'Leroy' and 'Lassalle') and his radio operator, Furet ('Mercier'). In Toulouse they joined the group set up by Bertaux. Other members of this group included Jean Cassou, in charge of subversive propaganda; Francesco Nitti, responsible for direct action; Jean-Maurice Hermann, formerly a chief reporter for the newspaper *Populaire* and now supervising the group's recruitment and organization; and Vanhove, a member of the Christian Syndicalist movement, whose duties involved collecting information and arranging logistics (one of his notable feats was to relieve the Compagnie Industrielle des Pétroles of some 10,000 litres of fuel!).

The following night it was Richard's turn to jump. Richard ('Ronsard') had been sent by Colonel Passy to set up another network and to find him suitable places for future parachute drops and aircraft landings.

On 19 September three more F Section men arrived, this time by sea. They had been obliged to make an appalling seventeen-day voyage on board HMS *Fidelity* because after the 12th the moon was waning, which prevented aerial operations. The trio were Georges Dubourdin ('Alain' or 'Dolan'), who was heading for Lyons to join Virginia Hall; Leroy, who was going to Bordeaux; and Francis Basin ('Olive'), who was to create a new group of his own as well as make contact with the Carte group, then being set up.

Carte, which was run by the artist André Girard, already included men of the calibre of André Gillois and Captain Henri Frager. The group was also in touch with General de Lattre de Tassigny and several officers in the Armistice army. A later recruit was Pierre-Guillain de Bénouville, a friend of Frager's, who had twice been imprisoned by the Vichy police. He had no sooner joined them than he found himself despatched to Geneva to establish a courier link with London via Switzerland, and to set up a system whereby funds could be sent from Britain through Geneva to the French resistance.

Operation Corsican, F Section's first successful supply drop – explosives, weapons and ammunition – took place on 10 October, near Villamblard in the Dordogne.[1] The reception committee was organized and led by Jean Pierre-Bloch. Four men made parachute jumps in the same operation, one of them Denis Turberville, who was dropped too far off course and was caught by gendarmes.

The gendarmes apparently found an address on Turberville which led the DST [Direction de Surveillance du Territoire, the French security police] to

1. There is still a monument in Villamblard commemorating the first SOE parachute drop of arms and men in the Unoccupied Zone, on 10 October, 1941.

launch a raid on the Villa des Bois, a safe-house near Marseilles. In fact, several other people might have been to blame for this unfortunate incident, but the truth of the matter has never been formally established. De Guélis had given the Villa's address to the four SOE agents because Turck had set up his base there. As a result of the DST ambush, most of SOE's agents operating in southern France were caught: the other three agents who had landed at Villamblard (all of them instructors in sabotage), J. B. Hayes, Jumeau and Le Harivel; also Robert Lyon, Roche, Jean Pierre-Bloch and his wife Gaby (Pierre-Bloch and his wife had gone to Marseilles to deliver the money sent from London in Operation Corsican,[1] Trotobas, Liewer ('Staunton') and Georges Begué. The month of October thus proved a particularly inauspicious one for SOE. The only agents still in place were Virginia Hall and Dubourdin in Lyons, Vic Gerson and Olive. It was a total catastrophe.

Olive reacted by setting up his own group, Urchin, maintaining his links with André Girard and Carte. (On the subject of Carte, M. R. D. Foot writes that 'a purist' might not in fact consider it to be one of F Section's circuits at all, but 'a distinguished French scholar [Hostache] counts it as one'.)

It was during the same month, October, that the Abwehr set off on a trail that would lead them to de Vomécourt. This was part of the La Chatte affair, already mentioned in connection with de Vomécourt; this will be discussed at greater length in a later chapter (see p.164) for it is a useful illustration of the dangers that SOE's agents had to face.

October also marked the start of joint parachute operations between the Free French army and SOE's RF Section, as a result of which many more agents were dropped in France. The first of them was Mansion – by now on his third mission – who landed on 3 October with a radio operator. But the precious suitcase was damaged and the operation had to be called off.

The next drop took place on the night of 10 October, when Donnadieu and his radio operator, Laurent, landed near Mimizan in Operation Barter. According to Passy their task was to make contact with 'a group that Begué and Forman had both mentioned', while Foot says their mission was to prepare a plan of attack on the Mérignac airfield. (But it should be noted that the British did not always know what Passy's secret orders were to his agents.)

On the night of 13 October, Joël Le Tac returned to France, this time by sea. He and his radio operator, Kergorlay, condenamed 'Joe' and 'Joe W' respectively, were part of the Overcloud mission, whose main objective was to arrange a radio link between London and a group in Britanny which had impressed Le Tac on his first visit there. Foot adds that another of Overcloud's objectives was to set up a covert ferry service between England and France using fast motorboats. This was later used by the Le Tac brothers, Fred Scamaroni, Labit, Forman and many others.

1. See Jean Pierre-Bloch's account of this affair in *Le Temps d'y Penser Encore*. The money totalled 1,150,000 francs, a huge sum in those days.

The same night, 13 October, there was another group: at La Martinette, near Fonsorbes; this was the start of the Mainmast B operation. Forman, the radio operator Periout and supplies of weapons and explosives were met by a reception committee comprising Labit, Bertaux, Fernand Bernard and four local students. It was a major operation, with an unusual aim, for Forman's orders were to make contact with a politically motivated network called Liberté; it was also the first such operation by the Free French intelligence section. Forman was to meet P. H. Teitgen in Montpellier on 18 October, and later François de Menthon in Lyons. These operations mounted by the Free French and the BCRA are worth mentioning here because they were very often dependent on SOE for logistic support and were mainly set up with Buckmaster's agreement.

One other noteworthy event that month was the arrival in London, on 20 October, of Jean Moulin, for Moulin – who had escaped via Lisbon – was to play a very major role in the future.

Finally, still in October, André Girard of SOE met Henri Frenay; but the meeting produced no useful result since Frenay was nervous about Girard's fierce hostility towards the Free French. Frenay also arranged to see General de La Laurencie in Lyons, in the presence of Allen Dulles, Head of OSS [precursor of the CIA] in Europe; but this meeting was equally unproductive. The Americans had agreed to recognize the General as overall leader of the French resistance, which was obviously unacceptable to Frenay.

On 9 November the radio operator André Bloch was arrested in Le Mans. He was tortured and later killed. Autogiro, the circuit planned by SOE's F Section and run by Pierre de Vomécourt, was thus deprived of any radio link with London.

Frenay and Pierre de Vomécourt had a meeting on 25 December, arranged by the lawyer Michel Brault. Although de Vomécourt was merely proposing that the British should supply Frenay's resistance movement, Combat, with arms and equipment, without infringing on its independence, Frenay refused to let SOE have anything to do with Combat.

Meanwhile Pierre de Vomécourt was desperately seeking some way of re-establishing contact with London. As we have seen, it was through Michel Brault – who knew the leaders of Interallié – that he met Mathilde Carré, 'La Chatte'. She agreed to transmit his message to London, and thus de Vomécourt was back in communication.

This is how Benjamin Cowburn sums up SOE's activities in 1941:[1]

> The casualty rate was extremely high. Almost all the agents sent to France in 1941 had been caught. I myself had managed to escape only thanks to an extraordinary series of events. I still had not been involved in any direct action. The equipment and

1. Cowburn, op. cit.

communications supplied for our early operations had proved sadly inadequate. But our achievements were by no means negligible. . . . Not only had we laid the groundwork for a network that would later expand enormously but we had also gained in valuable experience.

On 1 January, 1942, in a join operation between the RAF and the BCRA, Jean Moulin was parachuted into France. His codename was 'Joseph Mercier'.

A fortnight later, on 15 January, Peter Churchill made yet another trip to France, arriving by submarine just off Antibes.

In February the three SOE agents, Dubourdin ('Alain'), Robert Boiteux ('Nicolas') and Victor Gerson ('Vic') arranged to meet Jean-Pierre Lévy. This is Lévy's description of the ensuing series of encounters:[1]

> My relations with them were sometimes very cordial and friendly, but at other times we ended up having furious rows. Knowing that I had numerous contacts all over the area, they wanted us to join their organization, under their control. But in the France-Liberté movement, and later when we merged with Franc-Tireur, we were determined to keep our independence, both on a political level and in terms of outside control, particularly from a foreign government.

On the night of 3 February, the Le Tac brothers – Joël and Yves – returned to France again, this time by sea, and went to join the radio operator, Kergorlay. They had brought considerable supplies of equipment from England and were planning to revive Operation Overcloud. But a week later they were arrested, and the Germans destroyed the group they had set up in Brittany. All three men were sent to concentration camps in Germany.

Autogiro, meanwhile, was continuing to expand; as yet, Mathilde Carré did not know any real details about the organization. The de Vomécourt brothers were still recruiting new members, mainly personal friends who came from the world of politics or who were lawyers or senior civil servants, like Brune, Michel Clemenceau, Senator Landry, the Marquis de Moustiers, Gourdeau, Ribet the barrister and Antonini who was Secretary General of the SNCF railway board.

Then on 26 February, after several unsuccessful attempts, Pierre de Vomécourt managed to take Mathilde Carré over to England on board a motorboat.

Urchin, the circuit set up by Francis Basin ('Olive'), was also continuing to expand; it would soon include some thirty sub-groups all over the south-eastern corner of France, from Marseilles to Grenoble to Menton.

---

1. Quoted by Henri Noguères in *Histoire de la Résistance en France* (Laffont, Paris 1967–81); Vol. II of five.

Basin was gathering a vast amount of information. He was also setting up small units for direct action, and developing his contacts with other resistance organizations (whom he often supported financially). It was also Basin who made the arrangements for Emmanuel d'Astier de la Vigèrie to be taken to London: he was picked up by submarine on 17 April and delivered to Gibraltar, whence he was flown to England, accompanied all the way by Peter Churchill. Basin's headquarters at the Villa Isabelle were frequently visited by other resistance people such as Girard, Frager, Frenay, d'Astier, Colonel Vautrin and General Cochet. In April, Basin was finally sent a radio operator, Isidore Newman ('Julian'), who was landed by a small sailing boat. Newman was a particularly able man, hardworking and very brave. (He would be captured on a later mission, imprisoned in a deportation camp, and executed.)

Still in April, the submarine that had arrived to collect d'Astier had landed Victor Gerson ('Vic') off Antibes. Vic had managed to avoid being captured during the ambush at the Villa des Bois, and had escaped through Spain back to England. He now started to expand his remarkable escape line, helped particularly by General Martin, a Spanish Republican, who provided the group with all the *passeurs* it needed between Perpignan and Barcelona.

The same submarine had also landed another passenger: the radio operator Marcel Clech ('George 60'). His task was to join Virginia Hall in Lyons and set up a radio link for her. But first he went to Châteauroux to collect the transmitter set that Begué had hidden there shortly before his arrest.

April also saw submarines bringing Edward Zeff (another radio operator: Virginia Hall sent him to Dubourdin, who was running the Spruce network around Lyons), Menesson, Pertschuk and H. P. Le Chêne ('Paul'). Dubourdin set Menesson the task of reinforcing the Coq Enchainé movement and its clandestine newspaper. Pertschuk's job was to organize a new group, Prunus, and Le Chêne was to set up the Plane network, in Clermont-Ferrand and in Périgord. Le Chêne's brother ('Grégoire') landed by parachute a few days later, and joined Dubourdin as a radio operator. V. H. Hazan ('Gervais'), who made the jump with him, was specifically interested in active sabotage.

At the time of the April full moon, André Simon was parachuted into the Unoccupied Zone for a special mission: to organize Edouard Daladier's departure for London in a Lysander. But as we have seen, this mission was to end in failure.

Philippe de Vomécourt, in the south, was busy developing the Ventriloquist circuit. Meanwhile, his brother Pierre (now with the codename 'Sylvain') was returning to France for another operation; he made a blind parachute jump near Philippe's château at Limousin. By this time Autogiro had been partially disrupted as a result of Mathilde Carré's treachery, and Pierre's only way of communicating with London was by sending a courier to Virginia Hall in Lyons. Following the capture of one of his men while trying to cross the Demarcation Line, Pierre himself was arrested, at the same time as Jack Fincken (who had been dropped back in January to help his operation), Burdeyron, Du Puy and many other members of the group, notably Cottin. After a long struggle, and his own attempted suicide, Pierre de Vomécourt finally persuaded the Germans that the Autogiro agents should be treated as prisoners of war and not as spies. But the network itself, the only SOE network in occupied territory, had been totally destroyed.

In May SOE's RF Section carried out several missions on behalf of the BCRA. The Ali network, run by Maurice Andler, by now gaining strength in the Unoccupied Zone, was collecting virtually all the Vichy government papers and sending them to the BCRA; it also had close links with Achille Peretti in Corsica. One member of Ali was Philippe Roques, who was also one of Olive's top men in the Urchin network. On 24 April Gaston Tavian and a naval officer called Captain Mariotti were parachuted into France to join Ali, and Tavian (using the codename 'Tir') took charge of the group's active unit, with Joseph Piet as his radio operator.

On the night of 2 May Henri Labit made a blind jump at Sore in the Landes; he was to start up Operation Bass. But shortly afterwards, while crossing the Demarcation Line, he was captured. He tried to escape and shot at his pursuers, but they caught him again. A first-class agent, he killed himself by swallowing his cyanide pill.

On the night of 5 May three men were dropped in the Cher province – de Clay, Gauden and Bodhaine. Their task was to destroy the radio transmitter towers at Allouis, which the Germans were using to jam BBC broadcasts. On 9 may the mission was accomplished, with no casualties.

In June there was a major drop of men and supplies at Anse, near Lyons.

The following month there was a mass escape of all the SOE agents who had been arrested back in October, 1941, as a result of the Villa des Bois affair. They had been imprisoned at Périgueux, but on the night of 16 July they had just been moved to Mauzac prison camp in the Dordogne. Among those who escaped were Jean Pierre-Bloch, Georges Begué, Lazare Rachline, Raymond Roche, Michael Trotobas, George Langelaan, Jacques Hayes, Claude Jumeau, Jean Le Harivel, Francois Garel, Philippe Liewer and Robert Lyon – and with them went the camp guard who had helped to arrange the break-out. They escaped across the frontier into Spain on the night of 8 August. But the Guardia Civil caught them, and the whole party was interned at Miranda de Ebro until October, 1942.

On 20 July, one of Colonel Buckmaster's close associates, Major Bodington, was landed at Antibes by felucca. The object of his visit was to assess the progress of SOE networks in France. He was accompanied by Frager and one of SOE's women agents, Yvonne Rudellat. They were met by Olive, who put them up at the Villa Isabelle. Bodington's first move was to inspect the Urchin set up and then to meet Girard, head of Carte.

Alan Jickell ('Gustave') and Robert Burdett ('Nicolas' or 'Boiteux'), who had both landed in June, went to Lyons to join Virginia Hall. Jickell would later start a team of saboteurs who became very active in the Saint-Étienne area. 'Nicolas', meanwhile, was setting up another new group; notable among his recruits were Joseph Marchand, the perfumer, and Jean-Marie Régnier. Bodington, on his visit to Lyons, endorsed Nicolas's handling of Alain.

Two other British agents who created a new group for SOE were the brothers Alfred and Henry Newton. Philippe de Vomécourt didn't need them in his group, Ventriloquist, so they set up their own in the Haute-Loire region: Greenheart.

On the night of 1 July, SOE sent their youngest agent yet, Tony Brooks ('Alphonse'); he was still only nineteen years old. He made a blind parachute jump, landing near the château of Bas-Soleil. His job was to set up another new group in the south, with trade union members from the local railways. Aided by de Vomécourt and Bertholet – one of the oldest and most experienced men in RF Section – Brooks very quickly built up his new group, Pimento; made contact with scores of railwaymen, among them Léon Jouhaux and Yvon Morandat (whose brother Roger became one of their best agents); received a radio operator from London; and, thanks to the railwaymen, set up a strong and rapid courier service to Switzerland.

Following a brief visit to London, Ben Cowburn had returned in June, making a blind jump with an RAF officer, E. M. Wilkinson ('Alexandre'); it was their task to start up the Tinker group. Through Virginia Hall they managed to find their radio operator, Denis Rake, who had arrived back in May after landing by felucca. The three of them were now joined by Robert Heslop and crossed into the Occupied Zone to carry out their mission.

At the end of June, Raymond Flower ('Gaspard') was dropped to set up the Monkeypuzzle circuit, and was later joined by the radio operator Marcel Clech ('Bastien'). But Bastien found that Gaspard was doing very little, and he decided to act alone. He recruited a man who was to prove invaluable, Pierre Culioli ('Pierre Leclair'), and was soon joined by Yvonne Rudellat, newly arrived from England with Major Bodington.

At the beginning of July, Robert Leroy was parachuted into an area near Bordeaux. He had already made one visit to France in September 1941, when he worked with Olive. Now he was to set up the Scientist network. He was soon joined by Claude de Baissac ('David') and his radio operator Harry Peulevé ('Jean'), who were dropped blind on the night of 30 July, landing not far from Nimes.

After the Autogiro disaster, Buckmaster had come to the conclusion that it was better to operate several small groups rather than one large one. He began by asking Charles Grover-Williams ('Sébastien') to create one of these small groups, to be codenamed Chestnut, and advised him to avoid all contact with the survivors of Autogiro. One of Sébastien's first recruits was his friend, the racing driver Robert Benoist, who agreed to let his house in the suburbs of Paris be used as the group's command post.

Through Girard, head of Carte, Bodington met Colonel Vautrin, who was stationed in Nice as an officer in the Armistice army. Vautrin assured Bodington that a large majority of the soldiers were in sympathy with the Allied cause, and he agreed to make a secret trip to London in order to discuss things further at Headquarters. As M. R. D. Foot says:

> Girard persuaded both Peter Churchill and Bodington . . . that his organization had methodical plans in hand for preparing first sabotage teams, then larger guerrilla groups, and finally a private army some 300,000 strong that would join the Vichy armistice army at the right moment and help liberate France.

So on 2 October Bodington sent Buckmaster an enthusiastic report. In London the Chiefs of Staff were informed of this startling news. It was decided to send J. A. R. Starr ('Émile') to Nice, firstly to take charge of the Acrobat operation, and secondly to speak to Girard about what supplies would be needed for such a vast secret army. The British now began to see a way of outmanoeuvring de Gaulle, intractable as ever. They agreed to let the Carte agents use the BBC and American wireless frequences to broadcast to the Armistice army in France. Claude Dauphin and Jean Guignebert were nominated to make the programmes; but because of a last-minute hitch they were unable to do so. Jean Gandrey-Rety, who had left France on 31 August, was nominated in their place, and it was he who finally launched Radio Patrie.

In Nice, however, Starr quickly realized that Carte's ideas were impracticable. He spent ten weeks on a round of disappointing meetings, then in November returned by boat to England.

These were critical days on the south coast of France; indeed, Buckmaster was having to consider the possibility that Allied troops might soon be landing in North Africa. As a result, Peter Churchill was ordered into this sector to do whatever he could to help Olive. He was duly parachuted into the Montpellier region on the night of 27 August. But ten days earlier, Olive had been captured by the DST. So now, as well as creating the new group, Spindle, Churchill had to take over from Olive as head of Urchin. He in turn made the Villa Isabelle his base near Cannes. He found support from Experton, Malval, Marie-Lou Blanc ('Suzanne') – who was to organize reception committees for supply drops on the beaches – Newman the radio operator, and Raymonde Mennecier.

Bodington had earlier found some French industrialists who were willing to lend financial support to SOE. The deal was that they would give the money – in francs, of course – to SOE agents working locally; equivalent sums, in pounds sterling, would then be paid into English banks, credited to accounts that would be opened in their names.

There was one other notable parachute operation that August, involving

Henri Sevenet. He was dropped near Loches, where his duties were to form the Detective group and try to help de Vomécourt escape. One of the members of the reception team was Sevenet's own mother!

On the night of 1 September, two men boarded a small fishing boat at Cassis, bound for England: Frenay, representing the Combat movement, and d'Astier, representing the Libération movement. Together they were going to London to meet de Gaulle and discuss what could be done to unify all the various resistance groupings. Jean-Pierre Lévy, from the Franc-Tireur movement, was supposed to join them; he was due to be collected by Lysander with Jean Moulin. But the Lysander never arrived. Nor did the submarine which was meant to pick them up at the end of the month off Anthéor on the Côte d'Azur. However, F Section did manage to get Frenay and d'Astier to London eventually.

On 4 September, while being transferred by train to a prison in Lyons, Olive made a bid for freedom. But he was soon recaptured, largely because Girard had not been able to spare the men to help him (which demonstrates how much he must have been bluffing to Bodington).

However, Peter Churchill's new group was going from strength to strength. He was soon sent his own radio operator, Alec Rabinovitch ('Arnaud'), who landed blind at Grenoble; Arnaud rapidly proved himself a first-class agent.

Also in September, a sailing boat brought Sidney Jones to France; his job was to start up a small new group, Inventor, based in Marseilles and specializing in sabotage of railways and harbour installations. He was also to liaise with Peter Churchill and the Carte network. He quickly enlisted the aid of one of his friends, Dumont-Guillemet, then Pierre Picard as well. Inventor rapidly developed into a very efficient unit. For instance, when the Germans invaded the southern half of France that November, the saboteurs set fire to fifty goods wagons bringing food for the enemy in Marseilles.

Earlier that year SOE had sent Ted Coppin to Marseilles. Landed by felucca in May, this expert saboteur was to set up another small active unit with some local railwaymen, to attack local rail transport.

On 24 September the Headmaster team was parachuted into the Puy-de-Dôme. But forty-eight hours later the team leader – Captain C. S. Hudson – was arrested in Le Crest, at the home of the man responsible for his reception committee, Roger Werther; Werther was also caught. The radio operator G. Jones lost an eye when he fell off a bicycle – but his transmissions went on without interruption. Now only Brian Rafferty ('Dominique') remained safe, so this young Irish-born undergraduate boldly took over command of the group.

In Tours the Monkeypuzzle circuit had been having internal problems. Gaspard, fearing his home was about to be raided, had moved all his gear – arms, transmitter, papers, etc – to Yvonne Rudellat's house. But he hadn't warned her in advance, and her lodger tipped off the Gestapo. Yvonne

Rudellat herself only just managed to escape capture. She and Pierre Culioli had a furious row with Gaspard, who then informed London that 'Pierre' and 'Jacqueline' had gone over to the enemy and asked to be sent some poison that he could eliminate them.

Shortly afterwards, however, SOE became seriously disillusioned with Gaspard when he failed to organize the reception for a particularly important operation. This involved two women agents who were to be dropped by a plane flown by Wing-Commander Pickard, the ace pilot on this sort of mission. On 24 September Pickard flew over the dropping zone as arranged – but no one was there, so he returned to England. On the 25th London sent a radio signal ordering Gaspard to be there without fail the following night. But Gaspard had disappeared. Consequently the radio operator Clech was obliged to ask the 'traitors', Yvonne Rudellat and Culioli, to arrange the reception instead. Their arrangements went as smoothly as anyone could have wished. Now Buckmaster began to understand . . .

So the two women agents arrived safely, Andrée Borrel and Lise de Baissac. Andrée Borrel ('Denise') had been a member of the Carte group before leaving for Britain via Spain; taken on as an SOE agent, her mission now was in Paris. Lise de Baissac ('Odile'), on the other hand, was going to the Poitiers area to set up a rallying point, codenamed Artist, similar to the one that Virginia Hall was running so admirably in Lyons.

But Odile had to change course when her brother asked her to help him with Scientist, the network he was starting in Bordeaux; her job was to maintain contact between Scientist and the Prosper circuit.

In October, John Goldsmith ('Valentin') and Major Chalmers-Wright were landed on the Mediterranean coast by felucca. Goldsmith, using General Chambe as an intermediary, was to meet General Giraud to pass on the arrangements for his imminent departure. Afterwards he was supposed to go north to set up the new network, Attorney, between Amiens and Boulogne, which would specialize in sabotaging enemy communications. But Giraud wanted to make use of Goldsmith himself, to set up a sub-group for Carte in Corsica, and Buckmaster consented to this change of plan.

Chalmers-Wright, meanwhile, went to Grenoble to stay with a senior diplomat by the name of Gosse.

On 24 October Dubourdin was taken back to London by Lysander. Nicolas was therefore the only agent left in Lyons – apart, of course, from the indispensable Virginia Hall. He stepped up his contacts with 'neighbouring' agents such as Anthony Brooks, the Newton brothers and Le Chêne brothers; he also stepped up sabotage activity and arrangements for supply drops, distributing arms not only to the Francs-Tireurs et Partisans (FTP) under Marchand but also to non-Communist organizations like the Coq Enchaîné movement.

The same Lysander also took Ben Cowburn back to London with Dubourdin. Because Cowburn had not had a radio operator, he had been unable to expand his Tinker group in the Châteauroux area as he had planned; but he had sabotaged the power lines at the Eguzon dam and, in Châteauroux itself, the Debard factory making pistons for the Germans.

At his home, the Château de Bas-Soleil, Philippe de Vomécourt was arrested by the police. He was sentenced to ten years' imprisonment and taken to Saint-Paul prison in Lyons. But he had been sentenced as Philippe de Crevoisier, his middle name, so when the Germans invaded the southern zone he was able to avoid deportation to Germany.

Still in October, Major Francis Suttill arrived in the Occupied Zone to set up Prosper, the largest new network since Autogiro (now destroyed). Suttill, then aged thirty-two, was an international lawyer with a French mother. Buckmaster entrusted him with a very onerous mission: to establish another base, as quickly as possible, in Paris itself, in permanent radio contact with London; and then to set up further groups for SOE in the east, west and centre of France – in central France he was to take command of the Gaspard circuit. Gaspard himself had been asked to organize the reception committee for Suttill, but once again he shirked his duties; it was therefore Yvonne Rudellat, Andrée Borrel and Culioli who set out the landing lights on the dropping zone where Suttill had to jump. Suttill duly arrived – accompanied by a young jockey, a Frenchman by the name of Jean Amps – and warned the reception team to expect his deputy, Gilbert Norman, who was due to be dropped at the same place at the next full moon.

Assisted by Andrée Borrel, Suttill now started recruiting in Chartres, Melun, Orléans, Blois, Romorantin, Beauvais, Compiègne, Saint-Quentin – wherever he could find new people to join SOE.

On 31 October, Gilbert Norman ('Archambault') was dropped near Boise-Renard, as arranged, and was met by Culioli. With him was Lieutenant Roger Landes ('Stanislas', later 'Aristide') who was going to join Claude de Baissac in Bordeaux.

Ironically, Baker Street had given Norman the phial of poison that Gaspard had asked for to 'liquidate' Culioli – but since Gaspard was not on the reception committee, Norman gave it to Culioli himself!

At the end of October, 1942, while waiting for the Prosper group to become operational, SOE was setting up four other groups in the Occupied Zone: two in Bordeaux, run by de Baissac and Leroy respectively; the Chestnut group in Paris, a small independent unit set up by motor-racing enthusiasts; and another group started by two friends, the businessman Jean Worms and the Swiss Jacques Weil. Worms and Weil had been in touch with British Intelligence as well as with Virginia Hall, Olive and Peter Churchill, and the three SOE agents had arranged a felucca to take Worms to England that October. In London he was recruited by SOE and a few months later he parachuted back into France to organize a new group, Juggler, formed from his old group, Robin.

On 11 November the Germans invaded the so-called 'Free Zone'; this had been anticipated as a reaction to the Allied landings in French North Africa.

On the same day, Olive, who had been imprisoned in Fort Montluc in Lyons, was released by the prison commander, Colonel Granier, as a consequence of long negotiations with Virginia Hall. With Raymond Mennecier and Georges Liévin, Olive now went into hiding at Madame Gilbert's hairdressing salon in the Rue de la République, Lyons. Here they met Lazare Rachline ('Lucien'), who had been making plans for the Urchin group leader's escape, in case Colonel Granier did not keep his word.

When the Germans moved into the southern zone, the prison governor at Limoges released three SOE agents who had been caught there on 15 August: Heslop, Wilkinson and Rake. And as the invaders entered Lyons, Virginia Hall decided it was time she left France altogether – and she thus managed to avoid capture. According to M. R. D. Foot, the head of the Lyons Gestapo said that 'he would give anything to put his hands on that Canadian bitch'.

Colonel Buckmaster carried out as many operations as possible that November, before the Germans became too well established in the south.

On the night of 8 November a felucca landed five agents on the coast near Cassis; Major George Starr (whose brother returned in the same boat to London, following the semi-failure of Operation Acrobat), who was later to become famous throughout south-western France under his codename 'Hilaire'; radio operator Marcus Bloom, who went to join Tony Brooks, head of Pimento (Tony sent him to the Pertschuk group); Odette Sansom, who was to work with Peter Churchill (and later married him); Mary Herbert, who had been sent to work as liaison officer with Claude de Baissac (these two would also end up married); and finally Marie-Thérèse Le Chêne, wife of Paul Le Chêne, who joined the Plane circuit run by the two Le Chêne brothers.

On 17 November three agents were parachuted into what had been the Occupied Zone, landing to the south-west of Paris. One was Gustave Bieler, a Canadian, who had been sent to organize the Musician network. Bieler was hurt when he landed; but, refusing to be taken back by Lysander, he insisted on carrying out his mission.

The same night another two agents were dropped: Michael Trotobas ('Sylvestre'), who was one of the escapees from Mauzac prison camp, and his radio operator Staggs. They were to set up the Farmer network around Lille.

The following night, the Mauritius businessman 'Antelme' made a parachute jump over the dropping zone arranged by Monkeypuzzle. Buckmaster had given Antelme several important jobs. Firstly he was to contact all the resistance groups, whether pro- or anti-Gaullist; secondly, to get in touch with the business and banking communities to negotiate financial aid, both for the groups in need of cash and for whatever preparations would be made for the Allied landings; thirdly, to try to persuade Édouard Herriot to go to Britain. But in this last mission, Antelme was no more successful than any of those who had previously tried.

On 26 November Charles Hayes was dropped on a second mission: to reorganize the sub-groups belonging to Claude de Baissac's Scientist network in the Bordeaux region.

At the end of December, 1942, the Carte movement was running into serious difficulties. Girard, who was in command, was trying to remain non-political. He refused to acknowledge de Gaulle as head of the Free French forces. With British support he had arranged for a French radio station to be set up in London, Radio Patrie, which was in competition with the Gaullist radio programmes called 'Les Français parlent aux Français'. The leading figure in Radio Patrie was André Gillois, who was quite unaware of all the controversy.

By the end of the year, however, Carte had lost two of its most important elements, Frager and de Bénouville. Frager was critical of Girard for lacking the ability either to organize or to lead. He left Carte, which was struggling to maintain its base in Arles, and went to Marseilles to set up a new group with SOE support. De Bénouville, meanwhile, had finally managed to arrange a meeting between Girard and Frenay, with a view to forming a close link between Carte and Combat, the latter being the large movement Frenay had set up. Girard, however, was not to be moved; he still refused to accept de Gaulle's authority or the necessary discipline imposed by other resistance movements. It was stalemate. So de Bénouville decided to join Combat himself. Under the name 'Lahire', he now took over the Combat team in Switzerland.

Carte thus found itself almost completely isolated and impotent. All the high hopes that Bodington had built up around Girard and Carte had now collapsed.

This is how Henri Noguères summed up SOE's position in France at the end of 1942:

Autogiro, the network run by Pierre de Vomécourt, was conclusively out of action. Urchin, which had gone to ground after Basin's ('Olive's') arrest, had not yet resumed activities, although he was now out of prison. Ventriloquist had also come to a standstill after the arrest of Phillipe de Vomécourt. As for Virginia Hall, from the Heckler circuit, we have already seen how she had had the good fortune to put a frontier between herself and the Gestapo by the time the Germans invaded the southern zone.

Nevertheless, SOE was now well established in France and was still recruiting new members. In the northern zone, their work went on. Firstly there was Major Suttill's Prosper network, covering several provinces south of Paris, with its sub-groups Juggler (run by Jean Worms and Jacques Weil in the Paris area) and Satirist, which Octave Simon was running in the Sarthe.

Another group functioning in the Paris region was the

Chestnut group, set up by Charles Grover-Williams and Robert Benoist; but this was a much smaller group – much less vulnerable too.

Other groups included Raymond Flower's Monkeypuzzle, and Sevenet's Detective, both in Touraine, and Wilkinson's Privet in Anjou; Farmer, which had just been set up in the north by Michael Trotobas, one of the agents who had escaped from Mauzac; and Scientist, Claude de Baissac's group in Bordeaux.

Finally there had been two recent arrivals, J. Lodwick and Oscar Heimann, who had made blind parachute jumps on the night of 29 December. They had been given the job of sabotaging several factories in the La Rochelle suburbs. But the two men became separated and could not find each other after they landed. One was carrying the explosives, but only the other knew what the targets were; as a result they both travelled all over the country looking for each other and only met up again in Paris, whereupon they had a slight quarrel, then returned together to England via Spain.

In the southern zone, SOE still had the Spruce network in Lyons, which Boiteux ('Nicolas') had taken over from Dubourdin, and the Greenheart group in the Haute-Loire, which the Newton brothers had set up. Brian Rafferty, the sole member of Headmaster to remain free, was meanwhile doing his best in Clermont-Ferrand.

Still further south, around Toulouse and Montauban, Prunus and Pimento were still active, urged on by Pertschuk and Tony Brooks respectively. And finally, on the south coast itself, Sidney Jones's group Inventor was still functioning well in Marseilles, and Peter Churchill's Spindle in the Maritime Alps. Churchill would no doubt have had a simpler job if he hadn't also had to play the role of schoolmaster dealing with a particularly troublesome pupil – André Girard, better known by his pseudonym 'Carte', which was also the name of his group.

The year 1943 began with Operation Arquebuse. After several false starts, on 26 February the BCRA boss, Passy, was dropped near Lyons-la-Forêt. He was accompanied by Flight-Lieutenant Yeo-Thomas from SOE, whose codenames included 'Seahorse', 'Shelley' and François'. Their job was to make an assessment of resistance forces in France; obtain their allegiance to de Gaulle; co-ordinate their military and intelligence-gathering activities; and 'to consider whether and in what circumstances it would be possible to implement the setting up of a "central management committee", responsible for settling all civil matters'. Jean Moulin preferred to call it the 'Conseil National de la Résistance', and this was approved by de Gaulle. It was therefore a very important mission. At the same time the presence of an SOE officer demonstrated that the French service and the British service were working together in close harmony, which calmed the fears of certain French resistance fighters who had heard something of the disputes in London.

The two men went to Paris the following day and there met Pierre Brossolette, head of Operation Brumaire, at Claire Davinroy's home in the Rue de la Faisandèrie. While waiting for Jean Moulin ('Rex') to arrive, the leaders of the two missions Arquebuse and Brumaire – and their companion from SOE – spent the time laying the foundations for the Conseil National de la Résistance (CNR), an important landmark in the progress of the French resistance.

At the end of February Girard arrived in London, and was joined in mid March by Frager, to ask Buckmaster to settle the matter of their dispute. It seems clear that SOE had overestimated the importance of Carte. Learning that his wife and two of his daughters had been arrested, Girard did not return to France, but left instead for America (following a request to the Americans from Buckmaster). What remained of his network was restructured into small independent units specializing in sabotage, which were totally loyal to Baker Street.

As for Frager, he retained control of Donkeyman, the largest of the groups that had been set up within the Carte movement. He based himself at Auxerre and extended the sphere of his activities as far north as Normandy and as far east as Nancy. But while Frager had been away, the Abwehr had arrested many of the circuit's agents. Francis Cammaerts ('Roger'), who had been sent as Frager's assistant, was alerted by the radio operator Rabinovitch, and left Annecy for Cannes, where he started up his own group, Jockey.

Prosper, the network set up by Major Suttill and Andrée Borrel, was spreading rapidly; in fact it was now the largest SOE group in occupied France since Autogiro. One of its sub-groups, Butler, was being run by Bouguennec ('Garel') – another escapee from Mauzac – who had made a blind jump on 23 March with his radio operator, Marcel Fox ('Ernest').

The Monkeypuzzle circuit, in Touraine, now became another of Prosper's sub-groups, under the new name Adolphe. There had been serious internal problems in the circuit so Suttill put Pierre Culioli in command, as a replacement for Raymond Flower ('Gaspard') who was recalled to London. The energetic Culioli was to step up the group's sabotage activities, with particular help from Yvonne Rudellat ('Jacqueline'), Gérard Oury and Marcel Sauvaget. As Cookridge notes:[1]

> During March, 1943, alone, the railway lines between Orléans and Tours and Orléans and Vierzon were put out of action six times. Cautious estimates show that some 200 German officers

1. Cookridge op. cit.

and men were killed and wounded in these railway wrecking operations.

April was a gloomy month for SOE. Bleicher, who had been La Chatte's German boyfriend, managed to fool Odette Sansom and Bardet, passing himself off as an anti-Nazi officer by the name of Colonel Herni. Only the radio operator Rabinovitch was not taken in, and he sent a warning to London.

On the night of 14 April Peter Churchill returned to France yet again, this time making a parachute landing; Odette Sansom was on the reception committee that met him. Buckmaster had told Churchill about Rabinovitch's suspicions but Churchill didn't pay much attention. The following evening both Churchill and Miss Sansom were arrested by Bleicher in Saint-Jorioz. Thus at this time of rapid expansion, SOE had lost two of its best agents. Moreover, as M. R. D. Foot points out:[1]

> A number of unfortunate consequences followed [their] arrest; there would have been many more if Bleicher had done his job efficiently. Churchill had a habit of keeping old messages; some weeks later Rabinovitch, cautiously reconnoitring the scene of the trouble, was able to spirit away a suitcase of Churchill's that the Germans had overlooked which contained a pistol, parachuting gear, nearly half a million francs, and the deciphered texts of over forty messages exchanged with London by himself. A few messages were found on the captured pair. Churchill was carrying in a pocketbook in clear the telephone numbers of three of his Riviera sub-agents, one of whom – de Malval – was confronted some months later, when arrested at his flat in Paris, with a message from SOE's home station to Spindle which he had seen before; it said, as he later remembered it, 'On reaching the coast of France the agents who have come by felucca will proceed straight to the Baron de Malval, Villa Isabelle, Route de Fréjus'.

On 27 April it was the turn of Ted Coppin and Giselle, his courier, to be arrested. Nothing is known about their capture or their ultimate fate. No one ever saw them again. They hadn't talked, however, since the Germans arrested no other members of their group.

It was also during the second half of April that Bardet was arrested. He became a double agent, working for Bleicher. It is possible that he had been a double agent for some time, for his two escapes from German police – in November, 1942, on the Côte d'Azur and in January, 1943, in Aix-en-Provence – had seemed rather suspicious. What is certain, though, is that

1. Foot, op. cit.

because of Bardet's collaboration with Bleicher, Germaine Tambour ('Annette') and her sister Madeleine were also arrested. Their flat was used as a safe-house by Suttill and the Prosper agents.

At the time of the April full moon, the Prunus circuit was sent a new operator, Duchalard, a French-Canadian. But within a few days the circuit had been demolished by the German security police. Pertschuk, his radio operator Bloom and the majority of the group's members were caught in Toulouse. According to Foot, Pertschuk and Bloom had made numerous blunders.

Another arrest that April involved Roger Morandat in Lyons; he was the brother of Yvon Morandat, head of the Pimento group in Lyons. He gave nothing away. One of his agents, a police inspector by the name of Jean Dorval, somehow found time to enter Morandat's flat before the Gestapo got there and managed to destroy all the incriminating papers.

Brooks, head of Pimento, was keeping himself and his men very busy, stepping up sabotage operations particularly of railways in the Massif Central, the Alps and the Rhône valley. But his activities were hindered somewhat by the fact that the Prunus group had been destroyed, for Bloom had usually acted as his radio link with London. That April Brooks narrowly avoided capture when the train he was travelling on was stopped at a German checkpoint.

The other SOE networks were also stepping up operations, without interference from the Germans. In central and south-western France, the Stationer group under Maurice Southgate ('Hector') and the Wheelwright group run by George Starr were helping the maquis with supplies and instruction. In the south Roger Cammaerts was reconstituting Spindle. Ben Cowburn, who had returned to France for a third time, was setting up a new group, Tinker; he was now using the codename 'Germain' and his radio operator Denis Barrett called himself 'Honoré'. Around Rouen and Le Havre Philippe Liewer – another of the Mauzac escapees – was setting up the Salesman group with Jean Chartrand ('Dieudonné'). In the north the two groups Farmer (run by Trotobas) and Musician (Gustave Bieler) were systematically launching sabotage raids on railways, canal locks, electricity transformers, etc. In the Bordeaux area Claude de Baissac's Scientist group had found a grand total of forty-five separate dropping zones and landing sites for arms drops and Lysanders; he was supplying the entire region with arms and explosives and organizing a veritable feast of sabotage of all kinds, against high tension cables, fuel depots, enemy patrol boats, etc. Two other groups were concentrating on railway sabotage: Juggler, the group run by Jean Worms and Jacques Weil, which included nearly a dozen specialist units; and Butler, the group run by Garel in the Angers area.

During the spring of 1943 Prosper had continued to make excellent progress. It controlled a number of sub-groups spread across a major part of what had been the Occupied Zone – among them Satirist, run by the sculptor

Octave Simon in southern Normandy, still a relatively quiet area, where Suttill was hiding most of his supplies.

Working with him Suttill had several leading figures such as Yvonne Rudellat, Andrée Borrel, Culioli and Norman. He kept in close contact with local resistance workers, and was personally involved in several jointly planned raids. He was also supplying them with arms. Prosper, in short, was SOE's mainstay in the northern half of France. On the night of 13 May Suttill was flown out by Lysander to report to Buckmaster in person. In view of Prosper's achievements so far the head of SOE's F Section willingly gave Suttill everything he asked for, namely trained deputy agents, arms and other supplies. At the June full moon a total of 190 containers were dropped on the group's territory; this constituted a record for parachute operations in France. Most of them were received by Culioli.

But on 12 June several containers exploded on landing near the village of Neuvy. The Germans went on the alert, bringing in 2,000 men – including 500 SS guards – to scour the Sologne. Culioli decided a signal should be radioed to London telling them to stop parachute operations for the time being; but the signal, given to Déricourt, was apparently never transmitted. As a result, between the 12th and the 20th of the month, Culioli had to rush from one dropping zone to another to collect all the arms and munitions that were falling from the sky in such abundance!

On 13 June Suttill returned from London. Three days later he was followed by two Canadian officers: Frank Pickersgill ('Bertrand') and John Macalister ('Valentin'). On the 21st Culioli and Yvonne Rudellat set off for Paris with them in an ancient van with front-wheel drive. But after a vain attempt to pass through a German roadblock, they were arrested by the Gestapo. Both Culioli and Yvonne were shot and taken to hospital under armed guard, while the two Canadians were thrown into jail.

Suttill was very worried about his two friends and the Canadians. He started looking for them but without finding the slightest clue to their whereabouts. On the 24th he too was arrested, just as he was entering his room in a hotel in the Rue de Mazagran. He was taken to the Avenue Foch. The night before, Gilbert Norman and Andrée Borrel had also been arrested in the Boulevard Lannes. The Germans set up an operation using French collaborators – named Roger Dupré, Renée Lefebvre, Jacques d'Arcangues and Lucien Prévost – who pretended to be messengers from Suttill, and thus managed to recover the group's arms cache at Trie-Château. Several more arrests were to follow. The Prosper group had been annihilated.

There then ensued the strange affair of the 'pact of honour' that was apparently arranged between the Germans and the Prosper leaders now in custody. Foot and Cookridge give conflicting reports of this affair. It is certainly true that some sort of bargain was struck, by the Germans on one side and Suttill and Norman on the other. The bargain seems to have been that Prosper chiefs would tell the Germans where they were hiding all the arms supplies that had been dropped; in return, all the captured agents from the group would be treated as prisoners of war. In fact, what happened was that hundreds of French resistance workers were arrested and the Germans were able to recover most of the arms sent from London. Naturally the Germans had never for a moment intended to respect the bargain. Suttill, Norman, Andrée Borrel and the other Prosper agents were all sent to Nazi concentration camps and executed.

According to Cookridge it was Suttill who signed the pact, Norman merely initialling it at a later stage. But Foot is less definite; he says that 'there is no direct evidence that Suttill ever gave his personal consent to this arrangement, and plenty of evidence of character to suggest that he did not'.[1] However, Foot does not exclude the possibility that Suttill may have stood surety for the pact, but only after it had been negotiated and agreed by Norman. The truth of the matter will probably never be known. As Foot says, 'Prosper's downfall, tragic as its consequences were, was brought on in spite of their bravery by the agents' own incompetence and insecurity.' He goes on:[2]

> The circuit snowballed; its growth made catastrophe certain, and it was only a matter of time and chance before either one of the new untrained French contacts slipped up and fell into German hands, or someone changed sides, or the Germans stumbled on some fatal indiscretion, as in fact they did. From the start it had been poisoned; for Suttill's first contact in October, 1942, had been supplied by the notoriously insecure Carte organization, which the Germans had penetrated thoroughly in the spring of 1943: Germaine Tambour, the point of contact, in whom Suttill expressed great confidence in his first written report, was arrested in the third week of April – betrayed, in all probability, by the notorious Roger Bardet. Suttill himself, Amps, Norman, Andrée Borrel and Peter Churchill had all used her house as a letter-box and rendezvous; all of them but Churchill had used for the same purposes another flat in the same building, and so had Agazarian and his wife, Cowburn and Barrett, Bieler and Staggs.
>
> Ten agents in contact with one confidante was bad enough: there were worse errors. Jack Agazarian . . . who was still Suttill's second wireless operator, had been ordered to 'refrain from contacting members of any circuit apart from your own'. Nevertheless, when withdrawn in June, 1943, because he was too conspicious, he claimed to have transmitted for no fewer than twenty-four different agents . . . [including] Bieler, Antelme, Trotobas, Grover-Williams and Claude de Baissac, quite separate

1. Foot, op. cit.
2. Ibid.

— 134 —

organizers who would have had quite separate communications, had the shortage of trained operators not been so acute; as well as several of Suttill's subordinates and the staffs of the Butler and Juggler circuits Suttill was helping to launch . . . and two 'Vic' line sub-organizers who had nothing to do with F Section's business at all. What in fact was happening was that many of F's agents near Paris, particularly the Prosper ones whose work centred on the capital, were congregating there; in defiance of such security training as they had received, in defiance of elementary prudence as well, but in response to the desire for companionship with people who could share with them the secret of their identity and their mission. They made an intelligible, pathetic error; most of them paid for it with their lives.

As Foot concludes, 'the real wonder is not that Suttill and his friends were caught, but that it took so long for so many Germans to catch them.'

Buckmaster, however, was able to clear the matter up when he revealed something that Foot did not know. When he was in London, Suttill was summoned to a private interview with the Prime Minister, and Churchill had asked him to step up the networks' activities even if this meant disregarding the agents' personal security. And Churchill added: 'I must be able to show Stalin that we're doing our best to make the German divisions return from the East.'[1]

Meanwhile, throughout that summer of 1943, the SOE networks – minus Prosper – continued will all kinds of sabotage activities. For example, at the end of June, Trotobas blew up the locomotive sheds at Fives-Lille. And on the night of 3 July, Ben Cowburn and his Tinker group used plastic explosives to do the same at the locomotive sheds in Troyes-Preize (in liaison with local resistants: Dr Mahée and the railman Thierry from the 'Railway Resistance'); eight locomotives were destroyed and five seriously damaged.

Brooks and the Pimento circuit were intensifying their efforts to cause systematic disruption on the railway route used by German reinforcements and military supplies being sent to Italy.

But now Juggler, one of Prosper's sub-groups, was also destroyed. Worms and Armel Guerne were arrested in a restaurant in the Rue Pergolèze. Weil, who'd been late arriving, turned up just in time to see what happened; but he was able to escape, fleeing to Switzerland.

On the night of 22 July, 1943, Bodington was dropped to find out what had caused the Prosper disaster, and to try and regroup the survivors; Agazarian had been sent with him to act as his radio operator. But Bodington had made the mistake of asking London to let him go and see Norman – who, in accordance with the 'pact', was now transmitting for the Germans.

---

1. Letter to the author from Colonel Buckmaster (dated 17 October, 1984).

Bodington and Agazarian tossed up to see who would go and see Norman; chance decided on Agazarian. He was arrested, of course, at the rendezvous they had arranged. He was deported and shot at Flossenberg, six weeks before the war ended. Bodington returned to London on the first available Lysander. Baker Street now knew for sure that Prosper had been totally destroyed.

The Germans had another success. Pickersgill had been given the job of setting up a new group in eastern France called Archdeacon; but as we have seen, Pickersgill was among those who had been captured. He was taken in hand by a German SS officer – Joseph Placke – who set up the group in his place. For ten months SOE suspected nothing; the bogus Archdeacon group was sent fifteen major arms drops, collected by the Germans, and a sabotage expert – François Michel – who was arrested the moment he landed on French soil. A further six agents were dropped in March, 1944, and they too were captured. It was one of the Germans' most effective coups.

During the month of August, 1943, according to Cookridge, '138 Squadron completed 184 operations, dropped 66 agents, 1452 containers and 194 packages'.[1] These figures are clear evidence of the SOE networks' intense activity.

By the time Bodington returned to England on 15 August he had only been able to recover a few elements of the Prosper group, including the sub-group Cinema run by Garry and Marc O'Neill, who were working for Claude de Baissac. Lise and Claude de Baissac had left France with Bodington, handing over control of their group to Grandclément, whom Marc O'Neill had recruited. On 19 August a British plane brought Tony Brooks, Boiteux, Marchand, Madame Le Chêne and Vic Gerson back to England too. They were followed within a few days by Robert Benoist, from the Chestnut group (arrested on 4 August, he had leapt out of the moving car that was taking him to Avenue Foch); Octave Simon, from Satirist, who on four consecutive occasions had narrowly managed to give the Gestapo the slip; and Francis Basin, now released after his incarceration at Montluc.

Among those arriving in France at this time were Harry Peulevé ('Paul'), whose job was to set up a new group in liaison with the Corrèze maquis; Madame Cormeau ('Annette'), a radio operator for George Starr's Wheelwright circuit; Bouchardon, an assistant for Floege; and Cauchi ('Pedro'), who was on his way to join Rée's Stockbroker circuit.

In the summer of 1943, apart from dismantling the small Chestnut group, the Germans did not cause SOE any problems.

On 5 October SOE officially came under the control of the Allied Commander-in-Chief, Europe. In fact, however, it remained under Churchill's direct authority.

---

1. Cookridge, op. cit.

That same month SOE carried out several major operations. On the 10th Liewer's Salesman circuit attacked a metal-working factory run by the Société Française des Metaux in Deville-lès-Rouen, and on the 31st they destroyed the electricity sub-station in Dieppedalle. Other sabotage operations that month, involving other SOE groups, included attacks on the Cellophane factory at Mantes (1 October); the Alsthom factory at Belfort (1 October); the engine construction sheds at Five-Lille (3 October); the Lambiotte works at Premery, Nièvre (7 October); the SNCAC aircraft factories at Fourchambault (20 October); the Philips plant at Brive-la-Gaillarde (21 October); the Société des Électrodes in Notre-Dame-de-Briançon (24 October), etc.

On 19 September the Germans had arrested Grandclément in Paris, the man to whom Claude de Baissac had entrusted command of the big Scientist network in his absence. Grandclément was head of a regional branch of the Organisation Civile et Militaire (OCM), one of the resistance movements, and also head of the Armée Secrète, B Region; he thus belonged both to the internal resistance and to SOE. He was therefore a valuable catch for the Gestapo; they transferred him to Bordeaux, where the Gestapo chief, Dhose, subjected him to torture. This was the start of the so-called 'affaire Grandclément'. M. R. D. Foot writes:[1]

> Dhose appealed to Grandclément's honour as an officer and a gentleman, and rapidly convinced him that France's real interests lay with Germany's; international communism was the monster that threatened to swallow up both alike, and all the heritage of European culture with them, unless they combined to beat it down. Would Grandclément mind helping to free the Reich from the slight menace in rear his resistance groups represented, so that the vital battle in the east could go forward more easily? All that was needed was for him to indicate where Scientist's arms were stored; that done, of course his friends would be released.
>
> Grandclément fell in with this arrangement promptly, and led the Germans on a tour of secret arms dumps.

It should be pointed out that Grandclément had once been aide-de-camp to Colonel de la Rocque and that he might have been influenced by the latter's passionately anti-communist sentiments.

The Germans rounded up over 600 crates of munitions. However, they missed about ten tons of weapons which had been hidden by certain resistance workers alerted to the danger. In a few cases, for example at Lestiac, the arms dumps were fiercely defended by individual resistants, before succumbing to sheer force of numbers. The Germans actually kept

1. Foot, op. cit.

their side of the bargain and freed some 150 people who had been in custody. But Henri Noguères quotes Henri Gayot as saying:[1]

> Following the arrest of Grandclément and the denunciations he made, there were violent repercussions throughout the whole region, particularly for the movement called 'Honneur et Patrie'. Their chief, Prairial, was among those arrested – he had just been appointed head of the OCM's local civil branch – as were Lisiack, who ran the Armée Secrète, Raymond Bouchet, one of the original organizers, and almost all the movement's members. In total, twenty-one were shot and thirty-eight deported, twenty-four of whom would never return. Only General Félix, the local military chief, Major March, Julien and Grasset were able to escape.

The most obvious result of this treachery, as far as SOE was concerned, was the destruction of Scientist, which Claude de Baissac had turned into one of the largest SOE networks both in terms of the numbers of agents and in the operation they carried out.

The networks and sub-groups that had survived the Prosper disaster had maintained radio communications with London via the radio operator for Garry's sub-group, Cinema, part of the now defunct Prosper network. This was Noor Inayat Khan, the Indian princess, a young woman of great bravery, although somewhat naive. In October, 1943, she was arrested by Bleicher, following a denunciation (Foot says that the informer was paid 100,000 francs-£500). A few days later, even though she had not talked, Garry and his wife were also arrested.

The Farmer group, operating in the north and the Pas-de-Calais under Michael Trotobas's leadership, was making tremendous progress. 'Captain Michel', regarded as a particularly skilful agent, had recruited 1,200 members into his group and greatly increased their sabotage activities and other operations. On 25 November, 1943, the Gestapo arrested 'Olivier', one of Trotobas's subordinates, and Olivier talked. When the Germans arrived at his headquarters, Trotobas opened fire. He was shot, though not before he had killed the German leading the raid. But Trotobas had taken the precaution of arranging a system of deputies for each senior agent in his group, and his work was taken over by Seailles and Bayart. As a result, Farmer was able to continue functioning despite the loss of its charismatic leader. Indeed, a few days after Trotobas was killed, the group destroyed eleven locomotives at Tourcoing.

Also in November, Harry Rée ('César'), who was head of the Stockbroker group, concentrated on the 'blackmail' technique – that is to say, using

---

1. Noguères, op. cit. Vol. IV.

high-level accomplices to carry out sabotage operations on industrial targets. The raid on the Peugeot works, described above, was the first operation in France to use this technique. But it wasn't every industrial manager who had the sort of patriotic courage shown by Monsieur Peugeot. Foot says that the Michelin family refused to help sabotage their tyre factory at Clermont-Ferrand 'and the RAF consequently damaged it seriously'.

In the autumn of 1943 SOE set up a new group in the Limoges region. This was the Author group, under the command of Harry Peulevé ('Henri'), with the able assistance of Roland Malraux. Peulevé soon established good relations with the leading figures of the local branch of the Francs-Tireurs et Partisans movement, who were very active in the area, led by Georges Guingoin in Corrèze and André Bonnetot ('Vincent') in the Dordogne. The German troops in these parts included a large proportion of White Russians from Georgia, who had been forcibly conscripted into the Wehrmacht. Many of them were now deserting to join the maquis; Peulevé collected their German army uniforms, which his men then used in sabotage operations – notably when they destroyed the submarine base at La Pallice.

Another group, Salesman, under Philippe Liewer, which SOE had recently set up in the area round Le Havre, was also enjoying good relations with the local resistance. As early as September, 1943, Salesman had organized the first arms drop for their resistance friends.

In December, 1943, several important agents were being held at 84 Avenue Foch in Paris, headquarters of the German security police. Among them were Major Faye, head of the large Alliance organization (not one of SOE's groups), and two of SOE's leading agents: John Starr, whose brother George was head of the Wheelwright circuit in the south-west, and Noor Inayat Khan, the Indian princess. One cold night, the three of them managed to loosen the bars of the attic cells in which they were held and escaped over the rooftops. But when they reached the street, the Germans were waiting for them. Faye was tortured the following day, then sent to a concentration camp; on 28 June, 1944, he was sentenced to death by a military tribunal at Freibourg-im-Breisgau, and on 30 January, 1945, he was executed. Noor Inayat Khan was sent to Dachau and there, on 13 September, 1944, she was shot in the back of the neck. John Starr was deported to Mauthausen, but he was fortunate enough to survive.

Foot gives a rather pessimistic account of SOE's standing in France as at 31 December, 1943, just a few months before the Allied landings:[1]

> What worried SOE a good deal more than support of the Neptune assault was support of Overlord, the follow-through. There was no doubt that the sizeable secret armies SOE now knew it could raise were woefully underarmed. Far too many of

1. Foot, op. cit.

the arms chaches built up in northern and western France by Suttill and de Baissac had fallen into enemy hands through the Germans' inroads into Prosper and Scientist; Britanny was in chaos; George Starr, Heslop, Cammaerts were flourishing, but far away; Suttill was in prison, Rée in flight, Bieler in danger; Trotobas was dead.

However, as a footnote to Foot's overall assessment, it should be pointed out that by 1 January, 1944, SOE did have twenty-five fully operational and very active groups in France. Moreover, new groups were still being started, despite all the setbacks, and SOE was able to play a far from inconsiderable part in the course of the decisive year of 1944.

Between 14 and 20 January, 1944, a series of Anglo-French meetings were held in London to plan the various Allied missions, jointly known as Jedburgh, that would be launched in France later that year. Major Debesse, who was a member of one of the Jedburgh teams, sent a report to Colonel Passy in which he described their objectives very clearly – for though the Jedburgh operations are well known, the details are often poorly understood. Debesse said:[1]

> 1. Most of the teams will be sent to help various resistance groups that are already known to us. Their job is to arm these groups, turn them into a rallying centre for all the local resistance workers, and, with everyone thus assembled, carry out certain planned operations (particulars in the English note). Once these missions are accomplished and the new groups have been formed among the resistance workers, these teams will either return to the front-line units or continue fighting behind enemy lines. . . .
> 2. A very few teams, composed of specially chosen officers, will be sent to meet the leading figures of all the resistance movements and the maquis, to act as technical advisers and to maintain liaison between them and High Command. . . .
> 3. Some teams will be kept in reserve for special tactical operations against weak points in the enemy's rear, either where there are insufficient resistance units or where the intended mission is beyond the capabilities of such units. These teams will include paratroops to enable the missions to be accomplished.

But Major Debesse, a French officer, went on to express his fear that when the time came – in other words, just before the Normandy invasion, as well as during and immediately after the landings – all these 'paramilitary elements'

---

1. Quoted in Henri Noguères, op. cit. Vol. IV.

in the French resistance would fall under British control, partly because they would be influenced by 'the prestige of being visited by uniformed officers from London' and partly because it was SOE's agents who would supply the central active core, well trained, well equipped and above all well armed. And, in most cases, this is exactly what happened.

January, 1944, was a relatively quiet month for the SOE circuits. As always, successes alternated with setbacks. Several agents were caught: in Haute-Savoie it was Mesnard, head of Director; in Saint-Quentin, Bieler, head of Musician, and also his radio operator Yolande Beekman and his deputy P. R. Tissier, both of whom had but recently arrived; also Sonia Olschanesky, the last survivor from Juggler, and on the same day – 21 January – ten members of the Vic escape line circuit (but Vic had set up such a close security system that the Gestapo never managed to catch any other members of the group).

'Friend, if you fall, another will come from the shadows to take your place . . .' Arriving from Britain at the start of January, 1944, there came several new 'friends', including Claude Arnault and Anne-Marie Walters, who landed on the 3rd, to join Wheelwright; and on the 7th Captain George Hiller ('Maxime') and his radio operator Lieutenant Cyril Watney ('Eustache'). Hiller's task was twofold: his first mission was of a politico-military nature, to do with the Vény groups being set up by underground members of the socialist party; while his second mission concerned active sabotage.

Hiller and Watney were delighted to find Harry Peulevé, their former instructor at Beaulieu, on their reception committee. They were housed near Martel at the home of Jean Verlhac, regional head of the Vény groups. They rapidly started joint operations with Vény, while Watney found a safe location to keep his transmitter – in the Creysse town hall, where the council secretary was also a local resistance leader. He was thus able to continue his transmissions right to the end of the war.

On the night of 19 January the Ratier factories became the target of a major sabotage attack. This is Cookridge's account of the operation:[1]

> Hiller had been doing the planning, and when London sent a large supply of explosives, they went to work. Plastic explosives were fashioned into small limpet mines by Hiller and Watney at Jean Verlhac's *fromagèrie*. They had to be taken to the garage of Charles Gamade, at the other end of Saint-Céré, who was to drive a van at night to the vicinity of the Ratier works. Crossing the town, patrolled by German Field Police, was a problem. A Vény member, Dédé Saint-Chamant, dressed himself as a pastry cook, in white overalls and a chief's tall hat, and walked several times

1. Cookridge, op. cit.

through the town, holding a large tray with the explosives covered with a clean napkin above his head, as sellers of freshly made pastries do. Thus all the mines were safely loaded into Gamade's van.

The night of 19 January was almost moonless. Chapou, Yves Ouvrieu, another schoolmaster and Saint-Chamant drove to the factory. They entered it through a small back door, having obtained the keys from a foreman, placed their charges, and left without attracting attention, although the factory was heavily guarded.

Shortly afterwards, Figeac was shaken by a terrific explosion. Although the Ratier works stood well outside the built-up area, hardly a window in town remained intact. The 5,000 inhabitants gladly endured the loss when they realized what had happened. A thirty-ton press was lifted twenty-five feet and smashed to pieces; several machines that produced the precision blades of the aircraft propellors were destroyed; within minutes the whole factory was in flames. Production was never resumed during the war.

And, concludes Cookridge, 'Buckmaster sent Hiller and Watney a congratulatory signal'.

In February, 1944, the radio operator Roger Casa was dropped to join Brooks's Pimento circuit. But Pimento had been under great strain recently, as André Moch, Brooks's aide and appointed successor, had been killed in a altercation with the Milice, the French security forces.

That same month René Dumont-Guillemet and Diancono arrived to reinforce the Spiritualist circuit and Roger Landes came to inspect progress. Floege and Bouchardon were also flown back to France by Lysander, and Frager came by sea.

Frager had been in London to tell the SOE chiefs of his doubts concerning Déricourt. He suggested that Déricourt should be recalled to London. Earlier, Agazarian had already told Baker Street about Suttill's suspicions, and the previous July several groups had done the same. But Buckmaster and Bodington still had faith in Déricourt; Bodington though that if Déricourt was a traitor, he would have had him arrested during his recent trip to Paris. Besides, Déricourt had successfully planned and carried out a total of seventeen air drops involving twenty-one aircraft, thus helping forty-three people to return to France and sixty-seven to leave.

What really shook Buckmaster was a telegram from Georges Pichard ('Oyster') which reinforced these accusations. Now Déricourt was recalled to London. He and his young wife were collected near Tours by a Lysander on the night of 8 February. He would not return to France till after the Liberation. In June, 1948, he appeared before a military tribunal but was acquitted, chiefly thanks to Bodington's evidence. It does seem certain, however, that Déricourt had been in close contact with the Germans. Writing about this delicate subject, Foot says:[1]

> It is clear from interrogations of members of the notorious Rue Lauriston gang of Paris criminals, headed by Bony and Lafont, that gangsters were habitually hidden round Déricourt's landing grounds in the summer and autumn of 1943, with the task of trailing the agents who arrived.

March, 1944, saw the downfall of the Author circuit, which had been set up in Corrèze and was led by Major Peulevé. The latter was accused of blackmarket dealings by a jealous neighbour, and he was arrested on the Tulle-Brive road while he was in the middle of sending a signal to London. At the same time as his arrest, the radio operator Louis Bertheau, the police commissioner of Ussel, Charles Delsantie, and Roland Malraux, Peulevé's deputy, were also caught.

Foot's account of the German operations leading to the break up and capture of numerous groups and SOE agents, whose work would have been invaluable on the eve of the Allied landings, is here summarized by Henri Neguères:[2]

> It was in March, 1944, that the 'game' set up by Dr Goetz – who was responsible for the Germans' false radio messages being sent from Paris – was to reach its most remarkable and dramatic heights. Without going into all the details revealed by M. R. D. Foot – alarming and exciting though they are – we can sum up the consequences of these operations as follows.
>
> After having 'turned' Prosper's radio operator (Norman) but only with partial success, Goetz had been able to fool the Baker Street people by using the captured transmitter sets from three separate groups: Archdeacon, whose set had been picked up with Macalister and Pickersgill and had not given a single day's service to the Allies; Butler, whose set had been operated by Garel; and Phono (formerly the Cinema group, under Garry).
>
> Within the space of a few short months, SOE had delivered to the Germans, via these three 'phantom' groups:
>
> 1. Considerable supplies of arms, ammunition and miscellaneous equipment in numerous drops.
>
> 2. Substantial sums of money, meant either for the three groups themselves or for new groups that were never set up because their organizers had fallen into Goetz's three-part trap: in total,

1. Foot, op. cit.
2. Noguères, op. cit., Vol. IV.

8,572,000 francs, of which 2,585,000 francs arrived in the single month of March, in six separate drops.

3. Finally, and most important of all, twenty-one agents had been dropped (mostly in March) on the dropping zones arranged by the three 'circuits'. . . . The majority of them were British, but they also included Americans, Canadians, Frenchmen and two Mauritians. Most were seasoned group leaders, with months or years of experience behind them, or radio operators who had also proved their worth.

Ten of them became victims of the Archdeacon set-up: one sabotage instructor, François Michel ('Dispenser'); a four-man team with the task of setting up the Liontamer circuit near Valenciennes, namely Macbain, Finlayson (a radio operator) and the two Americans Lepage and Lesout; four group leaders, namely Rabinovitch, one of SOE's most experienced radio operators, who was about to launch his own Bargee circuit near Nancy, Woerther ('Woodcutter'), Pearson ('Pedagogue') and Defendini ('Priest') who was arrested at the agreed rendezvous; and finally the Canadian, Sabourin, who was sent to help Defendini, himself arrested when he landed at a dropping zone arranged through Archdeacon.

Four fell into the Butler trap: two who had been sent to reinforce the team, the Belgian Detal ('Delegate') and Duclos; and two others, both of them experienced men, Octave Simon and his radio operator 'Defence', whose task was to reorganize the Satirist circuit in the Bordeaux area.

Finally, seven agents sent for (or by) the Phono circuit were greeted when they landed – a little before the others, in February – by a reception committee which had come straight from Avenue Foch. They included, first, a four-man team made up of the Frenchman Alexandre, the American Byerley (a radio-operator); the Canadian Deniset (an arms instructor); and the Anglo-French Jacques Ledoux. The latter was meant to have started a new group, Orator, while his companions devoted themselves to Surveyor. Then, on the last night of February, three more were caught – the Mauritian France Antelme, the radio operator Lionel Lee, and a woman courier by the name of Madeleine Damerment.

These twenty-one agents thus delivered straight into enemy hands would all be deported, most of them to Gross Rosen, the others to Buchenwald or Mauthausen. And there they were all killed before the Allied forces arrived.

Foot is somewhat critical of the SOE staff in London. He comments that most of them continued to trust their radio operators completely. Yet the operators had been sending transmissions for the Germans ever since their arrest; they did their best to let headquarters know they were no longer free by making deliberate mistakes in their 'security checks', including errors in their signals which they were sure London would immediately detect as being false, and so on.

And, in the case of the Indian princess, Noor Inayat Khan, Foot concludes from the reports on her by the Beaulieu instructors that she should never have been sent to France at all; moreover, that the instructions she had been given were ambiguous and open to different interpretations.

In the Troyes area, Ivan Dupont ('Major Ivan'), head of the SOE group Diplomat, was taking in surviving agents from the now demolished Tinker circuit. On 15 March he sent a team of them to carry out a major raid on railway stocks at Troyes-Preize: fourteen tenders and locomotives were destroyed by plastic explosive.

In the west SOE had re-established the Clergyman circuit around Nantes, using men and supplies from the decimated Chestnut group. Clergyman was led by Robert Benoist, along with his radio operator Denise Bloch.

On 25 March SOE successfully sabotaged the hydro-electric plant at Ugine by destroying the engines of two auxiliary pumps; the plant was out of action for a week.

Also in March, SOE set up a new group, Scholar, in the R.1 (Rhône-Alpes) region; it later spread to the Ain and the Jura mountains. The group leader was Gonzague de Saint-Geniès and Yvonne Baseden was the radio operator.

Earlier that year, in the R.2 area, the small group Monk run by Skepper, Steele and Eliane Plewman had blocked the Marseilles-Toulon railway line to Italy, causing a derailment in the tunnel between Marseilles and Cassis. In January they had destroyed a total of thirty locomotives, and thirty more in March. But on 23 March Skepper was arrested, as was Villevielle, a resistance worker who had joined SOE. In the following days the Gestapo destroyed the whole group, setting a trap to catch first Steele, then Eliane Plewman too. Jack Sinclair, who was dropped on 6 March to join Monk, had landed to a reception committee organized by the Gestapo. The destruction of this very effective little group had been caused by a French informer; after the Liberation he was arrested, tried and executed.

But this area was of particular strategic importance – so important, in fact, that Buckmaster instructed a new group to be set up (Gardener) by three highly skilled agents: Boiteux (founder of Spruce), Cohen (who had been with Juggler) and Aptaker, a radio operator.

The new group did not take long to make its presence felt, operating in the same area as that excellent group, Jockey, led by the experienced SOE agent Cammaerts.

In the R.4 area, the centre of which was Toulouse, some of SOE's best agents were continuing their good work throughout the spring of 1944, including George Starr, George Hiller, Tony Brooks and Henri Sevenet.

In the R.6 area, the head of Stationer, Maurice Southgate, had been unable to secure the co-operation of the Michelin works managers for a small but efficient sabotage operation there. As a result, it was the RAF who intervened on 17 March. Five hundred bombers crushed the Michelin plant under a carpet of bombs. Unfortunately the operation also caused 19 deaths and 26 wounded; 30 buildings were destroyed, 300 others were damaged (100 of them seriously).

On 15 April Colonel Coulaudon ('Gaspard'), head of the maquis in the Auvergne, went to Montluçon to meet Major Maurice Southgate ('Hector', 'Philippe'), head of the SOE circuit Stationer, one of the biggest in the south. The two men decided to go ahead with 'Plan Caiman' (also called 'Koenig'). The idea behind the plan was to set up three secure bases for the resistance fighters: one at Mont Mouchet in the Margeride mountains, where the regional headquarters were, one in the Chaudes-Aigues region and one in Lioran. Southgate asked London to send arms, ammunition, transmitters and support personnel as soon as possible. So, on the night of 28 April, the two leading figures in the Freelance circuit were dropped – Major John Hind-Farmer ('Jean') and Lieutenant Nancy Fiocca-Wake ('Andrée'). A third member of the team joined them a month later – Captain Dennis Joseph Wake ('Denis'). In fact, however, on Roosevelt's recommendation, the Allies cancelled the plan.

In April SOE continued to step up operations with a view to the forthcoming Allied landings. This is how Henri Noguères summarizes their activities at this period:[1]

> First of all, more new organizers were arriving to set up more new circuits. Some of them were old acquaintances of ours – such as Philippe de Vomécourt, whose new circuit was contained within the triangle of Vierzon, Orléans and Blois, covering only a partial extent of the vast zone on which the old Ventriloquist circuit had spread its branches. Another old friend was Roger Landes, who returned to start up the new group Actor on the ruins of Scientist. Another was Rouneau, the Belgian who had run Racketeer; he was making an urgent trip now, landing by sea, to find out what had happened to cause the Bricklayer disaster after Antelme had been arrested. Yet others included Henri Borosh, in charge of starting the new Silversmith group alongside Robert Lyon's Acolyte; Régnier, who came to set up Mason in liaison with Marchand's Newsagent; and finally Corbin, the policeman from Bordeaux who was a friend of Claude de Baissac's. Corbin had had a miraculous escape from the consequences of the Grand-clément affair, and after attending a course in London he was now

---

1. Noguères, op. cit., Vol. IV.

back in France to start up the Carven circuit between Angoulême and Rochefort

For Liewer and Violette Szabo, dropped at the beginning of April, their mission was to be cut short; they were supposed to try and re-establish contact with the Salesman agents They soon realized, however, that they had no chance of rebuilding this circuit, and heard that the Germans had put a huge price on Liewer's head; so they returned to England after only three weeks.

Other new arrivals had come simply to reinforce the various teams, whose activities were now in full swing, or else to fill the gaps in their ranks caused by the Gestapo and Abwehr. This was the case for Brouville, sent to join Stockbroker in place of 'Pedro', also for Beau Clerk and Peter Lake, dropped to help Poirier, Peulevé's successor in Author (which had since become Digger), and for Beggar who was joining Minister

Out of all the agents sent to France that April, SOE archives show just one single trace of a serious blow: this involved the team composed of two Frenchmen, Captain Leccia and Lieutenant Allard, and a Belgian, Lieutenant Geelen. Dropped on 5 April on the borders of the Indre region, right beside the Cher, the team was codenamed Labourer and their task – Operation Beaudoin – consisted simply of blowing up the German headquarters near Angers just before the landings. Only a few days after they arrived, however, they were contacted by a double agent who took them to Paris and handed them over to the Gestapo. All three of them were executed at Buchenwald on 10 September, 1944.

It wasn't every SOE agent leaving London who was given a precise objective like Leccia and his unfortunate companions. But they had all arrived to carry out prompt action of one kind or another.

On 10 May Robert Lyon, head of the SOE group Acolyte, was arrested in Lyons. He escaped but was recaptured. Then he escaped again, while he was being transferred to Drancy, by jumping out of the train while it was passing through Villeneuve-Saint-Georges.

On 19 May, 1944, SOE formally approved the Bibendum plan set up by the BCRA. This plan, a successor to 'Plan Torture', was intended to use every possible means to delay the arrival of German armoured divisions, which would undoubtedly be sent to the new front created by the Allied landings. Regular communications were maintained in London between SOE and General Koenig's staff in order to co-ordinate operations in this essential area. (On 30 May Koenig was officially recognized by the Allied chiefs of staff as Commander-in-Chief of the Free French Forces.)

On 4 June, 1944, two officers from SHAEF (General Eisenhower's headquarters) – Colonel David Bruce, an American, and General Gubbins, the Englishman who had succeeded Sir Charles Hambro as chief of SOE in September, 1943 – paid General Koenig a courtesy visit. The intention was to make sure French High Command would not raise any objections if Supreme Allied Command decided, while Overlord was in progress, to use the BBC to send messages instructing operations to start up over the whole of France.

In June the Germans were alerted to the possibility of an Allied invasion by their intelligence units – and also by the systematic pounding of railway junctions and vital communications centres; in response they stepped up their brutal repression of resistance forces. Vast numbers of people involved in the resistance were arrested, and SOE was not spared. Thus Frager's group Donkeyman, operating in Normandy, was infiltrated by the traitor Raoul Kiffer; many of the members were arrested and the Germans seized several arms caches that had been built up from parachute drops. Also in June, the SOE group around Bordeaux, severely damaged by Grandclément's treachery, was strongly rebuilt by Roger Landes. His teams would go into action immediately after D-Day, taking over most of the operations in the south-west.

The operation launched in the critical sector of Calvados, before and during the landing, is here described by Marcel Baudot:[1]

> It was above all the FTP [Francs-Tireurs et Partisans] from the Vire region who led the action in the Calvados. In Lisieux and Orbec the SOE group Antoine and several FTP teams crammed all the main roads with mines. Other French resistance units attached to SOE – from the Michel group in Normandy – made their presence felt in Lisieux, Evercy, Beny-Bocage and Sourdeval. The largest was the Cesny-Bois-Halbout group, run by André Le Nevez who was working with the SOE team leader Renaud Dandicolle; they were well armed, thanks to three supply drops carried out at Cesny in September, 1943, and at Pierrefitte-en-Cinglais at the end of May and again at the beginning of June. This group cut railway lines and launched guerrilla raids on 6 and 7 June, but they were captured shortly afterwards. Before they surrendered, members of the Le Nevez group killed four German officers.

The repression did not bring operations to a complete halt, however. For example, on 10 June, the day of the Oradour massacre, Violette Szabo was arrested. She had been dropped on the 6th, at the same time as Liewer and Bob Mortier (back in April these three had tried in vain to rebuild the Salesman group in Rouen, which the Gestapo had broken). Here Georges

1. Quoted in Noguères, op. cit., Vol. V.

Guingoin tells the story of how this courageous young woman, an SOE agent, was caught:[1]

> While she and Jacques Dufour ('Anastasie') were driving to meet a contact near Salon-la-Tour, they ran into an SS ambush. Both armed with machine guns, they leapt into a ditch; but they were outnumbered and had to flee across the fields. Unfortunately, Violette fell, twisting her ankle painfully. Strenuously refusing to let her companion help – he wanted to carry her – the English girl bravely told him to save himself. With a superhuman effort, she held out against the pursuers, firing machine-gun bursts at them while Anastasie made a desperate run for safety. He managed to reach a small farm, owned by the Montintin family, and hid in a woodshed; three women of the house quickly covered him with logs and branches. They were just in time. An armoured truck roared into the farmyard and German soldiers jumped out, hurling questions at the family. The family pretended that they had seen a man running off along the railway line. Neither the house nor the outbuildings were even searched. Dufour was safe. Violette, however, was taken prisoner and sent to Ravensbrück.

At Ravensbrück on 26 January, 1945, Violette Szabo was shot.

It would be impossible to give all the details of the operations SOE carried out before, during and after the crucial weeks of the Allied landings. While it is difficult to evaluate them properly, their achievements were considerable: railway lines were cut, bridges destroyed, locomotives blown up, telephone lines cut, German command posts isolated, pylons brought down, roads mined, enemy columns attacked, etc. For example, the Normandy sub-groups of Donkeyman, the SOE circuit led by Frager, had managed to elude Parleani, local head of the FFI,[1] and threw themselves into non-stop vigorous activity: continuing to cut roads and railways, harassing the enemy, guerrilla tactics, etc. Among their successes were the derailment of a munitions train in the Bernay tunnel on 24 July, and on 29 July the raid on a major armaments stock at Livarot which they 'liberated'.

Occasionally, of course, there was some friction between the resistance workers and SOE agents. When the Germans raided the maquis band around Écot on 8 July, and killed their famous leader, Lieutenant Joly ('Valentin'), Ernest Floege ('Paul') from SOE, who replaced Harry Rée, decided that he himself shoud take over as military commander of the Monbéliard sector. But Colonel Maurin ('Devaux'), who was head of the FFI in Franche-Comté, decided to take over instead, making 'Paul' his assistant. It was a diplomatic solution.

1. Georges Guingoin, *Quatre Ans de Lutte sur le Sol Limousin* (Hachette, Paris 1974).
2. Forces Francaises de l'Intérieur.

SOE also knew how to balance its liabilities against its assets. The traitor Grandclément, who was being hunted down by 'Aristide' and his powerful SOE teams, was finally found by Meirilhac – sent to Bordeaux by the BCRA – at the home of one of his subordinates, Duluguet, who had been hiding him in Canauley. Meirilhac told Grandclément that a Lysander was being sent to collect him and take him to London. On 24 July Meirilhac, along with Dastet and other members of the group led by Borde ('Georges'), took Grandclément and his wife and Duluguet to a cave near Léognan and subjected him to a long interrogation. Finally Grandclément signed a document admitting that he had betrayed patriots and arms to Dhose. On the 28th Roger Landes ('Aristide'), accompanied by 'Dédé le Basque', Louis Campet and Max Paye, arrived to question him further. The traitor repeated his confession, pleading that he had been forced to work for the Germans. But he was executed, as were his wife and Marc Duluguet.

Claude and Roland Malraux, brothers of André, had long been members of SOE groups, Claude with Salesman, where he acted as Liewer's deputy, and Roland with Author, as Peulevé's assistant. Both men were to fall into enemy hands, Claude in March and Roland in May – at the same time as Peulevé.

It is not clear quite when André Malraux joined the fight. According to Foot, he was probably one of the FTP leaders in Corrèze, and according to Cookridge he was 'in command of the FFI region'. But Henri Noguères writes that 'it was not, in fact, until the spring of 1944 that André Malraux decided to take an active role in the resistance'. 'Colonel Berger', as Malraux was known, is said to have been in Corrèze, in the Dordogne, in the Tarn and the Lot. It was Peulevé who put him in touch with Hiller, who admired him as a writer, and Hiller helped to put him in touch with the Vény groups in the Lot. After the war Buckmaster said that Malraux had never actually been recruited by SOE.[1] When Malraux and Hiller were returning from a visit to inspect resistance units in the Tarn, they were ambushed by the Germans. Slightly wounded in the leg, Malraux was arrested and transferred to Toulouse on 23 July. When the Tarn was liberated he was released from Saint-Michel prison where he'd been held for nearly a month.

In July several SOE agents were actively working with the maquis bands: in the R.4 region, where the FFI was led by Ravanel; in Saône-et-Loire where SOE and maquis teams around Sylla and Corlay were continuing sabotage and guerrilla operations; in Vercors, where Frenchman Pierre Raynaud ('Alain') had been dropped by SOE in June, 1943, as deputy for Francis Cammaerts, leader of Jockey (that June Alain joined the FFI in Drôme, as commander of the 3rd Battalion); and in Allier, where the FFI were being sent sizeable arms drops in August thanks to the SOE group Freelance run by John Farmer and Nancy Wake.

1. According to Noguères, op. cit., Vol. V.

According to Cookridge the German General Elster surrendered on 10 September with nearly 2,000 of his men 'to the American General Macon and Commandant Philippe de Vomécourt of SOE', for the German troops now in retreat had been harassed incessantly by the FFI and Americans before being trapped beside the River Allier. They were caught like fish in a net, cornered between the Allier and the Loire.

Major Bodington, Buckmaster's deputy, was dropped into the Haute-Marne to join the Pedlar circuit. In this connection, Henri Noguères quotes Michel-André Pichard, Director of Military Operations, who was himself dropped on the night of 11 August:[1]

> Major Bodington had much to do in the northern part of the sector. In addition to the two units in Montier-en-Der that he personally was to lead, he had to supply arms to the FFI in Saint-Dizier. At my request he sent a battalion into the Chaumont sector, and when Chaumont fell he took over command of all the new units arriving in support: namely one unit from the Aube, another from the Marne, two from Saint-Dizier and one from Joinville.

On 16 September the whole department was liberated. This is just one of a number of examples that illustrate the excellent co-operation between SOE agents and the interior French resistance forces and Allies. This co-ordinated action was pretty widespread and undoubtedly helped the advance of the liberating armies.

This is how Cookridge sums up the combined efforts in the fight for Liberation:[1]

> During the last few weeks preceding the liberation, SOE and OSS [the American organization] intensified every effort to drop great quantities of arms, including mortars, bazookas and machine guns to the FFI. Several experienced SOE organizers arrived on their second and third missions.
>
> According to French sources, ninety Jedburgh teams were parachuted to the maquis after D-Day, with 300 French, British and American officers to provide commanders and instructors. According to SHAEF, the number of French, British and American officers thus employed was almost twice that figure. In addition, many units of Special Air Service, each consisting of thirty to sixty heavily armed, commando-trained men, were dropped to aid FFI units.

1. Noguères, op. cit., Vol. V.
2. Cookridge, op. cit.

It might be appropriate to end this chronological survey of SOE's activities, by no means complete, with one significant episode.

Major 'Paul' had created a huge army of maquisards on the Lomont plateau, assembling 3,000 men – all very well armed thanks to parachute deliveries that were being made almost every night. On 6 September the Germans launched an attack on them, for the maquisards were threatening their line of retreat. But the maquisards repulsed them. General de Lattre de Tassigny underlines the importance of this battle:[1]

> The most outstanding occurrence during this unstable stage prior to Liberation was at the eastern end of the Lomont mountain range, where Linarès made contact with an FFI group which, under the American Major 'Paul', had been holding this high plateau for three months, and the old fort that stood on it, despite its isolation and repeated attacks by the Germans. This admirable feat gave us an incomparable viewpoint over the Montbéliard plain and the 'watchdog' of the Belfort pass.

This Major 'Paul', born in Chicago in 1898, was none other than Ernest-Fred Floege, who had been parachuted into the field as a British SOE agent. Each morning he had the three national flags solemnly raised in front of his command post while a bugle sounded the 'Au Drapeau'. The bugler was Pierre Sellier, famous as the man whose bugle had sounded the ceasefire on the afternoon of 11 November, 1918, on the road from Capelle to Haudroy, thus marking the end of the First World War.

De Lattre, the 1918 bugler and the SOE officer who commanded the maquisards – what a remarkable analogy of the historical unity between different generations, Allies, regular forces, resistance workers and SOE agents in France.

1. General de Lattre de Tassigny, *Histoire de la Première Armée Française* (Plon, Paris 1949).

—— 2 ——

# THE SETBACKS

This outline of SOE in action has shown, alongside the exploits and achievements, the all too frequent setbacks and crises which Buckmaster's agents experienced, resulting for many of them in the supreme sacrifice.

These derived from the very nature of the work in which they were engaged, from high-level disagreements, from certain shortages of arms and other supplies, and above all from the enemy's actions, for the Germans had managed to infiltrate some of the networks and 'turned' some of the agents, as well as subjecting them to arrest, torture, deportation and death.

The question of direct action gave rise to much dissension within the French resistance.[1] As Henri Noguères says:[2]

> This was certainly the most fundamental problem in the spring of 1943. It was also this problem that apparently engendered the most serious misunderstandings. The BCRA, Jean Moulin and General Delestraint had initially opted for a wait-and-see strategy, not undertaking any premature action against the enemy and his installations. Their reasoning was that direct action risked inciting the Germans to reinforce their troops in France, thus making it more difficult for the Allied invasion to succeed. But Passy and Brossolette, when they made a special visit to France, had found it virtually impossible to prevent the resistance from going into action immediately – and not only those who were working for the 'militant' Front National and the FTPF [Francs-Tireurs et Partisans Français]. On 21 May, 1943, General de Gaulle settled the question by sending General Delestraint a personal and highly confidential message which explicitly said: 'We accept the need for immediate action.'

1. See M. Ruby, *La Résistance à Lyons.*
2. Noguères, op. cit., Vol. III.

Conflict was thus avoided between the French resistance and the SOE agents whom Winston Churchill had instructed to set fire to the occupied countries of Europe.

Here we should mention one theory that was fomulated long after the war was ended. According to Fuller[1] and Wighton,[2] Gilles Perrault raised the possibility of 'the Allies exploiting the resistance in order to deceive the Germans'. He was thinking particularly of Prosper, which Baker Street continued to use even though Buckmaster knew perfectly well that the circuit had fallen into German hands and that its radio operators had been 'turned'. Perhaps the Allies wanted the Germans to think they were planning an invasion on the Channel coast during the summer of 1943 – in order to keep as many German divisions as possible in France, while General Eisenhower was landing at Salerno (8 September, 1943)? Perrault himself concluded:[3]

> When they were finally completely sure that the enemy had discovered and 'turned' the radio operators, they decided that contact must still be maintained to make the enemy believe they had fallen into his trap . . . the communications lines that the enemy himself had set up would be used to trick him. But there was a price to pay. . . . It follows that some men were sacrificed deliberately.
>
> Twenty years later, is it not time to acknowledge this? For their sacrifice was not in vain. Today, now that the tears have dried and the wounds have healed, is it not possible to face the bitter truth? The resistance was the anvil on which both the Germans and the British struck their hammers, turn and turn about, but on which to some extent the success of the D-Day landings were forged.

If this was indeed the case, then the facts should be made known more plainly. Attacked not only by the enemy but by the Allies too – in the national interests, of course – the sacrifice paid by the SOE and resistance martyrs is that much more valuable.

This is consistent with another theory: that the Allies told the resistance the landings would be in the Pas-de-Calais, not Normandy. The resistance consequently mobilized all their units there at the end of May and in June, 1944, intensifying their efforts and suffering heavy losses. But the Germans did keep most of their troops in the Pas-de-Calais for more than two weeks, thus allowing the Normandy landings to go ahead successfully.

For his part, Pierre de Vomécourt, the first organizer parachuted into

1. Jean Overton Fuller, *Double Agent* (Pan, London 1961).
2. Charles Wighton, *Pinstripe Saboteur* (Odhams, London 1959).
3. Gilles Perrault, *Le Secret du Jour J* (Fayard, Paris 1964).

France by SOE in May, 1941, has categorically stated what he considered SOE's aims to be:[1]

> Although the long-term objective was to supply the French with the material means to participate in the liberation of their country, the immediate objective was to hinder the enemy's production capacity: to disorganize transport and delivery of vital materials, to sabotage industry and stocks, to cause deliberate errors in the planning of production schedules, etc. This form of action was admittedly not very spectacular, nor very well understood by certain people, but it was effective and it was also economical in terms of human lives.

This was certainly the original intention . . .

Following a long-established tradition, there was constant rivalry between the various secret services, sometimes more obvious than at others. It was impossible not to see this in London where so many separate intelligence units were based in such close proximity – American, British (not just the SIS itself but also SOE F Section and SOE RF Section) and the French BCRA as well.

Victor Chatenay acknowledged this situation in his diary, not without sadness:[2]

> Our different organizations do not understand each other. The British Intelligence Service, the IS, to which I belong, cannot stand the Gaullists. But me, I am a Gaullist, I shout it from the rooftops. They can't even get along with the British action groups [SOE], who are just amateurs – we call them saboteurs. On the other hand the BCRA, both the action side and the intelligence side, do not like the British intelligence agents going to France to cheat and to steal their own people by pretending to be from General de Gaulle, who is not exactly a friend of theirs and whom they thwart at every turn. They are slightly better disposed towards Buckmaster, who calls his group SOE or French Section, even though some of his people aren't all as tolerable as him. On the other hand, the English who worked for SOE's RF Section were just as loyal to the vision of a Free France as real Frenchmen.

It could hardly have been otherwise, considering that constant guerrilla warfare had been waged between the French and the British in London for

1. Pierre de Vomécourt, in a letter dated 'September–October 1960'.
2. Victor Chatenay, *Mon Journal du Temps du Malheur* (published Courrier de l'Ouest, n.d.).

four whole years, as General de Gaulle describes in great detail in his *Mémoires de Guerre*. Benjamin Cowburn confirms this particularly clearly:[1]

> General de Gaulle, quite understandably, wanted all secret operations on French soil to be his and his alone The BCRA's agents, recruited from French volunteers who had escaped from France, underwent special training courses at our secret schools and then returned to France on various different missions; intelligence, sabotage, organizing the Free French forces, propaganda, political and administrative preparation to establish a provisional government when the country was liberated, etc.
>
> No less understandably, British High Command – with overall responsibility for action against the Axis forces – wanted its own special agents in France, the largest of the occupied countries. The enemy forces there presented the most obvious threat, and the most decisive battles of the entire war certainly took place on French soil.
>
> The 'lack of harmony' between the British and French services in London prevented unity of command, with two 'competing firms' operating in the same field. The British, of course, supplied the BCRA with equipment, transport and reception facilities for clandestine transmissions; but they also allowed it complete liberty of action. The British service, for its part, recruited bilingual Britons as well as Frenchmen dissatisfied with the reception they had received from the Free French in London and who had chosen to join our ranks instead.
>
> This high-level lack of agreement was no joke to us and we tried to keep it from our friends. The excellent daily BBC broadcasts by Maurice Schumann, praising the way the Allies were all working together, was a great help to us in this respect.
>
> It sometimes happened that the two sides met each other in the field. One of my own 'contacts', for example, told me that a friend of his had joined a group whose leader was in touch with 'an emissary from London'. I had to explain to him that we were strictly supposed to stick to our separate divisions and that each of us had to obey our own immediate chief.
>
> The BCRA itself had problems, and, like us, suffered heavy losses.

The same impartiality is shown by Philippe de Vomécourt, for example, who also stresses the opinion of agents who actually operated in the field. He writes:[2]

> The differences of opinion between SOE and the BCRA in London (which persist in the publications of certain uncharitable

1. Cowburn, op. cit.
2. Philippe de Vomécourt, op. cit.

individuals) were hardly perceived at our level, and the political, diplomatic and international wrangling that went on in London, Algiers and Washington had very little impact on our activities. We thought it regrettable that Churchill, de Gaulle and Roosevelt did not see eye to eye about everything, if only because their disagreements caused us needless complications. On the whole we tended to disregard their bickerings – when we knew of them, that is; our sole concern was who was 'with us' and who 'against us'. I don't doubt that General de Gaulle . . . had the long-term interests of his country at heart.

It was more or less by accident that my brothers and I became responsible for groups that had been organized by the British government. If the Free French had accepted my brother Pierre's suggestion of setting up their own operations in the field, we would have been running pro-Gaullist circuits. The British had been first to see the value of an organized resistance force, and we were glad to accept the help they offered. The French were in no position to refuse such offers.

The SOE group organizers often found themselves in touch with the heads of Gaullist groups or other movements. We did not waste our energies on petty jealousies; we asked each other what had to be done and tried to give each other mutual support. We had the same objective, after all – to defeat the Germans and drive them out of France. It didn't matter whether a man was French or English, or even Polish or Spanish; and we didn't think much of someone who measured his own contribution in terms of the size of his group. The essential thing for us was to be able to act, and the English groups were luckier in the sense that we received the highest proportion of arms and supplies that were parachuted into France, at least until 1943. If a Gaullist group needed explosives, we did not refuse them. Pettiness is a characteristic of bureaucrats and desk-bound pen pushers, not of men who are face to face with the enemy.

Philippe de Vomécourt's words put the matter into perspective.

However, even in the field there were occasional problems between the British services – SOE included – and the French resistance groups. This is confirmed, for instance, in a communiqué issued by the leaders of the Mouvements Unis de Résistance (MUR) on 27 March, 1943, to all their branches:

The policy of the British Secret Service towards militant activists here in France is influenced by a certain conception of the role to which they think the French resistance organizations ought to confine themselves. They want to use the activists for their own tactical ends, to ensure an Allied victory but without giving any consideration to the political wishes of a majority of the French people or to the strategic potential of resistance movements. They view the resistance forces, both inside and outside France, as nothing more than an extra military body to be used for their own tactical advantage, without seeing it as an expression of French political will.

Any direct contact between active members, cells or local leaders and the British secret service agents, without prior agreement from above, will totally compromise the discipline, security and political integrity of the resistance movements.

Among our militant members there are many patriots who are not politically minded who explain, in all sincerity, that these contacts offer an effective way to join the common fight against the Germans. These militants do not realize that by acting like this, on their own and without any mandate, they are seriously damaging the cause of French resistance. For resistance to be effective, in design and execution, it needs to be strictly unified and disciplined under the direction of General de Gaulle. By acting on their own initiative, without considering the other movements or their policies, they can seriously prejudice the French cause and its future policies. While victory is the common aim of all the Allies, the form that this victory will take, once it has arrived, may differ, and it is important that France should then have all available means at her disposal and be able to make the most of all her rights.

It was not that the resistants were grimly determined to have autonomy, but they wanted a clear definition of French policy towards the Allies. They were willing enough to co-operate, but only from a secure knowledge of their own independence. Hence their precise instructions:

1. Militants from lower ranks, at both the provincial and the regional level, are expressly forbidden from giving any aid or any intelligence to British agents without specific authorization from regional headquarters. Offenders will be subject to immediate sanctions, especially those who without prior consent agree to help the British secret service. In short, all double-dealing is expressly forbidden.

2. Central command must be informed by regional heads immediately they hear of any contact between members and British agents. Contacts that have been established in the past may be allowed to continue, but central command must be

notified about them. Arms or other equipment that is offered may be accepted, but not the other way round.

3. All regional leaders, after checking with the provinces, will submit a general report on British agents' activities in relation to the resistance organizations.

4. Whenever possible, British agents should be informed that central command asks only to maintain or establish contact with them . . . but that they must not ignore the head of the resistance organizations.

Alban Vistel, who was civil and military head of the R.1 region at the time, summarized his worries and those of the MUR leaders:

It is all too easy for foreign agents to come and benefit from our hard work, to divert teams that we have formed and engage them in operations outside our control and for which we will ultimately have to take responsibility. With British agents who understand our loyal attitude, all is well. This is the case with some of the Buckmaster agents (who have helped the Coq Enchaîné movement), for the formation run by Dargand in the Ain. In other cases – all too often, unfortunately – the British agents will try to create a resistance that is subject to foreign control. The situation they create will present serious problems when fighting begins for the Liberation.

After the landings, the Executive Committee of the Mouvement de Libération Nationale (MLN) sent out a new warning on 20 June, 1944, 'to all regions and provinces' with a handwritten note indicating that the message should be 'passed on to the small group sectors':

Militant members at all levels are hereby reminded:

1. That any contact with agents from the British secret service, British War Office or any representative from a foreign service must be notified immediately to their direct superiors, and particularly that the MLN Executive Committee must be told about such contacts. Any failure to report a contact will be liable to immediate penalties, and may lead to expulsion from the movement.

2. That they are subject exclusively to the control of the French military and political authorities, at present the Liberation Committees and the FFI headquarters; if these authorizing bodies are unavailable, it is the duty of our members to obey only the regional and provincial leaders of the MLN and the CFL [Comité Français de Libération].

3. That no agreement may be entered into with British secret service agents, or with representatives from the British War Office or any other foreign service, unless it is in line with directives issued by central command, or by the MLN Executive Committee, the leader of the CFL, the headquarters of the FFI or the Conseil National de la Résistance. In case of dispute, only the orders of the latter shall prevail.

4. That any agreement which implies direct subordination to foreign military command or foreign intelligence agents shall be rejected forthwith. Of course, any supplies of arms, equipment or explosives may be accepted, on condition that the operations in question do not contravene the proper resistance authorities, and are not rendered on behalf of a foreign service, no matter which one, and that these operations do not take precedence over operations given to the FFI by the properly accredited authorities working under the orders of the provisional government of the Republic.

The Executive Committee draws the attention of our members to the responsibility they incur if they put themselves at the service of foreign forces, even Allied forces. The war we are fighting is a common cause, but in certain particular circumstances our interests may be divergent. Moreover, no one can know for certain whether we may follow very different paths. For this reason, our members are warned that they will carry a heavy responsibility by joining the ranks of a foreign intelligence agency. Our Allies have only to make their requirements known through the proper French channels – that is, the provisional government of the Republic, and its accredited representatives in France who are close contact with the resistance and in particular the MLN.[1].

These texts speak for themselves. Disputes would continue to occur, in some cases even after the final battles for the liberation had begun, on a local level. But as we have seen earlier, it was possible to arrange efficient co-operation between the British networks and the FFI. On the whole Buckmaster's agents were apparently more acceptable than those of British intelligence.

Nevertheless it remains true that there was high-level co-operation. Athough Colonel Buckmaster himself mentioned, in his interview of 9 December, 1981, the differences of opinion that he had had with the BCRA, he also made it clear that he appreciated the work and support of the French services, and he also expressed his high regard for their leaders. This was echoed by Pierre de Vomécourt when he wrote:[2] 'It is sad that M. R. D.

1. Quoted in Ruby, *La Résistance à Lyon*.
2. In a letter dated 'September–October 1960'.

Foot's book should recall the friction that existed between the SOE and the BCRA groups. Their differences were reduced, partly thanks to the passage of time and partly thanks to the efforts of certain heads of movements and resistance networks in France.' Colonel Groussard was even more emphatic on the subject:[3].

> I have nothing but praise for the British services. They were very competent, which is the most important thing. They were also very hard to please, but they knew they carried a heavy burden of responsibility. Brilliantly using the lessons of a very old and very rich experience, making slow but steady progress, they at all times gave us cause to value the work they accomplished. Moreover, we always knew where we were with them. I had laid down the principle, from the beginning, that my groups would only work with the Allies on a military level. We stood by this right to the very end.

Bearing in mind the inevitable tensions that arose from time to time between agents working under cover for different services in the same field, it does seem that the conclusions reached by Pierre de Vomécourt and Colonel Groussard reflect the feelings of most of those who were involved, likewise the historians who recorded these facts.

In the initial phase of SOE operations, agents came up against various difficulties, here described briefly by Pierre de Vomécourt:[2]

> The conditions under which the first agents were sent to France were often very hard: very little money, no food coupons, and a false identity card that could not be used to obtain ration cards in the proper way. Besides, none of the French contacts that London gave these first agents were at all useful (except for Begué, who was taken in and helped by Max Hymans). Finally, in Begué's time the only radio link with London was in the Unoccupied Zone, which meant having to cross the Demarcation Line each time one wanted to send a signal. Obviously, the excellent security rules devised in a peaceful office turned out to be somewhat theoretical for those who had been dropped into the back of beyond – sometimes thirty kilometres from the intended place – and with less than adequate means of living or communicating with London. We were forced to take risks the theoreticians would have deplored, risks that we ourselves hardly appreciated. Moreover, the lack of radio contact was to cost many of us very dear.

1. G. Groussard, *Service Secret* (Éditions de la Table Ronde, Paris, n.d.).
2. In a letter dated 5 September, 1966.

According to Cookridge, this difficult period lasted well into 1942, even into 1943. The shortage of munitions was particularly worrying:

> Buckmaster had to plead incessantly with his chiefs, and through them with the War Office, the Air Ministry and the Chiefs of Staff, for more aircraft and more arms.
>
> Thus 1942 was, in the main, a year of preparation, while 1943 became a year of consolidation. The number of circuits in France grew steadily, in the face of heavy losses in the Paris and north-eastern sectors. Because of shortage of air transport, only thirty-six agents and seventeen radio operators were parachuted into France during 1942, although additional dispatches were made by the cumbersome sea route from Gibraltar to the Côte d'Azur. The total quantity of supplies was very small: 2,265 lb of explosives, 269 Sten guns, 388 pistols, 856 incendiary bombs, paltry supplies of limpet bombs, clams and abrasive products for sabotage. Altogether only a little more than one ton of explosives was sent by air.

It was only in 1943 and particularly 1944 that the situation really began to improve, because of the preparations for Overlord and the growing participation of the US Air Force. Cookridge goes on:

> Every effort was made at Baker Street to persuade the powers that be – from Churchill to the Air Marshals – of the great upsurge in French resistance activities. SOE chiefs submitted detailed reports proving that tens of thousands of able-bodied Frenchmen who . . . had formed maquis bands in the mountains and forests, represented the cadres of a guerrilla army, if only they could be trained and armed.
>
> Churchill read these reports and in January, 1944, ordered the Air Ministry to make thirty-five aircraft available to SOE. He also wrote a special minute ordering that, in view of the plans for an Allied invasion of southern France, the maquis groups in that region should be armed first. His orders were carried out, but only after many delays and strong objections on the part of the Air Marshals, who disliked diverting to SOE planes that could be used in bombing operations against German industrial targets. . . .
>
> Even before the aircraft allocation improved, SOE and the Special Duties Squadrons made great efforts to increase deliveries. In August, 1943, alone, 138 Squadron completed 184 operations, dropped 66 agents, 1,452 containers and 194 packages – a record mainly due to excellent flying weather. SOE was also responsible for all air operations concerning de Gaulle's BCRA agents, and

more than 300 were parachuted into France. . . . 'From 1943 until August, 1944 [according to Professor Henri Michel] SOE and BCRA together arranged 8,651 parachute operations, in which 868 agents and 8,545 tons of supplies were dropped to the French resistance.'

Although it was not until after D-Day that the Special Duties Squadrons were equipped with long-range Stirlings, delivery was dramatically stepped up during the first six months of 1944. Until the third week in May, in addition to considerable quantities of explosives and ammunition, these weapons were parachuted into France: 45,354 Sten guns, 17,576 pistols, 10,251 rifles, 1,832 bren guns, 300 bazookas and 143 mortars. On D-Day these supplies and previous deliveries meant that 20,000 men were fully armed and some 50,000 additional men were armed in some degree.

If these figures seem a little optimistic, it is nevertheless true that in 1944 the initial shortages – of arms, ammunition, explosives etc – had given way to an abundance for the SOE groups and for the French resistance workers who had the good fortune to profit from them.

It should also be remembered that if some groups still went short of arms, other groups had been supplied with plenty – and handed them over to the Germans, as in the Prosper and Scientist circuits, whose leaders, Norman (perhaps) and Grandclément respectively, had done deals with the enemy, of which not only they but very many other resistance workers became the victims.

We should add that the SOE groups shared their arms and ammunition, during these times of plenty, with other French resistance fighters, including the FTP. M. R. D. Foot quotes a report dated 25 March, 1943, sent to SOE by J. F. A. Antelme, one of Suttill's friends. Antelme's report said: 'Germans are killed daily in the streets of Paris . . . Ninety per cent of these attacks are made with arms provided by us, e.g. to the Communists.'

If the supplies of arms and equipment left much to be desired, SOE's recruiting procedures were also open to criticism.

Cookridge, for example, cites the case of Pierre de Vomécourt and the trouble he had in being accepted into the Buckmaster groups. De Vomécourt had left Cherbourg in circumstances already described, to present himself to General de Gaulle and suggest to him his ideas for sabotage and resistance in France. The General gave him a cool reception, believing that de Vomécourt's plans would bring about German reprisals and that one of the worst consequences would be to create a widespread hostility towards operations which he himself was setting up. As Cookridge says,[1]

1. Cookridge, op. cit.

Sadly de Vomécourt turned to the British. But at the War Office his reception was even cooler. He was told there were no plans for sending secret agents and saboteurs to France. The only alternative open to him was enlisting as a private in the British army, with a prospect of having a commission awarded at a later date.

For some months Captain de Vomécourt kicked his heels in London, until he learned of a secret organization established by the British just for the purpose that he had discussed with General de Gaulle. During his many abortive visits to the War Office he had been treated kindly by Lieutenant-General Templer, who eventually gave him an introduction to Brigadier Gubbins, the newly appointed Chief of Operations of SOE.

That was how the French Captain Pierre de Vomécourt became 'Lucas', the first secret agent of SOE's F Section.

Pierre de Vomécourt himself commented on how SOE's slowness caused regrettable results; for instance, he mentions Michel Clémenceau, the politician with a famous name, who had let the British know he wanted to leave France by air to visit Britain and continue the fight there. Several months later Clémenceau had had no response and he was arrested by the Germans.

It must be said that SOE did not always have room to manoeuvre and that it had to struggle every step of the way to get aircraft and supplies from the Allied Chiefs of Staff – and also that the SOE groups were pursued incessantly by the Germans, often helped by traitors.

Of course the Nazis made use of traitors like Bardet. But a detailed study of the work of SOE's circuits shows that the German services were undoubtedly very efficient. This is proved by their penetration of the Prosper and Scientist circuits. Another case in point is the clever way the Nazis managed to fool Baker Street into believing in the existence of the Archdeacon, Butler and Phono groups, which they had built up to resemble the real thing (with the dreadful consequences described above).

One very typical case may serve to illustrate the pitiless secret struggle between SOE and the Nazis with their traps, double- or triple-agents, 'turned' radio operators etc, and that is the case of Mathilde Carré, La Chatte.

When war broke out, this young woman who was to become an exceptional spy had been a teacher in southern Algeria. Her husband had joined the army, and she never saw him again for he was killed in Cassino. She joined up as a nurse, and was sent to a front-line hospital in Italy. Following the Italian débâcle she found her way to Toulouse and there met a Polish officer by the name of Roman Czarniawski, who was with the Polish secret service. Together they went to Paris, and on somebody's recommendation they were invited to join the Interallié circuit. He took the codename

'Arnaud' and she the name 'La Chatte' (the Cat), which was appropriate enough because of her strange, wide-set eyes. Despite her small stature she was undeniably attractive. La Chatte worked hard for the Interallié circuit and provided them with valuable intelligence. At the end of October, 1941, a docker from the port of Cherbourg, half-drunk, confided to a non-commissioned officer in the Luftwaffe, Hugo Bleicher, leaning on the bar beside him, that he had supplied information to a certain Madame Bonnet for cash. Bleicher reported this to the Abwehr, who ordered him to investigate further.

On 3 November Bleicher arrested Madame Bonnet, and she admitted that she was working for a British agent called 'Paul': this was in fact Raoul Kiffer, head of the Interallié branch in Britanny and Normandy. Bleicher managed to 'turn' him. He was thus able to arrest another score of the circuit's members. On the 16th he found out the address of Interallié's command post, 8 Villa Léandre in Montmarte. On the 17th, the Interallié leaders were happily celebrating the first anniversary of the group's formation. On the 18th, at six in the morning, Bleicher arrested them. That night La Chatte had been staying with friends. She heard what had happened and returned to her lodgings in Rue Cortot to destroy some papers she kept there, whereupon she in turn was arrested and taken to La Santé prison.

The following morning Hugo Bleicher took her to the Hotel Edouard VII and gave her a splendid breakfast. He offered her a deal: 600,000 francs a month if she would agree to collaborate. She agreed without hesitation. It is hard to explain the reasons why she did this, after the courage she had shown previously. She said later that she had not been prepared to die at the age of thirty-two.

On 19 November, 1941, and on subsequent days, Hugo Bleicher arrested many more of Interallié's agents. La Chatte, who had been his mistress since the first night, accompanied him. It was she who appeared at the homes of the agents she knew. They opened the door readily enough for 'Micheline' (her official *nom de guerre*) and Bleicher had only to seize them.

Interallié had been decimated, but Bleicher wanted to do more: he wanted to use radio transmissions to deceive the British. With La Chatte's help he 'turned' the radio operator 'Marcel'. The first message, composed by Bleicher and encoded by Renée Borni, another young woman who had agreed to work for the Germans, was transmitted by Marcel. In the message La Chatte told London that there had been several arrests – hence the break in transmissions – but that Interallié was still functioning. From then on, La Chatte, or 'Victoire' as she now called herself, sent regular signals to the War Office – signals composed by the Abwehr. Bleicher had brought off a masterstroke. The British were completely taken in. Thus, in one notable case, on the night of 12 February, 1942, Bleicher was able to ensure a safe passage for the battleships *Scharnhorst* and *Gneisenau*, accompanied by the heavy cruiser *Prinz Eugen*, from Brest to the North Sea along the Channel without a shot being fired.

On 25 December, 1941, Victoire went to the George V hotel for dinner with the lawyer, Brault, and Pierre de Vomécourt. She was thus in direct contact now with SOE. Lucas, who had arrived seven months earlier, was cut off from London as his two radio operators had been arrested. He asked her if she would transmit messages for him, if Interallié would agree. She told him she would have to ask her friends.

Naturally Bleicher agreed. He was delighted to have this chance of infiltrating the SOE circuit whose activities had caused the Germans so much trouble. La Chatte introduced him to Pierre de Vomécourt, who was pretending to be a Belgian resistance worker with the name of Jean Castel. Pierre de Vomécourt has already told us something of his suspicions about La Chatte's treachery and how he turned her round again to work for him; and then how he divided his circuit into two: 'one part comprising the people who'd been "blown", who fussed about without really doing anything, and the other part comprising the parallel group with which no contact should be made unless Cottin, Burdeyron or myself were completely certain we were not being watched. This parallel group remained totally unknown to the Germans, or to Mathilde Carré, until the war was over.'

Ben Cowburn goes into this affair in some depth,[1] confirming Lucas's account and adding to it in places:

> One day, just before the New Year, I went out to lunch with Lucas, Roger and Gaston, and there met the heaven-sent young woman, Madame Carré. It was an enjoyable party in a splendid black-market restaurant. She was slim, good-looking, but very short-sighted. She talked about the disaster of Armand's capture – her Polish chief – and the consequent arrest of almost all the circuit's members, and of the luck that she, the radio operator and one or two others had had in not suffering a similar fate. She seemed very proud of her codename, 'Victoire', but admitted that she was often nicknamed 'La Chatte'.
>
> One morning at the end of January, Roger asked me to dinner.
>
> 'Lucas wants to talk to us. Can you get to the Étape by eight o'clock this evening?'
>
> All three of us arrived at the restaurant more or less together. Lucas was looking very serious. We ordered our meal and as soon as the waiter had brought the *hors-d'oeuvre,* Lucas leaned towards us and began: 'I've got bad news – very bad.' A pause. 'As you know, Victoire told us that when the Polish group was caught, she and some of her chums managed to escape . . . Well, it wasn't true. She was arrested too!'

1. Cowburn, op. cit.

Roger and I were listening very closely.

'Keep eating – it looks more natural!'

We picked up our knives and forks again.

'She seems to be able to come and go whenever she likes,' I commented. 'How did she manage to give them the slip?'

Lucas gave a heavy sigh.

'That's just it – she hasn't given them the slip. No, she's agreed to work for the Boches. She's a double agent, and she's betrayed us.'

My next question was obvious:

'But what about our radio signals? I suppose that was just a complete smokescreen?'

'No, they were real. You see, the Germans got their hands on the transmitter and the operator. They went on transmitting to London as if nothing had happened, and Victoire was a great help to them with their little game. She composed the right sort of messages. The texts that I wrote out and the answers we got back were all faithfully transmitted, but under the eyes of a German sergeant.'

It was certain seemingly insignificant details – a delay in sending a signal, a clumsy phrase – that had first caught Lucas's attention. Then one or two more serious things (the arrest of a friend, the way Victoire managed to produce false identity cards – the German signatures were authentic) had deepened his suspicions. Briefly, Lucas had questioned her very skilfully and in the end she gave in. After her terrible confession, rather than killing her and trying to escape, he decided it would be better to try and find out the extent of the damage and, since our little spy's contrition seemed genuine, he told himself that this might be a way to make use of her apparent vanity: she had been a wonderful double agent, so why couldn't she work for us? Lucas had bet on a winner: she accepted his offer without hesitation.

It was vital that London should be warned as soon as humanly possible. I expressed a wish to meet Victoire to interrogate her and get things clear in my own mind. Lucas agreed and promised to take me to see her the next day.

At the rendezvous I fould Lucas calm and serious and Victoire worried. She relaxed when Lucas told her I'd heard all about it, and the discussion began. Victoire described Bleicher, told us what position he held in the German counter-espionage service and explained his usual modus operandi . . . Then we came to the real problem. What should we do now? Lucas began to unfold his grand plan (I had agreed that he should tell her about it). So the Germans were counting on one big coup, were they? Well, we were going to let them think they were heading for a coup beyond their wildest dreams. Victoire would report to Bleicher that Lucas had finally confided that he was intending to organize a meeting in Paris of the leaders of all the main groups formed to date. The 'bait' for this imaginary conference was to be the presence of a British general, who would be sent to France secretly to spend a day or two in Paris and to give personal instructions for co-ordinated action. Afterwards he would return to London to report. Supposedly so that he could arrange this general's imaginary visit, Lucas had to go back to London on a motor torpedo boat arranged for 12 February. Then Victoire would offer the Germans a chance to bring off an extraordinary coup: to persuade Lucas to take her with him to England. When she returned to France, she would thus be able to give them a fund of information of the highest military value. What a master stroke! A female Abwehr agent going to London, taking part in secret service deliberations and drawing a British general into a trap, thanks to which the entire resistance movement would be destroyed! This was the fantastic plan which was meant to make the Abwehr's eyes light up. But of course our own plan – the real one – was slightly different . . .

When we got to London we would warn head office that the Polish radio set was in enemy hands and that the 'double-double-agent' was ready to start. Victoire would tell the British all she could about the German counter-espionage organization, and the British in turn would send out a mass of fake signals via Radio Bleicher. Once the arrangements had been made to our best advantage, Lucas and I would secretly return to France, each to continue with our own jobs, while Messrs Bleicher and Co would start telling each other that the British general was taking rather a long time to come. This was Lucas's machiavellian plan to transform disaster into sucess. Victoire had listened to everything without saying a word. When Lucas had finished speaking she said she thought the Germans would walk into the trap.

At our next meeting Victoire arrived with a radiant smile. The Boches had swallowed the bait and were already congratulating themselves at the though of the magnificent coup they were going to pull off.

As the appointed day approached, the final details were settled on both sides. Victoire reported that Bleicher had obtained permission from the governor of Brest that the beach patrols should be confined to barracks that night, to leave the way clear for us, and that orders should be issued to prevent any trouble being caused for the MTB, both when it arrived and when it left.

After two unsuccessful attempts, Victoire and Lucas finally set off on the night of 26 February, 1942. Watched by the Germans hidden behind some rocks, they climbed into the rowing boat that took them across a calm sea to the British MTB, and reached London without problems.

In London La Chatte was allowed to come and go as she pleased, but was closely watched. She told the British all she knew about the German secret service and volunteered one very valuable piece of information – the radio code that Bleicher had given her. The radio communications between Buckmaster and the phony Franco-Polish group in Bleicher's hands then continued for several weeks – to the Allies' great advantage.

Pierre de Vomécourt left London on 1 April, 1942, to fly back to France and continue his work. But he was arrested in Paris on the 25th.[1] Lucas's arrest led Colonel Buckmaster to have La Chatte imprisoned; she had served her purpose and would be of no further use if Lucas were forced under torture to reveal that Mathilde had been turned again. She was handed over to the French police in June 1945. Condemned to death on 7 January, 1949, she was finally released on 7 September, 1954, after a total of twelve years in prison.

This example of a 'double-double-agent' shows the complexity and the difficult work in which SOE's men and women were engaged. They suffered conflicts between leaders and services, sometimes badly supported and poorly equipped, constantly pursued by efficient special agents from the Gestapo or Abwehr, and often betrayed. Nonetheless they carried out their duties to the supreme sacrifice.

---

1. He was imprisoned in Fresnes, where he remained for eighteen months, ten of them in solitary confinement. The Germans had realized he was the SOE man responsible for the whole of the Occupied Zone. At the beginning of 1943, Major Roskoten told him he was to be sent to Germany and imprisoned in a fortress where potential hostages were being assembled. Lucas insisted that the same treatment should be given to the members of his circuit, threatening to kill himself if the Germans refused to comply. The German major took him at his word, for Lucas had already tried to commit suicide once; so in October, 1943, Lucas and all his British officer companions were taken to Colditz, while the other members of his group were sent to a specially guarded camp in Lübeck. He was liberated in 1945 by the Americans. Thus all the circuit's agents arrested as a result of Mathilde Carré's treachery were finally to return safe and sound in 1945.

# — 3 —

## THE SACRIFICE

Having volunteered to undertake 'terrorist' activity in territory that was in the hands of an arrogant, sadistic enemy, the SOE agent knew that he was risking his life at every turn; that a simple accident could put him out of business at any moment; that the Germans could throw him into prison, or torture him, or deport him to a concentration camp, or kill him according to their whims.

There would be no point in listing all the accidents resulting from aircraft take-offs and landings; these are natural aviation hazards. Many Lysanders and Halifaxes returned to base with damage caused by the German anti-aircraft batteries. Quite a few were actually shot down, such as the Lysander that had brought 'Roger' on 9 February 1944, or the one piloted by Arkel on 5 August, 1944, south of the Loire. Several pilots working for SOE had to make crash landings when they were on a mission. But as far as we know, none of them ever lost his aircraft on French soil as a result of a crash or for mechanical reasons.

Accidents were bound to happen, however. On 17 December, 1943, two Lysanders piloted by Hankey and MacBride were trying to land in foggy conditions on the same strip; they crashed and both pilots were killed.

Parachute operations also gave rise to a few problems. The operation at Anse has already been mentioned. On 1 June, 1942, at two in the morning, six containers and two SOE agents were dropped; the containers landed on the edge of the Azergues, getting caught in the branches of some poplar trees, and were only recovered with much trouble. The two agents landed in the village of Anse itself. Although Nicolas (Robert Burdett) managed to hide and later reached Lyons under his own steam, his companion Patrice (Robert Sheppard) was less fortunate; he landed on the roof of a house next door to the gendarmerie and was promptly arrested.

On 28 June, 1942, Alfred and Henry Newton were dropped near Limoges together with their radio operator, Brian Stonehouse. Their job was to set up the new group, Greenheart, but they had to hide out in some woods, going several nights without food while they waited for the chance to recover their radio sets, which had got caught by the parachute lines in the treetops. In the end, however, they were to complete their work successfully.

J. Lodwick and O. Heimann, on the other hand, who were dropped blind on the night of 29 December, 1942, had landed so far apart that they never managed to find each other and had to abandon their mission.

Sometimes it was the unforeseen accident that happened. Claude de Baissac and his radio operator, Harry Peulevé, were parachuted blind on the night of 30 July, 1942, near Nïmes. But the aircraft which had dropped them had been at too low an altitude and both men suffered injuries – de Baissac a broken ankle and Peulevé a broken leg. Fortunately they were found by local patriots who looked after them and helped them avoid capture.

There were many other accidents like this – which is not so surprising when one considers the conditions under which they had to jump. Take the case of Gustav Bieler, for example, one of SOE's Canadian agents. He was dropped south-west of Paris on 17 November, 1942, with orders to create the Musician group. He landed badly, suffering serious spinal injuries; but he very courageously refused to be taken back to Britain in a Lysander. He was secretly given medical treatment and after several weeks he resumed work and managed to accomplish the task he had been given. But because he had not received the proper medical help, he was to remain crippled for the rest of his life.

Claude Jumeau was killed accidentally when making his second parachute jump.

Ben Cowburn has written about one jump he made in May, 1942, when he landed right beside a high-tension electricity line and sprained his ankle very badly. Not only that, but he was about sixty-five kilometres from the intended spot. But he too managed to continue with his mission, despite the damaged ankle which made him limp and caused him terrible pain.

In some cases, the physical courage shown by SOE agents went even further. On 2 May, 1942, Henri Labit was dropped in the Landes. He was supposed to go to Bordeaux, but the Germans caught him when he was crossing the Demarcation Line. He fired at them, but they were too many for him and they had motorbikes. On the point of being captured, he swallowed his cyanide pill. This was by no means an isolated case.

It also happened that sheer bad luck played a cruel trick on the secret agent. For instance, the first-class SOE agent Peulevé, head of the Author circuit in Corrèze, was arrested because a jealous neighbour informed on him – as a black-marketeer! But as we know, he was eventually able to regain his freedom and he rejoined the fight.

Sometimes, too, agents who landed on French soil were greeted by reception committees organized by the Germans, as a result of informers or because someone had been forced to talk. On 29 February, 1944, Renaud (France Antelme), Mechanic (Lionel Lee) and Martine (Madeleine Damerment) were dropped from a Halifax between Chartres and Rambouillet. All were captured on landing. Renaud and Mechanic were executed at Mauthausen; Martine and other SOE women were shot on 13 September, 1944. Altogether the Gestapo caught eighteen SOE agents in this way, in the course of five parachute operations.

On top of these sometimes tragic accidents and misfortunes came the usual risks inherent in any kind of clandestine activity – that is to say, capture and the consequences: prison, torture, often deportation or execution.

The clandestine agent was constantly menaced by the possibility of arrest. But sometimes luck was on his side. SOE agent Robert Burdett (Nicolas) tells of one particularly bizarre trick of fate:[1]

> After six months in the Lyons area I now had a fair number of friends, teams of agents and men trained for sabotage operations . . . As I had three flats in different suburbs of Lyons, there was always some safe place for me to go. This particular night, we'd had the curfew at six o'clock and I spent the evening in my flat reading and making plans. It wasn't until nearly nine o'clock that I realized the police were in the middle of searching the district. Too late to move: in the street I would be picked up straight away. The streets were being combed by lorries full of German troops and French police. In my flat I had about fifty kilograms of explosives and a transmitter set. But the die was cast; there was nothing I could do but wait and see what happened. As well as the explosives and the radio set, a courier had arrived from Avignon with messages to tap out on my transmitter. The courier, a young woman, had been worn out after travelling all day standing on a bus, and she was now sleeping in the room next door.
>
> I tried to read, but was far too worried to concentrate on whatever the book was. It was not until two in the morning that I heard someone knocking on the doors of the flats below mine. My heart was beating at twice the normal speed, my mind was racing with thoughts of what sort of sentence I would get . . .
>
> My explosives were hidden in a little cupboard under the window, a place where one normally kept coal and logs for the fire. The explosives were covered with bits of kindling and if these were moved it would be impossible to miss the explosives; they would never escape even a simple search. And my transmitter was in a big drawer in my bureau, so I had no hopes of avoiding trouble.

1. Quoted in Courvoisier, op. cit.

Shortly after I'd heard the first noise in the building, someone knocked at my door. I opened it and found myself facing two plain-clothes French policemen and a third man in uniform holding a revolver which was pointed at me.

'We've come to search your flat,' one of them said, and while the plain-clothes men started searching, the one in uniform kept me under guard, his revolver covering me all the time. I did my best to look calm but my nerves were in a terrible state. I felt the search would never end. They looked everywhere, and I still don't know how I stood the shock when they opened the log cupboard. They were, I think, very wary about soiling their white hands, for they didn't deign to touch any of the logs. They slammed the cupboard door shut without noticing anything unusual. They went on searching and came now to the bureau. They opened one drawer after another – and then the one where the transmitter was. I couldn't watch, it was too much to bear. When I heard the drawer being closed again, and realized they hadn't found anything, I could hardly believe my luck. In France, as in England, everyone had to observe the blackout. My flat was very dark, the transmitter was only small, and it was hidden right at the bottom of a very deep drawer. It was undoubtedly this that saved my skin. Then the policemen noticed the young woman, just woken by their rummaging.

'And what about her?' one of them said. 'Is she over sixteen?'

'Yes,' I laughed, 'she's about thirty!'

But I wasn't yet rid of these gentlemen. They started going through my papers. At that stage I was using the name 'Robert Léger' and my job was 'mining engineer'. One of the policemen asked me if I gave out many driving licences. I wasn't sure what he meant but I said: 'Yes, quite a few.' Later I discovered that in Lyons it was the mining engineers who gave out driving licences. One of the policemen started laughing and made a few comments on the book I'd been trying to read while waiting for them. It was a detective story!

'Ah well,' he said, 'if you like detective stories, you've done all right tonight!'

The bulb in one of their pocket torches had gone, and I gave them a spare one of mine. We parted the best of friends, considering the circumstances, although the one in uniform had never for a second let his revolver stop pointing at me.

But it wasn't everyone that had the luck Nicolas had.

According to tradition, security regulations strictly forbade SOE agents from writing down the address of the French people who were to take them in, or even the address of a place of safety in case of an emergency. One typical example: a disregard for this rule was to cause a disastrous setback which Cookridge here describes briefly:[1]

On 10 October, 1941, a team was parachuted in the Dordogne, north of Bergerac, and received by Pierre-Bloch. Codenamed Corsica, its members were Jack Hayes, Claude Jumeau, . . . Jean Le Harivel, a radio operator, and Denis Turberville, who landed a mile away from his comrades, lost contact and was picked up by Vichy gendarmes the next day. Baker Street had given the Corsica team and several agents already in the field the address of Christophe (Georges Turck) at the Villa des Bois in Marseilles as a safe-house. Turberville carried a note with his address when he was arrested, and Vichy police waited there when the three 'Corsicans' arrived.

One by one the agents were trapped at the villa: Robert Lyon and Pierre-Bloch, the French socialist *député* enlisted by Jacques de Guélis, and on 24 October Georges Begué also. The débâcle was complete when two agents who had arrived with Ben Cowburn – the radio operator André Bloch on 9 November at Le Mans and Michael Trotobas at Châteauroux – were also arrested. Despite torture André Bloch kept silent and was shot a few weeks later.

With the capture of the 'pianists' Begué and Bloch, the radio link was gone, and all SOE agents were cut off from Baker Street.

This masterly ambush might have been even more dramatic if it hadn't been for Philippe de Vomécourt's cautiousness. He had felt from his first encounter with 'Christophe' that the man was not the sort to inspire confidence. Shortly afterwards, several SOE agents were arrested, which increased his suspicions, as he wrote in his book:[2]

Not knowing what had led to these people being arrested, I decided that all of us who were in the region should leave immediately for the south, including the Châteauroux chemist whose shop had been our first letter-box.

We agreed to go to Marseilles by different routes. Some of us would go via Châteauroux and Lyons, other via Toulouse and then along the coast. No two people were to take the same train. We would meet up at a rendezvous near the Marseilles docks.

'And above all,' I said, 'don't go to the safe-house in Marseilles

1. Cookridge, op. cit.
2. Philippe de Vomécourt, op. cit.

(C. was there). Use the telephone. Give them the password and ask someone to come and pick you up. Whatever happens, don't go there yourselves. Just wait, nothing else. I'll be there at two o'clock.' I fixed the rendezvous as the terrace of a café, everyone agreed, and my final words to them were: 'Don't go to that safe-house.'

I arrived in Marseilles a few minutes past one, and went straight to the rendezvous. Or rather, I went into the café opposite, to keep an eye on the place. There was no one there, nothing to make me think the place was being watched by police. I decided to make the telephone call: I gave the password and got the right response. I recognized C.'s voice.

'Where are the others?' I asked.

'They're here,' C. said.

'Why didn't they wait for me?'

'We've got something very interesting here. Come as soon as you can.'

'I don't know where the house is – send one of the others to meet me.'

'But you've been here before.'

'I've forgotten the way. Don't give me the address, we might be overheard.'

'All right, I'll send someone.'

'Good. Tell him to come to the second rendezvous.'

We arranged to meet at four o'clock in case one of us was delayed.

No one came. I was surprised and very worried. There had been a lot of us leaving Châteauroux; it wasn't right that I should be the only one here. At four thirty I telephoned the safe-house again.

'What's happened?' I demanded.

'Nothing – we just haven't been able to send anyone. Sorry.' That wasn't very convincing, I thought. 'Come as soon as you can,' he repeated.

I didn't bother to tell him again that I didn't know where the villa was. 'I'm awfully sorry,' I said, 'but I can't come now. I've got a lot to do. I must go back to Paris. I've got to catch a train in a few minutes. I'll be back in a day or two.'

I did, in fact, have things to do, both in Nice and in Monaco. I went there by train. Then I caught the train back to Marseilles and as soon as I arrived I phoned the villa again.

'Hello?'

'Who's this?'

I gave the password and got the wrong response – just slightly wrong, but enough to alert me. I asked a few simple questions, but the man avoided answering them, and went on urgently:

'Come on, hurry up – we're all waiting for you.'

I wasn't sure about this. I had to try and find out something definite.

'Has Gilbert turned up?' I asked. 'Gilbert – the one who was due to come by submarine?'

The answer came back straight away: 'He's here; he's waiting for you.'

I didn't know any Gilbert and there had never been any submarine.

'All right, I'm coming. I'll be there in twenty minutes.'

Twenty minutes later I had left Marseilles.

Long experience of the clandestine way of life and all the traps had saved Philippe de Vomécourt. But over twenty other people had been captured.

Apart from outright treachery, there was always the risk of someone informing on an agent. This was how Jean-Bernard Badaire came to be arrested. Someone must have told the Gestapo all about him because they knew he'd been Philippe de Vomécourt's deputy, and even that they had recently met. Furious that the circuit's leader had escaped their trap, the Gestapo tortured Badaire repeatedly in their efforts to learn de Vomécourt's whereabouts. He was beaten all over, kicked in the stomach, thrashed with riding crops, coshes and clubs, hung by the feet, etc. Several times the Germans made him kneel with his face to the wall, hands manacled behind his back, and told him he was about to be shot. He also suffered the torture of being plunged into a bath and held underwater until he nearly drowned – and every time he lost consciousness his torturers revived him and started all over again. But Jean-Bernard Badaire never talked, and Philippe de Vomécourt was never at risk. It wasn't until several years later that he learned that Captain Makowski, parachuted by SOE, had killed two Gestapo men trying to catch him, and this within forty-eight hours of his arrest.

For his part, Philippe de Vomécourt writes in sober vein about the death of his brother Jean, who was effectively murdered by the person who informed on him:[1]

He underwent the usual interrogation sessions, and denied any involvement with his brother Pierre's activities. Naturally Pierre himself and Roger too had both denied that Jean worked with them. In fact Pierre was about to be released by the examining magistrate when the police received a letter denouncing him; the

1. Philippe de Vomécourt, op. cit.

letter, posted in eastern France, thus brought a new element into the case and my elder brother was promptly deported to a German concentration camp.

He suffered the same fate as hundreds of thousands of others, forcibly deported like him, herded into trucks like cattle on the way to the abattoir, for a journey from which they would not return. Beaten, kicked, exhausted and starving, he clung desperately to life. His head shaven, his body emaciated, wearing his ghastly striped uniform, he stood up to the Germans armed with whips and cudgels with magnificent courage. When he was sent to work in the mines he contracted tuberculosis; but he was given treatment and he recovered. However, he never left the hospital where, thanks to his knowledge of German, he was made the senior orderly; he was still there as the Russians were approaching from Oranienburg-Sachsenhausen and when the Germans gave orders for the camp to be evacuated.

Jean stayed where he was with the men who were too weak to leave. When liberation became imminent, the Germans decided to liquidate all who had witnessed their bestiality; Jean must have been able to hear the distant thunder of Russian guns while they pushed him alive into the furnace of the crematorium.

Was the informer ever aware of the tragic consequences of his evil deed? How could human beings who had a conscience possibly do such things?

There is no eyewitness, no historian who will ever be able to set out the long list of secret agents who fell victim to treachery or denunciation.

The routine was much the same in all French prisons, even before the Occupation, as Jean Pierre-Bloch shows in his autobiography. First of all the new prisoner had to be processed:[1]

> If you are being thrown into jail, no matter where, there are always the same formalities to begin with. My companions and I were duly taken to the office where this ceremony unfolded. A man was waiting for us, his képi pushed casually back, a pipe in his mouth, a bad-tempered expression on his face (I learned later that this was the prison governor, Dupuy). One of the warders, furious at being 'put out' at such an unsocial hour just for a band of outlaws, made his disgust very plain.
>
> 'Line up against the wall!' the governor roared.
>
> The search was starting. The guard worked me over with scrupulous care. My pockets, the hems of my clothes, my shoes,

1. Jean Pierre-Bloch, op. cit.

the lining of my jacket were all examined. My inside pocket held photographs of my children. I protested, but in vain; the only response I got was:

'You won't need those now. Get your clothes off!'

Once we were undressed he made us go into the showers. One after another we were invited to give our fingerprints. I'm sure I went through this business at least a dozen times before my jailers felt they were really satisfied. Then it was my turn to face interrogation.

'Name and identity?'

'Pierre-Bloch, member of parliament, local councillor, reserve officer.'

They stamped the form, added my height and weight – and that was me finished. They let me have my wedding ring back; this was permitted by the rules. Two minutes to get dressed again. Then we were taken back to the governor's office, where the stove was giving off a frightful stink (at least, it might have been Monsieur Dupuy's pipe), then took us round the corridors – dreary, dead, dank corridors; prison corridors.

The guards took us to the cells and put four of us in each one, though they were obviously intended just for one man. And then for the first time we were allowed some rest. There were some sort of straw mattresses; after several tries we managed to find room for us all to stretch out. Our first night in prison had begun. Unfortunately I was too hungry to sleep, and too cold as well; the slop bucket in one corner made the whole cell stink; and my own thoughts were not exactly comforting. I'd have liked to know what the examining magistrate really thought of our activities; I'd have liked to know if my wife was being held in the same conditions as me . . .

At last the night was over. In the morning the guards gave us back our shoelaces and ties. It was no doubt considered necessary that prisoners should recover the attributes of 'civilized life' before appearing in front of a magistrate.

Before taking us up before the magistrate for another session of questioning, the guards chained us up. I couldn't stand this insult, and started shouting.

'We aren't wild animals, you know! I'm an officer and I refuse to be treated like a criminal. I haven't even been convicted!'

The helmeted guards who were to escort us simply stared impassively ahead.

'It's nothing to do with me, you know,' said the guard who was putting the chains on me. 'It's up to the magistrate to decide.'

There was nothing we could do but let the escort take us where they would. The women followed us, also surrounded by guards; women were no doubt regarded as particularly dangerous . . .

'I can't have you released from the chains,' said the magistrate blandly. 'That's a matter for the gendarmes to decide.'

Then he got down to business. More questioning about our identities. We were informed of the charges against us.[1] And the 'dialogue' didn't last long. They herded us together again, for transit through the corridors. This time I really blew up. The guard walking placidly beside me said:

'Calm down, lad.'

'Don't you speak to me like that! Can't you even make the effort to speak to us politely?'

He shrugged his shoulders and they took us back to our cells.

In those happy days, I suppose that all the prisons were packed to bursting point, that they were all like the Périgueux jailhouse – holding four times the usual number of detainees.

The 'workshop', a room used both as a canteen and as sleeping quarters, which was meant to hold about fifteen prisoners, currently contained forty or fifty. But in our case, like the first night, we were kept four or five to a cell for the whole time we were detained.

Not the least of our troubles was finding outselves caged up, in a broom-cupboard only three metres square, along with common criminals, pimps and rogues of all sorts and kinds. It was exactly the same in the women's quarters; Gaby found herself among resistance heroines, abortionists and whores . . .

Right beside me was Major Breuillac, an officer who had been awarded the Légion d'Honneur, and the Croix de Guerre with palms, handcuffed to an army deserter . . .

As far as I know, none of this was peculiar to Périgueux.

Reveille was at eight thirty. It might seem generous to the point of culpable weakness to let wrongdoers like us sleep in, long past a time when honest folk were thinking of going to work; but in reality, the official reveille didn't affect us much because at that time we were shut up in our cell, being devoured by vermin.

Health facilities were minimal. There was in fact only one tap, out in the courtyard, which we were supposed to use in groups of fifty! And then the tap iced up and we had to do without water for more than three weeks. In the canteen we were allowed one cup of soup – which, of course, we had to pay for. Then we were taken to the 'work cell' where, incidentally, I never did see any work being done; we must have seemed a dismal, inert bunch of men, I

1. All were charged with offences against the State.

daren't say resigned. The hours spent in prison are the longest and the most brutalizing – in the literal sense of the word – even to the most hardened individual. One daren't think of anything definite or immediate. And yet one never stops waiting and hoping.

The prison rules allowed us to take a ten-minute walk in the courtyard every day at eleven o'clock, and whatever the weather – sleet, wind, rain – to me those ten minutes seemed a happy escape. To get out at last, away from the thick unbreathable air in the cells and work room; to see something other than the sordid walls of my cage, the greasy dank corridors; to get away from this inhuman – or hardly human – throng of prisoners en masse, whatever they were like as individuals. A little courtyard with a patch of sky, and who cared if it wasn't blue. Without being a Verlaine, how we stared at that sky *par-dessus les toits!* But even this short recreation was very uncertain, for our guards, outnumbered by their 'customers', couldn't always find time to take us out. So the twenty-three hours and fifty minutes of imprisonment often lasted for a full twenty-four. And those ten minutes made more of a difference than the mathematical one . . .

Then they gave us a bowl of sops, brought by soldiers from a nearby barracks or some guards' mess or other, I don't know where. In this we were luckier than the 'civilian' prisoners, who were nourished by the tender care of Monsieur Dupuy; they received a little hot water garnished with bits of swede or half a dozen beans.

We also got 200 grams of bread, a dish of vegetables and – once a week – forty grams of meat which I seldom managed to swallow.

In such conditions it should come as no surprise that the mortality rate was very high. In one month, December, there were seventeen deaths due to 'insufficient nourishment'. That's what life was like in Vichy prisons.

Six thirty was the official bedtime and the beginning of our torment. We had to hand over all our clothes to the guard. I don't think I can find the words to express it properly: those long hours of night in our squalid blankets, wide awake, scratching ourselves, hunting fleas up the walls and in the straw mattresses. The torment lasted from six thirty at night to eight o'clock the next morning, more than half the day. It is still for me, and I suppose for my companions, the most enduring and the most nauseating memory of all. I'm not sure whether the system has really changed today . . .

And yet this description of cell conditions in the Vichy regime's prisons would look idyllic to those resistance fighters who came to know the Gestapo jails.[1]

The foregoing examples have shown how resistance workers were beaten and tortured. Philippe de Vomécourt cites several typical cases. After his arrest on 13 November, 1942, he was taken to prison in Limoges:[2]

> Before I was taken for interrogation I saw a young man called 'Kiki' Glasner who was helping the police with their enquiries. He had been accused of conspiring to blow up the headquarters of Darnand's SOL [the French security police], although he had been arrested before any crime was committed.
>
> Two men and a young girl, members of his group, had arrived in Limoges ahead of him. One of them had put the explosives in his pocket and, for some unknown reason, the charge had gone off while they were in a public garden. The man had died; his companion had one leg almost severed at the thigh, the other leg broken; and the young girl, too, had been seriously wounded. The two survivors were in police custody and the wounded man had been subjected to interrogation, during which a policeman had 'accidentally' leaned on the man's broken leg. This very effective means of persuasion had permitted them to catch a fourth member of the group, who was due to arrive from Lyons that very night; a second 'massage' produced a detailed description of Kiki Glasner, whom the police went to pick up at the station as he got out of the train.
>
> All this had happened just before my arrest. When I saw him, Kiki was being subject to the 'spade torture', also called the 'coal shovel'. He was made to kneel by the shovel, then the policeman casually stepped on the handle so that the shovel's metal rim was raised, digging into Kiki's leg just below the kneecap. Anyone who has ever been hit below the kneecap can imagine what agony it would be if a steel blade cut into them there. Kiki's face was ravaged with pain, but he didn't break.

After the Unoccupied Zone was invaded on 11 November, 1942, the Gestapo took charge of hunting down resistants and secret service agents. Their methods were far more 'accomplished' than those of the Vichy police.

In order to extract confessions and information which they could use to make other arrests, the Gestapo first offered money and immunity as a

1. See M. Ruby's books, *La Résistance à Lyon* and *La Contre-Résistance à Lyon* (L'Hermés, Lyons 1979 and 1981).
2. Philippe de Vomécourt, op. cit.

reward for treachery. If this didn't work they threatened the detainee's wife, children and parents. If this didn't work either, they turned to physical torture and subjected their victims to abominable brutalities. Some prisoners were made to stay kneeling for hours on end on a three-legged stool, and the torturers sometimes climbed on their prisoner's shoulders. Or the prisoner might be suspended by the arms, forced up behind his back, until he fainted. Or he was kicked and beaten with fists, with the butt of a revolver, with cudgels, with coshes. They often used bludgeons to beat a man's genitals, or pliers to pull off a woman's nipples. They filed down teeth, pulled out fingernails, they burned the prisoners with cigarettes or soldering irons. They slit the soles of his feet with a razor blade then forced him to walk on salt. They subjected him to electric torture. And so on. If he still refused to talk, they isolated him in the 'dustbin', a terrible dungeon room, small, dark and airless, and deprived him of food or drink or sleep (some dungeon cells, without windows, were so small that the prisoner couldn't even lie down; in other cells the lights stayed on, night and day, without interruption).

But the most common form of torture was the bathtub, already mentioned above. It was invented by a Parisian, Georges Masuy. It consisted of forcing the prisoner into a bath of icy water, his hands manacled behind his back, and holding his head under water until he was on the point of drowning. If he fainted, they dragged him out of the water by the hair and threw a pan of cold water in his face. If he still refused to talk, they pushed his head under again. All this was interspersed with beatings. Sometimes the poor wretch, almost staring death in the face, would be offered a hot cup of coffee or tea; then, if he still decided not to talk, the torment would begin all over again, and go on interminably.

The Gestapo's range of tortures was unlimited. A last example is taken from Philippe de Vomécourt's description of the fate reserved for SOE agents:[1]

> Jacques was a radio operator. Dropped into France in 1943, he had only a few weeks of freedom before being caught near Moulins. At Gestapo headquarters in Clermont-Ferrand he suffered the usual treatment to make him reveal his code; the Germans would thus be able to pretend to be him and to intercept his radio messages. But when their beatings and kickings had failed to produce the desired result, they moved on to another terrifying form of torture. With Jacques tied to a chair and his hands manacled, they brought a flame close to his right eye, then blinded him with a steel spindle.

Naturally, like prisoners the world over, they were obsessed with thoughts of escape. 'Jacques', bleeding and handcuffed, seized the opportunity when

1. Philippe de Vomécourt, op. cit.

his tormentors left the room briefly to break free from his chair and jumped out of a second-floor window. And, incredible as it may seem, he managed to give his pursuers the slip, hiding in a courtyard. Rescued by a gallant blacksmith, he was later able to reach a local group of maquisards.

The most spectacular mass escape of SOE agents is related by Jean Pierre-Bloch. He and his friends had been interned in the Mauzac camp, a concentration camp which had been set up when the Cherche-Midi prison was transferred to the so-called Unoccupied Zone. This is how he described the escape:

> Our escape was the combined work of my wife on the outside and Georges Begué on the inside. My wife, who had been given 'provisional liberty', appeared at the camp each week with a basket of books, food and clean linen. She would leave with the previous week's dirty linen. This innocent arrangement – it was in any case watched over by the guards – had become a part of the camp routine.
>
> My wife was in charge of arranging the escape. This involved her getting in touch with the network to find those who had taken over from us. She also had to find one or more of the exterior guards and persuade them to become accomplices; these guards were nothing to do with the camp itself, they were auxiliaries who patrolled the perimeter fence, carrying weapons and always following the same route. The auxiliaries were poorly paid; many of them were refugees from Alsace. Their zeal for supporting the Vichy régime was not infallible; and Gaby, who after each visit would spend the rest of the day in the only hotel in Mauzac, used to have coffee with them, talking to them and even trying to show them that an Allied victory was a certainty. She got to know one guard in particular, who combined his patrol duties with those of running a bar not far from the camp. Soon two other men also began to look fairly 'co-operative' . . .
>
> One day my wife told me that Curly had the whole operation in hand. He had arranged a safe hiding place and a car for the great day . . . Everything was ready!
>
> We were up to date with our crawling practice. We had been training each morning during the physical exercise sessions, English fashion, crawling about on the ground between the barbed-wire fencing, under the eye of an almost admiring guard.
>
> We urged Georges Begué to do his best to make us a key. We helped him by covering the noise of his tools by bellowing the most obscene songs at the tops of our voices, for several hours at a time. Georges regarded his key – made from tins of top-quality

sardines in tomato sauce – with the anxious tenderness of God contemplating his creation.

But when he tried to open the lock, between two patrols (we had timed them), our efforts were in vain.

And when my wife returned, she made us even more impatient: 'It's all ready,' she told us. 'There will be no particular risks except at the frontier. Someone will meet you in Spain.'

'And what about the guards? So far there's only one who is likely to help us.'

'No, there are two now.'

'How will we know the second one? We can't afford to make a mistake.'

'You won't have to talk to them. But I've arranged a way for them to communicate with you. They'll bring you notes in tubes of aspirin, and you can reply in the same way. Always deal with the guard you know, he'll pass on messages to the others.'

This precaution produced a 'happy' error. The last key that Georges made functioned marvellously well. The two escape props – V-shaped wooden trestles, the same artist's work – were ready. I wrote down all the details of the escape plan and the necessary instructions, slipped the note into a tube of aspirin, and tossed the little torpedo to the guard I was sure of. Gaby was due to come in two days' time.

'Well!' she said, as soon as we could talk in peace. 'We've certainly had a narrow escape! That tube you sent to Welten the day before yesterday . . .'

'Yes?'

'Welten didn't see the second guard that day; he went to the guards' cloakroom in the mess and slipped the aspirin into his friend's jacket pocket – only he'd got the wrong jacket!'

'Who found it?'

'The mess sergeant. He wanted to talk to me when I arrived.'

'You told him you didn't know anything about it?'

'Of course I did. He wasn't really convinced, though. But he's offered to help you escape himself – because he likes your face and because he wants 50,000 francs.'

'Oh no, not him too!'

'Yes, I'm going to give him fifty halves of 1,000-franc notes. He'll stand watch for you. When the car arrives, he'll let you know if the coast is clear by flicking on his cigarette lighter. All you have to do is tell him which day.'

The last days of waiting were particularly long and wearisome. Our escape was decided for the night of 16 July.

My wife's final visit, with the children, on 14 July, was rather sad. She gave me a sleeping pill for those of our companions about whom we weren't very sure. For the first time, her nerves got the better of her and she started crying. Then we parted.

The 16th was the longest day I've ever known. At last it was night. The moon began to climb. It shone brightly over the surrounding countryside and on the barracks; as bright as the night of the parachute drop at Villamblard.

Georges Begué tried the key for one last time. Pigeonneau had decided not to come with us. His lawyer had assured him the charges against him would be dropped.

There were eleven of us left on the escape party. We started drawing lots to see who would go first. I drew third place.

'Gentlemen, who's forgotten to go to bed?'

'No one. There's already a dummy in each bed.'

'Are we all here? It's almost time.'

Pigeonneau and Breuillac were watching the guards patrolling the camp. They had just returned to the guardroom. The door opened without a creak. But there was no signal telling us we could leave. What was going on? A bit late, our look-out appeared. The first man was already creeping out. He crawled quietly, slyly, soundlessly towards the barbed-wire fencing. The two V-shaped trestles, which Georges had set up a moment earlier, barely raised the wire fencing. The guard Welten whistled and tapped his stick from time to time on the wire; he managed to make more noise than us. One by one we slipped under the fence, hearts beating. As I crawled underneath it I caught my clothes on the barbed wire and was ripped from top to bottom. A little later I noticed I was bleeding profusely.

'Is that everyone? Ten, eleven . . .'

There had been thirteen of us altogether, including the guard[1] and the mess sergeant who was leading us. We'd done it in exactly eleven minutes.

'Let's go then!'

We certainly didn't waste any time covering the three kilometres separating us from the car.

Seated in the Citroen, hidden away in a hollow, Curly was waiting for us with Raoul Lambert – a pilot who'd been one of the founders of the Libération-Sud movement, and who played a very brave part in helping to arrange this escape, as did Lucien Rachet.

How fifteen of us managed to get into that car defied all the

---

1. This was the guard whom Madame Gaby Pierre-Bloch had recruited; he had agreed to help the escape plan on condition that afterwards he would be able to get to London to enlist with the Free French.

rules of capacity. But it must be the laws that are wrong, for we succeeded in getting in, squeezed together fraternally and reducing our vital space with heavy sighs and foul profanities.

Curly was meant to drop us about fifteen kilometres further on. The day was beginning to filter through the light morning mist. When he dropped us, all thirteen of us, in the middle of a stretch of heather, it was six thirty. We waited in the dew for about an hour before we saw him reappear.

We organized ourselves into a line and strode out into the forest, using tracks and mysterious paths. It took us nearly three hours to reach our hiding place – a dilapidated, abandoned house and barn, but with admirable organization someone had prepared for our visit. *Biscottes*, jam, soap, razors – in the thirteen days we were there, our friends helped to give us back a new sense of our identity . . .

Jean Pierre-Bloch and his friends had thus found the road back to freedom – and to the possibility of resuming their patriotic work.

After the Germans invaded the southern zone on 11 November, 1942, escapes became much more difficult, apart from the organized escape lines (particularly the SOE line run by Vic). The Gestapo and French collaborators mounted a vigilant guard from then on. All too often, the secret agent or the resistance worker would come to know their cruelty; or were deported to Germany and life in a concentration camp, that realm of suffering and death.

Throughout this history of the Buckmaster circuits we have seen that SOE agents were killed – caught by the enemy and shot while landing, or during an arrest or an attempted escape. Radio operators were killed with their earphones on. Others died in the Nazi concentration camps – either from a bullet or by hanging, or as a result of illness induced by malnutrition.

Death was also due to an occasional cruel stroke of fate. Thus Cookridge tells the story, for example, of the case of 'Lucien':[1]

Among the many SOE agents who arrived during the final stages of the war in France was a young count, Maurice Gonzague de Saint-Geniès ('Lucien') who parachuted with Yvonne Baseden ('Odette'), an English W/T operator. They set up a small circuit in the Jura, next to Heslop's, and their main task was the reception of arms for the maquis. While storing a large supply dropped from US Flying Fortresses, they were surprised by a German raiding party and hid in a loft. At first the Germans found nothing. Then one of the SS men, giving vent to his frustration,

1. Cookridge, op. cit.

began to fire at random. A bullet went through the trapdoor of the loft and hit Saint-Geniès in the head, killing him instantly. Blood trickled through the trapdoor frame and was spotted by the SS men. They found the dead organizer and arrested everyone present, including Yvonne Baseden (who hitherto had been taken for a local girl). She was sent to Ravensbrück but she was eventually freed by US troops – one of the very few SOE inmates to survive this extermination camp.

The same author gives examples of other tragedies – such as the case of Robert Benoist, the motor-racing champion who arrived in March, 1944, in the company of Denise Bloch ('Ambroise'), to resuscitate his old group. During previous missions he had several times barely managed to avoid capture. He found his old friend and racing rival, Wimille, and both men set about reorganizing a circuit west of the capital, numbering at least 2,000 well armed members of the FFI. Hearing that his mother was dying, Benoist hurried back home to the family château – where the Gestapo were waiting. He was deported to Buchenwald and was hanged. Denise Bloch was also captured and put to death in Ravensbrück.

Cookridge also cites the case of Alec Rabinovitch ('Arnaud') who on his second mission arrived in France on 2 March, 1944, accompanied by the French-Canadian, Roger Sabourin, to set up a new group in Nancy. They were parachuted into a dropping zone controlled by Germans. The Germans realized Rabinovitch was a radio operator who had given them the slip once before, at Saint-Jorioz; they deported him to the Polish extermination camp at Rawicz. Sabourin, meanwhile, was sent to Buchenwald, where he was hanged on 9 September, 1944.

The English author also reports the tragic fate of certain SOE agents in the very last stages of the war:

On 8 August, 1944, just two weeks before the liberation of Paris, 180 prisoners, all selected for extermination, were herded on a train bound for Germany. Between Paris and Châlons-sur-Marne, the train was attacked by Allied aircraft, probably because a British pilot assumed it was a German troop transport. The engine and the track were damaged and near Châlons the prisoners had to change to army trucks.

One of the prisoners was Wing-Commander F. F. T. Yeo-Thomas. His recollection of the journey is limited to that of two of the trucks, one containing thirty-seven SOE and French prisoners, the other a number of women, including several SOE agents. . . . The two army trucks stopped at Châlons and again at Verdun. Then the trucks continued to Saarbrucken, where the prisoners were taken to a prison camp for 'refitting'.

Here Cookridge quotes from a book by Bruce Marshall:[1]

The men were chained in groups of five. The chains were in the shape of an X, in the centre of which was a ring fitted to a pair of handcuffs, which were fixed round the ankles of one prisoner so as to force him to take short, shuffling steps. At the extremities of the chains were more handcuffs which were fastened to the ankles of the four others in the group. To prevent them from using their hands to keep their balance the prisoners were no longer attached to one another in pairs by their wrists, but each man's hands were shackled separately. In these cumbersome fetters, they were marched to the distant latrines and, as they tripped and stumbled, were kicked and beaten with truncheons, coshes and fists by the SS men. In the latrines, where fat slimy worms crawled among the overflowing faeces, they were forced to relieve themselves in these chained groups.

'Yet this was only a transit camp to Saarbrucken,' continues Cookridge. 'The journey ended at Buchenwald, the concentration camp near Weimar':

The SOE officers who arrived with Yeo-Thomas were Denis Barrett, Robert Benoist, Pierre Culioli, Henri Frager, Émile-Henri Garry, Desmond Hubble, Kane, John A. Mayer, John McKenzie, Harry Peulevé, Maurice Southgate, Arthur Steele and George Wilkinson. Already in Buchenwald were several other SOE officers including Christopher Burney, Maurice Pertschuk and Alfred and Henry Newton.

On 24 August, 1944, Allied aircraft bombed the Gustloff armament factory outside the camp, where many prisoners worked. Several bombs fell on the SS barracks, killing eighty and injuring 300 SS men. There were also heavy casualties among the prisoners. According to German sources, 400 were killed and 1,500 wounded, many of whom, receiving no first aid or surgical treatment, died.

As a retaliation for the Allied bombing raids, the camp commandant, SS Obersturmbann-Führer Pfister . . . ordered executions of British and French 'terrorists', all of them officers of SOE and BCRA. On 9 September sixteen prisoners were marched to the 'Tower' [i.e. the scaffold] and hanged. Among the SOE men were John Macalister and Frank Pickersgill . . . Émile-Henri Garry, Robert Benoist, Arthur Steele, John McKenzie, John Mayer, Charles Rechenmann, François Garel, and Desmond

1. Bruce Marshall, *The White Rabbit* (Evans, London 1952).

Hubble and Kane of the RF Section. On 4 October another batch
of twelve was taken to the execution yard and hanged. Amongst
them were Denis Barrett, Henri Frager, George Wilkinson,
Albert Dubois and Pierre Mulsant.

Wing-Commander Yeo-Thomas told me that all of them were
hanged from hooks in the wall of the crematorium and left to die
by slow strangulation. Harry Peulevé, too, was called on the
loudspeaker to report. But he had exchanged his prison garb (as
had Yeo-Thomas) for that of a dead French prisoner and had
become No. 76,635, Marcel Seigneur. The body of Seigneur was
sent to the crematorium as that of Peulevé.

Executions took place at regular intervals and many thousands
of prisoners were hanged (or shot in large groups) right up to the
end of the war. Maurice Pertschuk ('Perkins') who had been
'Eugène', commanding the Toulouse circuit at the age of
twenty-three in 1942–43, was hanged on 29 March, 1945, only
five weeks before Germany's surrender.

Other SOE agents perished in the concentration camps of
Dachau, Sachsenhausen (where Francis Suttill, the commanding
officer of Prosper, was hanged on 21 March, 1945, having been
held as a possible hostage until almost the end of the war),
Oranienburg, Torgau, Blankenburg, Lutzkendorf, Ravensbrück, Natzweiler, Rawicz and above all at Grosrosen, in Silesia,
and at Mauthausen in Austria.

Dachau, an all-male concentration camp when I was an inmate,
later contained a compound for women prisoners. On 13
September, 1944, Noor Inayat Khan ('Madeleine'), Eliane
Plewman ('Gaby') and Madeleine Damerment ('Martine') were
executed there.

A few SOE members were miraculously able to return from these
concentration and extermination camps. One was Jean-Bernard Badaire.
The Gestapo hadn't managed to extract any information from him and sent
him via Compiègne to the Neuengamme camp. As No. 39,343 he was there
submitted to the special treatment reserved for political deportees (the
'three-star regime'). And it was there that he met the man who later became
the famous Commissaire Chenevier.

Like most former deportees, Jean-Bernard Badaire recalls only with
extreme restraint the cruelties to which he was subjected in the camp's main
block. He has spent his whole life ever since his release trying to forget the
atrocious events he witnessed there. His personal situation improved slightly
when he was sent to join a work party at the submarine base at Bremen, for
this great port was being systematically bombed by the Allied air forces and
Badaire had to take part in clearing up operations. He retains particularly

painful memories of being forced to work in the 'quarry', where the SS instantly shot any unfortunate prisoner who momentarily stopped digging or pushing trucks about or transporting beams and girders. Badaire was one of the very few people to survive this work party.

In the spring of 1945, before the Allied advance, the Germans decided to evacuate the camp. Some of the prisoners were shipped off to Sweden – and were sunk by the RAF; chained together in the holds, many of them were drowned. Incredible as it may seem, however, some did manage to escape and swam towards the German coastline – where the SS shot them even before they could land. Another group of prisoners was sent to Sandbostel camp by train. On 6 April, 1945, they were herded into padlocked wagons, each man being given a slice of bread and a few grams of margarine. The train set off, was machine-gunned several times, but arrived at its destination on the 13th. After seven days of hell in that convoy of death, with no water and no food, the SS finally opened the doors. The casualties were horrific. In each wagon, only four or five men were still alive. And those who were not strong enough to join the column marching to the new camp were slaughtered on the spot by the Nazis.

But Jean-Bernard Badaire and Charles Chenevier survived these inhuman trials – and luck, at last, was about to smile on them. Only a simple barbed-wire fence separated their new camp from Stalag 10B. At night, in a landscape strewn with corpses, the men from Stalag 10B helped Badaire and Chenevier through the wire fence and gave them military uniforms. Luck was transformed into miracle when Badaire found out that the French officer appointed leader of the POWs in Stalag 10B was none other than Colonel Albert, who for years had shared a dormitory with Badaire's father in Oflag 10B. Thanks to this extraordinary coincidence, Badaire was particularly well looked after by the other POWs. A week later, on 20 April, 1945, he had sufficiently recovered to escape from the prison camp, taking advantage of all the confusion following the German retreat, and he reached the British lines. He advised them on how to liberate the camp and the stalag. It was in the camp that he celebrated – if one can use that word – his twenty-second birthday.

Youth and a few lucky breaks had permitted this SOE soldier's life to be spared. Others were not so fortunate.

The horrors awaiting the SOE agents deported to Nazi concentration and extermination camps, and others who suffered the same misfortune, were later described in a first-hand account by Dr Jean Rousset, the SOE agent from Lyons known as 'Pep'. Arrested in his surgery on 7 November, 1942, horribly tortured by the Gestapo, he spent a year in an isolation cell in Fresnes prison. He was then deported to Germany, first to Neu-Bremen, then to Buchenwald, where he remained for a year and a half. On 11 April, 1945, the American Third Army liberated him.

In Buchenwald, Dr Rousset was sent to work in the camp hospital, which comprised two wards, one large and one small; he worked in the main ward as a specialist in skin diseases. The camp's medical facilities were supervised by a surgeon who was a captain in the SS, assisted by a lieutenant from the medical corps and a male nurse who was a sergeant. None of these three ever did anything but look after their 'fearful paperwork'. Occasionally the SS surgeon would send for Dr Rousset and the four other inmates who had medical training for a consultation – but only on administrative matters. In reality the camp's medical service was in the hands of the prisoners themselves. As Dr Rousset later wrote: 'You could say that, in effect, all the official SS medical staff knew about their wards and the big camp was what the man responsible for the main ward felt like telling them.'

The following extracts from Dr Rousset's book[1] clarify the fate of the unfortunate wretches who wore the striped uniform of Buchenwald slaves – firstly on the subject of transportation:

One day in January 1945 we heard that a prison train had arrived at the station. During the midday break, we were asked for volunteers to go and help the sick people on the train – something that had never happened before. We duly volunteered, along with five or six Russian and Polish orderlies (none of whom had any real medical training). The spectacle that awaited us was more horrible than anything one could imagine. Because of the scarcity and poor quality of coal, the trains could no longer climb the incline between Weimar and Buchenwald. The wagons had therefore been towed uphill in several batches, now spread out along the tracks. The wagons were all open to the sky. Each of them held about a hundred detainees, all in ragged clothing, stiff with cold and covered with snow. They had been travelling for nine days, after three days' hard march through the snow, in the course of which many of them had died. The only food they'd had for six days and five nights was 1,500 grams of bread. Even then, some of them had not received their proper share, for the bread had been thrown at them like animals. Only the lucky ones had managed to catch a bit; what fell on the snow and mud of the wagon floors was trampled underfoot, for they were so tightly packed that no one could bend down to pick it up. It was only with the greatest difficulty that the prisoners managed to get out of the wagons and onto the platform alongside; as for those who were in the wagons stopped on sidings outside the station, they simply did not have the strength to jump out onto the ground, although fortunately the cinder tracks were covered with a thick

1. Jean Rousset, *Chez les Barbares* (Imprimeries Réunies, Lyons, n.d.).

layer of snow. When those who were mobile had managed to get out, the wagons were still full of corpses and dying or very sick men. Out of 5,000 men in that train, 470 were dead. One whole wagon was full to the brim with bodies. When we opened the doors they didn't even fall out; they had frozen together, one on top of another, the gaps filled in with hard-packed snow and ice.

But the real drama had not yet begun; this was to take place on the station platform. We hastened to find anyone still alive and bring them out. A wasted effort – there was no means of transporting them to the camp. From noon till half past five, we moved them on two little wooden sledges which could barely carry two men. Prisoners in the camp kitchens sent us a handcart; but it took eight Russians to pull it and only managed to do two trips in the time. We had no hypodermics, nothing to treat all the cardiac cases; we stood helplessly by, unable to do anything but watch our comrades as they rolled in the snow in agony.

The unfortunates who could still walk dragged themselves towards the camp, littering the road with blankets, billy cans, clogs, convict caps and dying men, all the way to the shower block. When the shower block was full to overflowing, the column of men was directed to Block 12, which was being rebuilt (it had caught fire after an incendiary bomb had landed on the neighbouring DAV factory, dropped by the RAF on 24 August, 1944) and still had no doors or windows. The building became so crammed with the new arrivals that during the night the floor collapsed into the cellar (this was the only building that had a cellar) and with it went screaming groups of prisoners, about eighty of whom died of suffocation or were seriously injured by falling timbers. No one went to help them and it was not until the following day that any of us learned about this new disaster.

Many of the very sick who had been on the train were dumped in the crematorium yard, where the SS guards also piled the bodies of those who had collapsed between the railway line and the showers. Long into the night the cries went on, in every language except French: 'Comrades! Come and help us, we aren't dead!' In the end the icy snow sealed their thin mouths and the snow laid a shroud over these new corpses as on the others.

We had left the station at five thirty and on the way back to the camp we'd had to follow in the new arrivals' path. We kept stumbling over bodies, which lay amid a trail of abandoned possessions, dropped by people at the end of their strength. The scene was like a battlefield. All this was under grey skies in the depths of winter.

Dr Rousset also describes the reception procedure when new inmates arrived at Buchenwald:

> The illness our jailers feared most was undoubtedly typhus. It was a constant struggle to control this Number One enemy.
>
> For the French at least, the struggle began even before we left our own country. In Fresnes, no one paid much attention to the parasites infesting the cells. We were kept in a separate cell all year, each with a single blanket heavily infested with lice. As we were being held secretly our complaints were in vain; it was three months before we even got a shower – and afterwards, all we had to wear or dry ourselves with was that same blanket. But the day we left there was a big offensive. We were given soap and allowed to take a shower and all our clothes were fumigated. Except – rules being rules – our hats, any leather or rubber items such as braces or sock suspenders, and whatever meagre possessions we kept wrapped up in our blankets. Slightly less smelly, we now found ourselves, for the first time in a year, shut in a cell with five other people; but it was one of the reception cells for new arrivals, and it was teeming with bugs. This was where we had to spend the whole day from eight in the morning until six at night. So much for German efficiency!
>
> On arrival at Buchenwald everyone had to be deloused. First they confiscated all your personal possessions, if any: jewellery, watches, fountain pens, wallets, money, everything. Then you were stripped of your clothes. All you had to do now was parade in front of the SS, who after examining your backside then stuck their hands in your mouth with a tongue-depressor (always the same one) to make quite sure you weren't hiding anything. Then they opened the door into the 'barbershop'. With electric razors plugged in at the ceiling, the barbers had the job of ridding the new arrivals of every hair on their heads. They needed a stepladder to help them reach. I should add that trainloads from east and west were massed together on arrival, everyone jostling everyone else in repugnant proximity, while the barbers worked in hobnail boots; typhus was rife among them, and the mortality rate was high. It would have been surprising if it had been otherwise. German efficiency . . .
>
> Next, disinfecting in a tub of cresyl. It began as a five per cent solution when the first man went in, but the orderlies supervising these ablutions added water from time to time, to top it up, so one can imagine how diluted and filthy it was for the one thousandth or two thousandth person to be disinfected. German efficiency . . .
> When everyone from the barbershop, eyes watering from the

cresyl, had been gathered together under the showers, the water was turned on. But people were so tightly packed that there was no question of anyone washing himself; it was a lucky man who managed to get wet all over! In the next room there was one small bit of cloth like canvas for a score of men to dry themselves with; and later on there wasn't even this chance of getting dry because the cloths ran out altogether. There remained one last prophylactic rite to face; the application of a solution called Cuprex, supposedly a parasiticide but anyway terribly irritating. When we arrived it was applied with a hose aided by air compressor; later the job was done simply by brushing the stuff on the areas round the armpit and groin, dipping the brush into the caustic liquid from time to time.

The prophylactic treatment for new inmates was so inefficient that we found lice on them even as they came out of the showers, when theoretically they should have been free of all parasites. When we ourselves arrived, in 1943, after the Cuprex treatment we were given dreadful clothes; but at least they were clean. Later on, in spite of confiscating and sharing out clothes among those who were still alive, there were never enough. As a result, while new arrivals were being deloused, the clothes they had just removed would be taken away for disinfecting and then redistributed at random. Leaving aside the repellent aspect of having to wear someone else's filthy clothes, possibly someone with dysentery, there was also the chance of catching typhus. The inmates charged with disinfecting clothes were obliged to stuff them to overflowing into the fumigating stoves. Under these conditions the gases simply could not circulate properly; afterwards the lice were just as active as before. German efficiency . . .

On the subject of washing facilities Dr Rousset had this to say:

In the big camp there was only one washbasin in each block. A row of sinks against one wall was for washing mess-tins. In the centre there were two – I repeat: two – circular troughs with a series of taps for personal hygiene. In the small camp, the facilities were even more primitive as there was only one long trough in each block, often outside, and this had only three or four taps (for 1,600, and towards the end 2,400 men!). The tented camp too had just the one trough, equally exposed to the elements, next to the latrines. The water was turned on in the morning at reveille, again at midday for half an hour, and again for one or two hours in the evening. There was nothing with which to dry oneself and a soap substitute (the size of two or three lumps of sugar) was handed out once a month – if at all. Showers were allowed every three or four weeks, in the same sort of conditions described above. A change of shirt was provided once a week in 1943, once a fortnight in 1944, and during the last six months no one was able to change at all. In April 1944 the underpants ran out. In all the time we were there we received just one pair of socks – when we arrived!

Those who suffered from dysentery received no more changes of clothes than anyone else, of course. In the small camp, where the disease was rife, the men were merely told to wrap themselves in a blanket while their trousers dried out. Those poor wretches had to consider themselves lucky if some brute of a German block commander or his Polish slave did not decide to wash them down outside with a hose . . .

On 27 March, 1962, when summoned to give evidence to the Commission d'Histoire de la Guerre (1939–45), Dr Rousset described the discipline imposed on Buchenwald inmates:

I was one of the first French people to arrive and was given the number 28,360. Before me, the few Frenchmen who'd arrived were Communists from the International Brigades, followed by people who had actively opposed the Occupation – officially 14,000 of them, though I knew of only two still alive. A Czech prisoner who spoke a little French told us the camp regulations: a mixture of standing orders for barracks and special rules for trouble-makers who were thrown into the glasshouse. The military discipline was worse than childish, it bordered on the demented. We had to stand to attention in front of the SS, keep our hands out of our pockets when walking round the camp, take our caps off when approaching the line of bricks at least thirty metres from the watchtower by the camp gates and put them on again only after passing the outer line of bricks. We had to attend rollcall bare-headed, when everyone had to be present, even those who had died that day. When we walked past Hitler's stone eagle, at the camp entrance, we again had to remove our caps.

The worst aspect – I would call it the criminal aspect – of camp discipline is well enough known. The death penalty was invoked for even the smallest misdemeanour: not only for attempting to escape or outright disobedience but also for a minor infringement of rules. They suspected everyone of plotting mischief and regarded us all as potential trouble-makers. Whipping was the mildest punishment – fifty lashes on the buttocks.

Dr Rousset also told the Commission about the camp's internal administration:

> When I arrived there had just been a major shake-up in the camp's administration; I personally witnessed only one outrage, and that was one of the less horrific. Basically the camp was administered by common criminals, specially appointed inmates who wore a green triangle; they had the job of telling the other inmates what to do, so they could belittle and humiliate the political prisoners (who wore a red triangle). The 'politicals' were completely at their mercy – not just their dignity but their very lives depended on the whims of these rogues. But abuse was piled on abuse at every level of the camp's internal organization, merely to satisfy the sadistic nature of murderers appointed heads of blocks or of work parties. There was no attempt to use the skills of the political internees, who would inevitably replace the real criminals one day.
>
> Of the German political prisoners at Buchenwald, the vast majority were Communists. There was hardly anybody from the Social Democratic or Catholic Centre parties, though some leading figures from the latter party were interned, like von Papen's secretary. In my time, therefore, the camp's internal organization was basically in the hands of Communists. They were idealistic and full of good intentions. On reflection and with the passage of time, as the memory of those incompetents begins to fade, I think I can honestly say that their discipline was meant well and had to be accepted, for it helped to save lives in the end and thus rendered the daily martyrdoms more acceptable.

Dr Rousset then came to his own working conditions:

> I was assigned to work in the camp infirmary – I can't really call it a hospital – in the Aussere Ambulanz section, officially as a medical orderly but unofficially as a senior specialist. Like all the other doctors, no matter what nationality, I shared the same lot as everyone else where food and accommodation were concerned. But to me it also seemed fairer to my compatriots – and more prudent, too, with Communists running the camp's internal organization – not to take advantage of all the little extras so eagerly pursued by doctors of other nationalities: a bed in the ward, at the expense of someone who really needed to be in hospital; a faked affliction to let me draw extra rations; a warm coat at the expense of someone working outside in the cold. As a voluntary member of the proletariat, the Communists adopted

me into their ranks and treated me like an old soldier. As one of the doctors, everyone regarded me favourably, whatever their nationality. They called me a real internationalist. They appreciated the way I made an effort to learn Russian.

On the medical front, the situation Dr Rousset describes was incredible:

My one great quarrel with the medical administrators was over the recruiting of doctors. When I arrived the prevailing notion was that any of the comrades could become a doctor; he could learn the business from the old hands. I therefore found housebuilders, a cobbler, an ex-sailor and an office clerk all setting to work with the lancet and the hypodermic needle.

In his evidence to the Commission, Dr Rousset described some of the punishments commonly inflicted on the prisoners; here is just one example:

They once ordered us all to assemble to watch a young Russian being punished. The session was held at night. The prisoners formed a square in the camp yard. The barracks floodlights were on, casting a bright patch of light that was bordered by row upon row of pale, ragged, skeletal figures. The unfortunate man was sent for – he was being held in a cell without a single stick of furniture, just the concrete floor – and brought out to the centre of the square where a table now stood. The interpreters recited the charge against him: he had been in the workshop and was supposed – I repeat, supposed, for I shall never for the rest of my life believe what an SS man says, and anyway the others told us he was lying – to have stuck out his foot and tripped up one of the guards. The two Poles now stripped the young Russian of his cotton trousers and tore away the couple of bits of sacking he used against the cold, then tied him up and made him bend across the table. The Polish officer stepped forward with his riding crop and started to lay into him – fifty strokes without stopping, grunting all the while like a man felling a tree. After about the twentieth stroke, the Russian gave a terrible unearthly scream; otherwise the silence was broken only by his torturer's panting. It was a bleeding and inert bundle of rags that was dragged back to the cell, under the eye of the grinning Polish officer. The next morning the SS guard we called 'the big bastard', a giant of a man, kicked him out of his cell and tried to whip him into running round the fire trough with us. But the unfortunate Russian collapsed, unable even to stand. He was viciously dragged and kicked across the ground by this giant we called 'the big bastard' and by another guard, a Feldwebel with intellectual pretensions. Then they took him back to his cell. A few days later, without once being allowed any medical attention, he died. The tortures inflicted on this young Russian seemed quite gratuitous and designed solely to impress the Nacht und Nebel [German commandants].

Dr Rousset was well placed, as the SOE doctor in the camp, to witness one particular barbarous practice: that of repeatedly taking blood donations from old or disabled prisoners for the benefit of the German army:

> Every three weeks these poor wretches were called to Room Two. Here, under SS control, the medical staff had to take excessive donations of blood from each man – at least 200 grams, often 350 or even 500! We took part in this butchery only the one time, just long enough to prove how useless we were at making a veinous puncture. Our victims gave only 10–20cc of blood and so slowly that it would have tried the patience of a saint.
>
> There were about 2,000 of these unfortunate disabled inmates. All were totally incapable of work. Among them were blind men, one-armed men, one-legged men, very often men who had been mutilated in one or other of the wars, like the tank corps lieutenant or the philosophy graduate, both of whom were known throughout the camp; also old men like gallant old 'Father' Labussière de la Flèche who at seventy-eight was the oldest Frenchman there, the Czechoslovakian who was eighty-three, Professor Maspéro from the College de France, and hundreds of others. The SS found their presence in the camp intolerable and did their best to get rid of them. They began by asking for volunteers for a simple little job, easy to do sitting down – rolling strips of absorbent gauze (or some substitute) into bandages; they said the volunteers would get the same food rations as other workers. In spite of all our efforts to dissuade them, these poor men were even more worn out than ordinary inmates by hunger and the terrible overcrowding that prevented anyone from lying down to sleep for more than one night in six, and many of them did volunteer, including some of the French. But none of them came back; transferred to another camp, the poor devils were exterminated there. Next the SS wanted volunteers to help with meteorology experiments. They were sent to the Dora extermination camp. The remainder were forced to strip – this in the middle of winter – and all the clothes they had been sent by their families, such as coats, jerseys and socks, were taken away. They were left with only one shirt, one pair of

trousers, one jacket and their clogs. And as they could never change them, these rags were all they ever had to wear. For weeks on end, the whole camp could see the buttocks of a French general, a hero of the 1914–18 war when he had been one of the famous 'broken lances'. Yet many of them clung stubbornly to life; so the SS denied them any sausage or margarine and their rations of soup and bread were reduced still further.

It was from these walking corpses, shivering with cold and stupid from lack of sleep, that we had to take blood – to help the wounded of the great Reich! In order that German hypocrisy should not be too obvious the 'donors' received supplementary rations each month: about 100 grams of sausage, of which up to eighty per cent was starch!

Some of Dr Rousset's evidence refers to matters that are still debated today:

At Buchenwald, healthy individuals were inoculated against typhus. This was done in one of three different ways: firstly by transferring infected lice from sick men; secondly by injecting an infusion made from crushed infected lice; and finally by taking direct infusions of blood from those who had the disease. This last method proved the most effective and was the only one retained. By the time we entered the camp they had perfected their technique. A healthy prisoner would be conscripted for the experiment and immediately inoculated. Usually, following orders from his SS masters, Arthur would inject anything from 0.1cc to 0.5cc of blood, taken from someone already suffering from the disease, if they were trying to produce an incubation period of fourteen days, or 2cc if they wanted a seven-day incubation. Two half-wits were kept as permanent guineapigs for any experiments the SS wanted to do. In fact Block 46 was twinned with another block, No. 50, where they were researching all sorts of inoculation treatments and vaccinations. When they thought they'd made a 'breakthough' in Block 50, the deadly activities in Block 46 were redoubled.

Prisoners were specially selected to test the experimental treatment. For about a fortnight they were given a decent diet including milk, butter, eggs and sugar. Then a high proportion of them (eighty to ninety per cent) were inoculated, thanks to the guineapigs, and all of them – whether sick or in reasonable health – were kept under supervision while the value of the product and possible side effects were assessed. When we were looking after the Poles, the treatment consisted of a single injection of 1,200cc of a 'serum' which had to be injected into a vein 'at high speed';

the supervisor was particularly insistent that it should be done very quickly. All of them caught typhus and died within forty-eight hours.

When they started testing the vaccine, the prisoners were of course vaccinated first, then a fortnight after the last injection of vaccine they were inoculated. At the same time, a number of control patients were infected so that the relative progress of the typhus and the vaccine could be studied. Death began to occur within ten days of inoculation. People responded according to the strength of the vaccine being tested. We had mortality rates in the region of eighty to ninety per cent, but it's also fair to say there were five to eight per cent who survived. Not that this was any use to the survivors, for once the experiment was over they were killed – the usual method in our block being an injection of carbolic acid. In July, 1944, for instance, these medical experiments cost the lives of 156 prisoners.

According to Dr Rousset, out of 250,000 French political prisoners, only 32,000 survived to be repatriated. He cites some of the mortality figures at Buchenwald:

In January, 1945, out of an average population of 61,000 prisoners, 6,477 died. In February the average population was 62,000 and 5,614 died. In March the average was 82,000 and 5,479 died. These were official figures, which we were given by the senior medical commandant in person during our weekly meetings. It can therefore be said that, given the average rate of death from illness in the first three months of 1945, the camp would have been completely wiped out in little more than eleven months.

Of course this rate was not constant. It went down in summer and up in winter. It also varied with the number of epidemics. Above all, the death rate fell when there was a large intake of new prisoners, and soared when the new arrivals were survivors from the death convoys. Finally, we must not forget the effect on the death rate of mass executions – like the one in October 1941 when 6,000 Russian POWs were put to death in the 'Pferdestal', the sinister stable block. The previous August, 100 unfortunate tuberculosis patients were murdered by injections of Evipan. But after the winter of 1944–45, these executions no longer affected our figures; they were carried out at the railway station before the prisoners reached camp. Deportees in three rail convoys from Buna, Myslowitz and Czenstochau died in this way: as night fell they were surrounded by a cordon of SS guards, then the SS doctors and orderlies opened the wagons and gave everyone, without exception, a lethal injection. The camp commandant spent the whole night at the crematorium, until the last body had been disposed of.

But enough of this catalogue of horrors. Suffice it to say that many SOE deportees died of exhaustion or illness, if they weren't slaughtered in cold blood.

Dr Rousset was finally able to return home, physically exhausted after his long imprisonment, during which he had done everything humanly possible to relieve the terrible experiences of his companions. An active member of the resistance, an SOE agent and a personal friend of mine, he died a few years later.

Mishaps, prison, torture, deportations and execution: this was the fate of many of SOE's agents; this was the price they had to pay for their fight against Nazism and the debased ideology by which men ultimately became mere executioners.

Pierre Vourron had joined the resistance at the age of fifteen, in February 1944. A member of the SOE group 'Nicolas', he was wounded while on a liaison mission, arrested by the Germans and deported to Buchenwald. He told of his inhuman experiences in a small booklet entitled 'Prisoner No. 85,295'. He has kindly authorized this retelling of the story of how the SS evacuated the camp when the Allied armies were advancing. On 7 April, 1945, 9,000 deportees, and another 4,000 on the following day, were marched off to an unknown destination. According to German figures, during the course of this exodus, 12,000 of the 13,000 unfortunates were to die. Here is how Pierre Vourron tells his story:

> Shouts and yells suddenly made us jump: 'Los! Los! Schnell! Raus!' [Move, move! Quick! Outside!]
>
> A company of SS men with dogs on chains were coming from the big camp and spreading out in the direction of the infirmary and the small camp.
>
> We were rapidly encircled and made to go straight towards the alley on the extreme right leading to the rollcall quadrangle. I didn't have time to think what was happening; I was pushed, shoved, swept along on this human tide. I tried to get free, I tried to think of a reason to return to the barracks.
>
> There was a human barrage blocking off each of the transverse lanes. All holding hands, groups of kapos [heads of blocks] and Vorarbeiter [barracks leaders] prevented the inmates from getting through into the main camp.
>
> I was pushed along by the crowd which was now moving in

small groups. We followed the same route as the day we had arrived, but on foot. During the march to Weimar, several shots were fired. Laggards were being killed on the spot.

At Weimar station, a long train was waiting: about forty animal wagons both covered and open to the sky. We were forced to climb into wagon number 24. Inside a space had been cordoned off by two railway sleepers.

Sixty of us went to the right, fifty to the left. All sitting down, legs apart, knees touching shoulders, lined up like sardines in a tin. Impossible to move! Imagine sixty people in a space measuring three metres by five.

The empty space in the middle of the wagon was occupied by two armed SS guards. Every nationality was there: Hungarian Jews with gaunt faces, Russians of all ages, Belgians, Czechs and about thirty-five of the 110 Frenchmen in the camp.

Where were they taking us and why? No answer. Some people thought we were heading for the front to dig trenches; others said we were being taken to an extermination camp. Nobody knew for certain.

As night fell we were each given half a loaf of bread, about 500 grams. The wagon doors were shut from the outside and then chained up. The two SS men were shut in with us. They settled down comfortably with their guns trained on us. A strident whistle and the train set off into the darkness of the night.

Despite the hunger pains gnawing at my stomach, I took a decision that was to save my life. I crumbled about threequarters of my bread into pieces and spread them among my pockets. Dawn appeared to us in the form of a dim light filtering through the two openings at either end of the wagon. Thin faces, pale and terror-stricken, emerged from the mass of arms and legs in the wagon. The abrupt jolt as the train braked had thrown everyone on top of each other. There were cries of pain and someone was grumbling: 'Ow, get off! Move! You've been sitting on my leg for the past two hours . . . I'm sore!'

The man to whom these words were addressed made an effort to move, but he couldn't – for the simple reason that there wasn't a single square centimetre of empty space. On my side, too, we were still squashed up, still in our rows. The train didn't stop, however, but moved on again. The guards removed food from their knapsacks and calmly started eating.

Someone in the centre of the wagon got up and went to stand near the SS. On his left arm was the word 'Vorarbeiter'. I thought he was the one I'd seen at Buchenwald. His triangle was marked with an H (for Holland).

How had he dared to disobey orders? We were expressly forbidden to stand. One of the SS threw him a bit of bread. He thanked the guard effusively and gave him a salute. It was grotesque. One of the guards told him to watch over us and point out anyone who moved. Proud of his new duties, the man started making remarks to us. His shifty looks earned him the approval of his new bosses. It was pathetic. How could someone like that taunt us so cheekily? His behaviour was inexcusable, yet under the circumstances none of us could blame him . . .

At dawn on the third day a frightful scene met our gaze: three hideous skulls with buck teeth and open eyes were staring at us, dead. The first three bodies, dead of exhaustion, worn out by suffering or perhaps simply smothered during the night by the Ukranians wanting more room to stretch out.

My neighbour muttered; 'It's not over yet. This is just the beginning.'

The SS, not in the least put out by this sight, were chatting to each other. Soon the complaints began, first polite requests, then louder. One voice, then two, then ten were asking for a drink: 'Wasser! Wasser! Water, water . . .'

The words rose in the poisoned air like a litany. Some gave up, too exhausted by the effort. Others went on chanting: 'Water . . . Water . . .' Three days without food or water – it wasn't possible! The SS started to get nervous and kept threatening to shoot us. The Dutchman was only waiting for the order; he got up, trampled over the outstretched bodies and hurled himself at the poor wretches, kicking them in the face. For a while all was silent.

The day before we had heard something about 'Leipzig'. Today the SS were talking about 'Chemnitz'. The train was slowing down. Through gaps in the walls we could see the roofs of houses. With a metallic shrieking of brakes the train came to a standstill. A sign read CHEMNITZ. Was this the end of the journey?

The sound of boots outside. A guttural voice: 'Number twenty-three? Number twenty-four?'

Our wagon was number twenty-four. The SS guards shouted, 'Alles in ordnung!' (All's well.)

But there were the three corpses. The thought of getting a little water kept us calm for a while . . . Unfortunately, some hours later, the engines gave a long blast on the whistle and announced our departure. Through a hole in the wall the SS guards had just enough time to pick up a bag of provisions.

'Give us something to drink! . . . Something to drink, for pity's sake!'

The voices repeated these words incessantly, begging. No one asked for food. It was thirst, a terrible thirst, that was drying up our mouths. Our breathing was hoarse. We no longer had enough strength to talk. We didn't care much about dying – we only wanted a drink of water, water . . .

The filth, the corpses, the desiccated breath filled the air with an unbearable stench. My eyes opened in horror as I saw what one of my companions was doing. He was Italian. He was urinating into an old sardine tin and drinking it in little gulps. Never, but never, could I have done that, in spite of the painful burning in my throat. That night the complaints began again, in a hallucinating refrain.

I was aroused from my torpor by gunshots. An ear-splitting scream broke the night, then there was silence. All we could hear was the rattle of the wheels and the usual tackety-tack of the rails.

'. . . Thirsty! Something to drink! Water! . . . *Wasser! Aqua! Woda!*' Everyone wanted water and was asking for it in his own language. The SS men were unmoved by anything.

We had come to the dawn of the fifth day. The scene was appalling. Blood covered the walls. The guards had opened fire at random, killing five men. One of the Poles had been hit in the head; a Russian was licking up the blood that was dripping onto the floor. The Dutch *Vorarbeiter* had been killed. We had a bit more room to stretch out our cramped legs. I turned my head to keep from looking at those dead men with their awful death masks. I rested my burning lips on a metal bar and felt a momentary well-being. The SS guards were undressing; taking off their shirts they started examining each other for lice.

The wail of an air raid siren reached our ears through the foul air. A noise of brake-blocks on the wheels; the wagons shunted into each other; several bumps; we were motionless. We could hear other engines puffing. We were in a marshalling yard. The guards looked worried. If the station was bombed they would die. The soldiers escorting us ran for shelter. We distinctly heard the distant roar of aircraft. Our guards banged on the door. No one answered. They were prisoners like us.

The marshalling yard was not bombed, however. When the alert was over we heard a door being opened and realized that at last the SS were going to give us something to eat and drink. There was the sound of chains, a padlock being opened, and then the gust of fresh air hit us like a kiss. The guards jumped out onto the track. While one kept an eye on us, the other went off to relieve himself. Afterwards they asked for two volunteers to empty the slops bucket which had been put in the truck for their use. Two Russians stepped forward. Despite the long privations, they managed to climb out of the wagon without apparent effort. Three or four minutes later they returned and got back into the wagon, collapsing among the living dead and the corpses. The open air had not lessened their thirst.

The guards were relieved by two older SS men, presumably reservists. In answer to a question put by one of them, we caught the words 'Pirna' and 'Dresden'. Outside from time to time we could still hear the mournful cry of agonized prisoners. *'Wasser! Water! Woda!'*

Four volunteers were appointed to take the corpses out. I was one of them. We took each dead man by the legs and dragged him along the stones lining the track. All six trucks had a foot-plate piled with skeletal corpses, a hideous tangle of arms and fleshless legs, a parcel of bones in which glassy eyes glittered. We made four journeys.

I took advantage of a momentary inattention by one of the guards to pretend to adjust my shoes and snatched up a handful of dandelions, hiding them under my jacket. Back in my place I seized these yellow flowers and devoured them greedily – leaves, roots and earth, everything. The Russian beside me did the same. The whistle blew, the engine snorted, there was a hiss of compressed air. *'Ansteigen!'* [All aboard.]

Thirst: always that lacerating, tormenting thirst, which made your tongue swell. I tore a metal button off my shirt and began to suck it: the illusion of a little freshness! I didn't think any more about the crumbs of bread in my pockets. Besides, they had been scattered about during the night when I turned over twenty times to ease the pain caused by contact with the floor.

Night surprised us in the same condition. The SS men were no longer watching us. What was the point? What could we do, these skeletons from whom the least effort drew groans of pain? When the wagon was lit up by outside lights, our brains registered a terrifying sight: shaven heads, hollow cheeks in which eyes were made bigger by suffering, open mouths showing blackened teeth, these dying human beings. We were in hell. Life only held by a short breath.

Yet another morning without water. Still more corpses. Two Italians, three Russians, yellow as the colour of the urine they had drunk. For those of us who were still alive, we had a pair of leg bones to use as a pillow. The train slowed down and stopped. The SS didn't show any special concern. A short stop perhaps? In looking for a few crumbs in my pocket I pulled out a fag-end, a souvenir of Buchenwald, a canteen cigarette. It was Russian tobacco, Makorka. I decided to put it in my mouth, perhaps I might suck it for a bit. One of the Ukranians breathed: 'Give it me, give it me, Frenchman!' I handed him the stub, heard him strike a match. At that very moment a voice from outside called to the guards.

'*Poste Vierundzwanzig?*' (Number twenty-four?)

'*Alles in ordnung.*'

'*Wer hat hier Geraucht?*' (Who's been smoking?)

The two SS men on duty looked at each other. The officer sniffed the air and repeated his question, looking at our group. The Ukranian raised himself on one elbow and pointed a finger in my direction. 'The little Frenchman.'

I felt that my last hour had come. I looked at the officer who was staring at me. One, two, three seconds . . . All of a sudden he seized the Russian, stood him up and pushed him towards the door. He held him with his left hand and with his right hand he fired a bullet from his pistol into the man's neck. He collapsed like a broken doll and toppled onto the track. Without a word the officer left.

I remained there, stunned, asking myself by what miracle I was still alive. Why had he killed the Ukranian, not me? The effort of thought gradually subsided. Thirst, water, a whistle blast, the grinding of wheels, we were off again . . .

My French comrade who looked about fifty years old had not once so much as shuddered since we left. You might have thought he was indifferent to everything around him. His head, hanging forward, wobbled from right to left with the rhythm of the wagon as it went along. The other Frenchman, younger, leaning back against the side wall, big mouth wide open, eyes fixed, let words flow from his mouth without ceasing and without meaning. Sometimes his expression became more cheerful; perhaps in his mind he was seeing water, masses of water . . .

I sank into total lethargy. I heard raindrops pattering on the roof; a hole was letting the water drip into the wagon. I opened my mouth and let it soak my face. Water, water at last! I came to; I was panting; my throat was on fire. I had been dreaming – but for how long?

The train stopped. Shouts just outside: '*Schweinerei! Tod-schlagen!*' All the yelling suggested that something new was up. The doors of the wagon crashed open. An army lieutenant asked if we were all dead. Shaking his head the guard made it clear that some of us, unfortunately, were still alive.

The lieutenant leapt at us, screaming and kicking and lashing out with his whip, and forced us all towards the door. 'Listen,' he told us in German. 'Fifteen terrorists including five Frenchmen have slipped onto the track. They took out a plank from the floor of the wagon and they've escaped.'

'*Schauen!* Look, there they are!'

'Bring out all those still alive in Wagon Twenty-three,' he shouted.

'*Gut.* Now count them all.'

'Thirty-three men.'

'Watch this,' he said to us. 'This is what trying to escape will cost you.' Five soldiers armed with machine guns fired several steady bursts. Our comrades were riddled with bullets, bathed in a sea of blood.

The SS returned to their places. The train started off again. There was no emotion among us. Death – after all, we were living with death. For them it was today. In an hour or two, or tomorrow perhaps, it would be for us. The cries were no more now than feeble croaks: 'Something to drink! . . . *Wasser!* . . . Water!'

No, there would never be any water. In the distance the cannons were thundering – the Russians perhaps? No, impossible, since we're dead. Liberty! What's the use. We're going to die. Who are these two soldiers watching us peg out – are they men or animals? When I was small I once saw a fierce dog with eyes like theirs.

I fell unconscious again. It was bitterly cold. The doors of the wagons were half open, the two SS men were looking out at the passing countryside. We were going very slowly. There was no need to chain the doors closed, we were already considered corpses. Some pattering noises made me lift an ear. Was this just another figment of my imagination? No, it was raining . . .

White houses appeared, another scene opened before us. I tried to read a name on a wall: PILSEN. Were we in Czechoslovakia? The train stopped. A few yards from the houses, some civilians in colourful garb were watching us. The rain was pouring down now and huge droplets were falling through the holes, bouncing off the floor and splashing us.

'*Poste zwanzig?*'

'*Alles in ordnung.*'

My old French friend had also noticed the freshness in the air. He stared up at a corner of the ceiling and watched the droplets. He seemed fascinated. He forgot the rules of prudence: 'Standing is strictly forbidden.' With a superhuman effort, propping himself up against the wall, he managed to get to his feet. He held out his sardine tin and collected a few drops of rain.

Twice the tin was filled with the life-giving water. Three shots rang out. The tin disappeared. His hand a mass of blood, my comrade fainted. Some brute jumped into the wagon armed with a big stick. He came straight at us. With all his strength he lashed out with his club. Blood splattered everywhere. He kept on and on, battering the corpses and near-corpses. I was dead. I was dying. My head was bursting. I must have been covered in blood.

'Where am I?' Perhaps it was just by speaking aloud that I realized I was still alive. My eyes were shut with congealed blood. With a trembling hand I tried to prise open my eyelids. Oh, my head . . . An agonizing pain flashed through my brain.

One more effort, and I half-opened one eye. Corpses stretched out, not a sign of life. Was I really still alive? Gently I touched the old Frenchman's face. He was still warm. He was alive. His hand was still bleeding, and his face was bleeding. Beside him lay two smashed heads, brains hanging out. Where were we? The SS had got out of the wagon, so we must be stationary. A soldier threw several buckets of water in, to wash away the blood which was thick on the floor. I raised myself on my elbows and murmured 'Water, water . . .'

The soldier left his bucket of water in the middle of the wagon. How to reach it? The bucket was two metres away. I lifted one leg, then the other. I was lying on my back. I tried to roll over onto my stomach. I fell back again immediately. I caught someone's leg and tried to pull myself forward but in vain.

'Water, water . . .'

Fascinated by this bucket, I started to crawl towards it. Another metre to go . . . Another fifty centimetres . . . Another twenty-five . . . I stretched out one hand. My head fell into the water, I drank slowly. As the liquid went down my throat I felt life being born in me again. I lay there, stretched out beside the bucket.

On the floor I found a can of food that the guards had left behind. I put it in the bucket and, still crawling, tried to get back to my corner. After an agonizing effort I finally reached my old companion. I tried to pour some water into his mouth but it spilled down his shirt. Was it the contact with the cold? He came to and understood. He pounced avidly on the can of food and emptied it in one gulp.

'Thank you,' he murmured with a sob. His feverish hand sought mine. 'Listen, my little one, I'm going to die but you – you'll get out of it all right. Remember, Charles Boucaud, 119 Rue Franklin in Angers. Angers, Maine-et-Loire. Repeat it,' he said.

I repeated it.

'You'll tell my wife how I died? Eh? You will tell her . . .'

'Yes, I'll tell her. But you're not dead yet!'

'You'll tell . . . my wife . . . my son . . .'

He rambled on. The efforts I'd made had broken me. I had a terrible pain in my stomach, my head was on fire. I lost consciousness.

The sun's pale rays lit up the sides of the wagon. There was a strange noise; it was getting louder. I'd been lying on some bodies. I dragged myself towards the still-open door. What an odd sight! Women, children, old people were standing around arguing with our guards. What was all the fuss about? They had a funny accent. Oh yes, I remember, we're in Czechoslovakia. They were all talking very animatedly and gesticulating furiously. The crowd dispersed but reassembled a few moments later, their hands full of bread and butter. The children were carrying pitchers of water.

The SS made these good people put the impromptu meal down in front of the train and forced them at gun-point to leave. What happened next was too awful for words. The Germans sprinkled the bread with petrol and set fire to it. When it was all burnt, the guards shut the doors. With that final barbaric act, our last hope of survival had gone. I looked among the dead for some sign of life, some other living being, but all I could see was glazed, bony bodies. In my corner, my old French friend seemed to have fallen asleep for the last time. I touched his brow. He was still warm. I leant against his shoulder and waited for death. My last thought was of God . . .

Two days later, the Allies arrived. By some incredible miracle, Pierre Vourron – although unconscious – was still alive.

There is little one can add to this poignant story to evoke the suffering of SOE agents and their comrades in arms when they were captured by the Nazis.

Many of SOE's men and women had known misfortune and mishaps, overwhelming odds and denunciation, prison and torture, deportation and execution. Inspired by a burning, idealist notion of patriotic duty, they had chosen to join the underground fight, summoning up all their strength, wits, stamina and nerve. Secret agents are wont to say that their war was 'a gentleman's war'. If there is an aristocracy among those who make the ultimate sacrifice, these people certainly belonged to it. From the moment they joined up their lives were constantly under threat. If they sometimes achieved astonishing success, their constant companions were suffering and death. Such was the price they had to pay for volunteering.

# ——— E P I L O G U E ———

During the Second World War the SOE networks spread not only across the whole of France, but also the other occupied countries of Europe, even the Far East. In this survey of SOE's work in France we have seen how remarkably effective the actions of a mere handful of men and women could be – and, which is also striking, how very young most of them were.

The exact number of SOE agents in France is still disputed. H. Michel writes that there were 393, of whom 119 were executed or killed while carrying out their duties.[1] Cookridge reckons there were 480 agents, 130 of whom were captured and only twenty-six of those would survive.[2] H. Noguères comments that of all the 1,600 agents sent to France, only twenty-seven were awarded the DSO.[3] André Courvoisier, after examining various different sources, concluded that:[4]

> In 1942, twenty-six new SOE circuits were set up on French soil under Colonel Buckmaster's control. In 1943 there were twenty more; in 1944, before the landings, another thirty-seven. In total, therefore, eighty-three circuits had been in operation, of which nearly fifty were still functioning on D-Day; and, between 1941 and 1944, SOE's Baker Street staff had sent over 500 agents to France.

Cookridge talks of 'seventy to eighty circuits' and goes on to point out that 'many of them had several *sub-réseaux* and as often as thirty local groups and cells, sabotage equipes and reception committees'. He also mentions 'the thousands of brave men and women of the French resistance who sheltered

1. H. Michel, *Les Mouvements Clandestins* (PUF, Paris 1961).
2. Cookridge, op. cit.
3. Noguères, op. cit.
4. Quoted in Ruby, *La Résistance à Lyon*.

SOE agents, helped them in many ways, worked as couriers, "letter-boxes", receptionists at dropping zones, saboteurs' and so on.

As for Colonel Buckmaster himself, the head of SOE agents in France, he declares:[1] 'From June, 1944, onwards there were fifty-three groups in communication with us, from all over France. . . . I had 480 officers working for me, 440 men and 40 women. The casualty rate was exactly twenty-five percent: we lost 120 agents.' These then were the official figures. But Colonel Buckmaster was apparently counting only those who went to the special training schools in Britain before being sent on active operations in France. Like Cookridge, however, we must also take into account the thousands of ordinary men and women from the resistance movements in France who helped SOE's agents. After all, that wasn't so many when one considers that they were facing the entire German army.

The resistance would still have existed even if SOE had not. But in the fight against Nazi Germany and her allies, the role that this active service played was clearly very important.

Pierre de Vomécourt recalls the pioneers, of whom he was one:[2]

> The first SOE agents in France began by 'cleaning the windows', so to speak, and thus letting London know what life in France was really like. But above all, these first agents gave the English proof that there already existed a resistance, and that it was only waiting for someone to come and help. With virtually no means at their disposal these pioneers did perform a useful job – not very spectacular, perhaps, but indispensable in terms of SOE's later developments. Moreover, and this is the crucial point, they launched a technical sabotage movement, thus providing increasing numbers of anonymous Frenchmen and women – each working in a particular sector and concentrating on a particular task – with a chance to cause daily interference in the pro-German industrial effort.

This sabotage work was developed and, after the Allied landings, increasingly took on a more specifically military aspect. At a cost, as we know.

Finally, for all that there were so few of them, the SOE circuits achieved widespread success. This is André Courvoisier's brief summing up:[2]

> The Buckmaster circuits can be credited with half the successful parachute operations into France, and more than half the total arms supply drops: 3,733 successful drops in all, bringing a total tonnage of 5,007,000 kilograms and comprising 104,536 Sten

1. Buckmaster interview, 9 December, 1981.
2. Pierre de Vomécourt, op. cit.
3. Quoted in Ruby, *La Résistance à Lyon*.

guns, 409,224 grenades and 307,023 kilograms of explosives. SOE operations made an enormous contribution to the enemy's constant insecurity. Moreover, the French resistance as a whole was able to benefit from the creation of SOE's circuits, as they helped to spread the burden of Nazi attentions; and finally, SOE's people provided valuable weapons-training for the maquisards.

Colonel Buckmaster himself lays equal stress on his agents' two main aims: on the one hand, to shake the German war machine by stepping up sabotage of economic and military targets (the latter especially from the spring of 1944); and on the other hand, to equip the French patriots with arms and explosives and give them instruction and training. By way of illustration, Buckmaster cites the example of the German armoured division, stationed at Hendaye, which was unable to reach the Normandy battlefront in time because of all the sabotage action and ambushes set up by French resistants and SOE agents. (Buckmaster made a personal visit to France at this critical stage; a bomber flew him into the Jura, which the maquisards had liberated, and he returned to London on the same aircraft twenty-four hours later.)

After the war, General Eisenhower made a celebrated speech in which he said:[1]

> Sabotage caused effects beyond the capacity of the Allied air effort, delaying all German divisions moving from the Mediterranean to Normandy, and forcing extensive enemy detours, with the consequence that they arrived, if at all, too late and not in fighting condition, or in a state of extreme disorganization and exhaustion.

And, concluded the Allied Commander-in-Chief:

> I consider that the disruption of enemy rail communications, the harassing of German road moves, the continual strain placed on German war economy and German security services throughout occupied Europe by the organized forces of the resistance, played a very considerable part in our victory.

With these words, the Allies' supreme chief paid a proper tribute to the activities of SOE's specialist saboteurs. They had, as Winston Churchill ordered, 'set Europe ablaze'. The price they paid was much courage and intelligence – and terrible losses.

It is only right that history should not forget the part they played – shadows fighting in the shadows. Equally that history should record what exceptional results can be achieved, even in the most difficult circumstances, when volunteers are motivated by sheer idealism – the ideals of freedom and human dignity.

---

1. Quoted in Cookridge, op. cit.

# —— BIBLIOGRAPHY ——

Writing a complete history of SOE is a difficult undertaking for the documentation is particularly scarce. The 'service' archives are practically non-existent.

Fortunately, however, several former members of the Buckmaster groups have published books about their experiences. These include:

Colonel Maurice Buckmaster: *Specially Employed* (Batchworth Press, London 1952)

Jean Pierre-Bloch: *Le Temps d'y Penser Encore* (Jean-Claude Simoën, Paris 1977)

—: *Jusqu'au Dernier Jour* (Albin Michel, Paris 1983)

Peter Churchill: *Missions Secrètes en France* (Presses de la Cité, Paris 1967)

Benjamin Cowburn: *No Cloak, No Dagger* (Jarrolds, London 1960)

Philippe de Vomécourt: *Les Artisans de la Liberté* (Éditions PAC, Paris 1975)

André Courvoisier: *Les Réseau Heckler* (France-Empire, Paris 1984)

Jean Rousset: *Chez les Barbares* (Imprimeries Rénuies, Lyons n.d.)

Pierre Vourron, 'Matricule 85,292' (privately published, n.d.)

I have also been privileged to hear from numerous members of the Buckmaster circuits, and several leading figures have given me their own personal accounts as well as showing me certain vital documents. Notable among these were:

Pierre de Vomécourt, the first SOE group organizer to be parachuted into France, to whom I owe a special debt of gratitude for helping to explain many points.

Jean-Bernard Badaire, president of the Fédération Nationale Libre Résistance (Amicale des Réseaux Buckmaster), who very kindly agreed to let me interview him on 28 June, 1984, and who has given me enormous help.

Dr Jean Rousset, 27 March, 1962.

Robert Sheppard, the famous 'Patrice', a senior SOE agent.

Jean Régnier, from Lyons, a generous associate, who visited London to attend a special training course before being parachuted back into France as an SOE officer.

All their first-hand information and autobiographical accounts constituted the basic documentation, the materials thanks to which this book has been written.

I have also drawn certain detailed information from more general books about the Second World War, notably the following:

Henri Amouroux: *La Grande Histoire des Français sous l'Occupation* (Laffont, Paris 1984; six volumes to date).

Winston S. Churchill: *The Second World War* (Cassell, London 1949, six volumes).

Sir Hugh Dalton: *The Fateful Years* (Frederick Muller, London 1957).

Sir Colin Gubbins: 'Resistance Movements in the War', in the Royal United Services Institution's *Journal*, Vol. XCIII, No. 570 (1948).

Colonel 'Rémy': *La Ligne de Démarcation* (Librairie Académique Perrin, Paris 1964–65).

Passy (Dewavrin): *Deuxième Bureau Londres* (Solar, Monte Carlo 1947); *10 Duke Street* (Solar, Monte Carlo, 1948); *Missions Secrètes* (Plon, Paris, 1951).

Two British historians have made a special study of SOE's operations.

M. R. D. Foot: *SOE in France* (HMSO, London 1966).

E. H. Cookridge: *Inside SOE* (Arthur Barker, London 1966).

But Foot admits that he was not allowed to interview former SOE agents and that he had to be content with consulting only those files that had been carefully selected for him by the Foreign Office. He acknowledges that his study is incomplete.

Cookridge was able to make use of wider documentation; but he had to wait several years before publishing his book, as the British government was long opposed to the divulging of certain documents (he was even obliged to remove certain passages from the English edition).

I have however, quoted several passages from both authors, particularly Cookridge, where they were able to provide original information.

Finally of course, there is Henri Noguères' *Histoire de la Résistance en France* (five volumes, Laffont, Paris 1967–81), a monumental work of reference for all serious students of the subject.

For a more detailed bibliography, see M. Ruby's *La Contre-Résistance à Lyon* (L'Hermès, Lyons 1981).

The Buckmaster groups were unique, created and directed by the British. Their relationships with their opposite numbers in the Free French were not always good. In fact, the British government usually worked out its plans without consulting the relevant Gaullist authority. The British tempted certain individuals, even whole resistance groups or bands of maquisards, with offers of money or arms if they would agree to accept British control. But agents were lured away by both sides. Hence the tension and conflict. This also helps to explain why there remains a certain resentment among those who worked in the French resistance towards those who did consent to serve in SOE's ranks, under foreign command.

As Jean Pierre-Bloch has remarked:[1] 'At one time it was an unpardonable crime to have worked with the British.' And he went on:

> In spite of the fact that so many died or were deported, not one single member of the groups belonging to SOE's F Section under Colonel Buckmaster, was made a Compagnon de la Libération. We even had to fight for them to be given the Resistance medal, and that was only granted with bad grace.

With characteristic fairness, Colonel Buckmaster said on 9 December, 1981: 'Our relationship with Passy, the French BCRA chief, was excellent.' And it is true that, because the two heads of service held each other in high esteem, their organizations were better able to co-operate. This was vital considering the need to share out the targets set by Allied High Command – and the few aircraft that were available for parachute operations.

However, even today, SOE agents are very often considered by those who served under General de Gaulle as part of a separate resistance. Many tried to dissuade me from getting interested in this subject on the grounds that SOE was a trouble-ridden organization. Nothing could have provoked my curiosity more; and an objective study showed me that even if certain allegations were not totally without foundation, it is certainly true that no other special service has such a record of operational success and acts of bravery. A clarification was necessary. May this book contribute to it.

1. Pierre-Bloch, op. cit.

# —— INDEX ——

Bardet, Roger, 131–2, 134, 164
Barrett, Denis, 132, 134, 188, 189
Barter, Operation, 117
Baseden, Yvonne ('Odette'), 145, 186–187
Basin, Francis ('Olive'), 116, 117, 119–120, 121, 123, 124, 127, 128, 136
Bass, Operation, 121
'Bastien' see Clech, Marcel
BBC, 26, 62, 74, 76, 77, 123, 156
BCRA (Bureau Central de Renseignements et Action): relationships 14–16 and note 1, 19, 52–3, 153, 155, 156–7, 160–1; operations, 119, 121, 147, 150, 156, 162–3
Beaudoin, Operation, 147
Beekman, Yolande, 141
Beggar, 147
Begué, Georges (George Noble), 17 note 1, 57, 161; (1941) operations, 19–20, 21, 27–8, 57–8, 113, 115, 117, 174; (1942), 69, 120, 121, 183–5 passim
Belfort, 137
Benoist, Robert, 122, 129, 136, 145, 187, 188
'Benoit' see Cowburn, Benjamin
Bénouville, Pierre-Guillain ('Lahire'), 116, 128
Bergé, Captain, 10
Bernard, Fernand, 118
Bernard, Victor, 9
Bertheau, Louis, 143
Bertholet, René ('Robert'), 114, 122
'Bertrand' see Pickersgill, Frank
Besnier brothers, 23
Bibendum, Plan, 147
Bieler, Gustave, 127, 132, 134, 140, 141, 171
Blanc, Marie-Lou ('Suzanne'), 123
Bleicher, Hugo, 131, 132, 138, 165, 168, 169
Bloch, André ('Draftsman'), 27, 115, 118, 174
Bloch, Denise ('Ambroise'), 145, 187
Bloom, Marcus, 127, 132
Blum, Léon, 35
Bodington, Major, 76, 121, 122, 123, 135–6, 142, 151

'Boiteux' see Burdett, Robert
Bonnet, Madame, 165
Bonnetot, André ('Vincent'), 139
Borde ('Georges'), 150
Bordeaux, xii, 11, 126, 129, 132 see also Actor and Scientist groups
Borni, Renée, 165
Borosh, Henri, 146
Borrel, Andrée ('Denise'), 125, 126, 130, 133, 134
Bouchardon, 136, 142
Bouchet, Raymond, 138
Bouguennec ('Garel'), 130, 132
Bourne-Paterson, 56
Brault, Michel, 29, 118, 166
Breuillac, Major, 179, 185
Bricklayer group, 146
'Brigitte' see Hall, Virginia
British Intelligence Service, see Special Intelligence Service
Brive-la-Gaillarde, 137
Brooks, General Dallas, 8, 35 note 1
Brooks, Tony ('Alphonse'), 122, 127, 129, 132, 135, 136, 145
Brossolette, Pierre, 130
Brouville, 147
Brumaire, Operation, 130
Brune, Charles, 26 and note 1, 31, 119
Buchenwald concentration camp, xii, 71, 144, 147, 187, 188–9, 191–200, 201
Buckmaster, Col Maurice: background and enrolment, 12–13, 14; responsibilities and relationships, 7, 15–16, 63, 154, 155, 160, 162, 212, 213; with trainees, 54, 56–7; (1941) operations, 76; (1942), 122, 125, 126, 127, 169; (1943), 97, 130, 131, 135; (1944), 142, 145, 150
Burdett, Robert ('Boiteux'; 'Nicolas'): (1942), operations, 41–3, 71, 72, 75, 77–82, 83, 84, 119, 121–2, 125, 170, 172–3; (1943), 136; (1944), 145; Spruce circuit, 66, 68 and note 1, 129
Burdeyron, Noël ('Gaston'), 20, 25, 30–31, 114, 120, 166
Burney, Christopher, 188
Bussière, August, 69

Frenay, Henri, 28, 118, 124, 128, 129
Furet ('Mercier'), 116

Gandrey-Rety, Jean, 123
Gardener group, 59, 145
'Garel' see Bouguennec
Garel, François, 115, 121, 143, 188
Garry, Émile-Henri, 143, 188
'Gaston' see Burdeyron, Noel
Gauden, 121
Gaulle, General de: appeal to France, 33,
    105, 123; relations with organisations,
    10, 19, 52, 129–30, 153, 156; and
    Churchill, 14 note 1, 15, 52, 157; with
    Pierre de Vomécourt, 17, 163; Op
    Savannah, 10
'Gauthier' see Vomécourt, Philippe de
Geelen, Lieutenant, 147
Genébrier, René, 26–7 and note 3
'George 60' see Clech, Marcel
'Georges' see Borde or Fox, Marcel
'Georges 53' see Zeff, Edward
'Germain' see Cowburn, Ben
'Germaine' see Hall, Virginia
Gerson, Victor ('Vic'), 69, 91, 114, 115,
    117, 119, 120, 136, 141
'Gervais' see Hazan, Victor
Gestapo, 43, 70, 108, 109, 137, 164,
    181–2, 189
Gilbert, 43
Gillois, André, 116, 128
Girard, André, 116, 117, 118, 121, 123,
    124, 128, 129, 130
Giraud, General, 15, 69, 125
Girin, Paul see Plessis, Pascal
Giselle, 131
Glasner, Kiki, 181
Goetz, Dr, 143
Goldsmith, John ('Valentin'), 125
Gouin, Félix, 115
Gourdeau, 23, 26, 119
Grand, Major-General Laurence Doug-
    las, 7
Grandclément, 136, 137, 148, 150
Greenheart network, 70, 122, 129, 171
'Grégoire' see Le Chêne, Peter
Gross Rosen concentration camp, 144,
    189

Groussard, Colonel, 161
Grover-Williams, Charles ('Sebastien'),
    122, 129, 134
Gubbins, Major General Sir Colin, 6, 9,
    148, 164
Guélis, Jacques de, 56, 59, 64, 115, 117,
    174
Guérisse, Dr Albert, 11
Guerne, Armel, 135
Guignebert, Jean, 123
Guingoin, Georges, 139, 148–9
'Gustave' see Jickell, Alan

Halifax, Lord, 5
Hall, Virginia ('Brigitte'; 'Germaine';
    'Marie'), 38, 64; (1941) operations,
    64–6, 115, 117; (1942), 67, 69, 70, 71,
    89, 120, 122, 125, 128
Hambro, Sir Charles, 9, 148
Hayes, Charles, 128
Hayes, J. B., 117, 121, 174
Hazan, Victor ('Gervais'), 68, 120
Headmaster group, 124, 129
Heckler circuit, 68
'Hector' see Southgate, Maurice
Heimann, Oscar, 129, 171
'Henri' see Menesson, Jean or Peulevé,
    Harry
Herbert, Mary, 127
Hérin, Jules, 23
Hermann, Jean-Maurice, 116
Herriot, President Édouard, 64, 72–3,
    127
Heslop, Roger, 122, 127, 140
'Hilaire' see Starr, Maj George
Hiller, Captain George ('Maxime'), 141,
    145, 150
Hind-Farmer, Major ('Jean'), 146
Hitler, Adolf, 3
'Honoré' see Barrett, John
Hubble, Desmond, 188, 189
Hudson, Simon ('Charles'), 70, 124
Hymans, Max, 20 and note 2, 22, 35,
    113, 161

Interallié, 29, 30, 34, 64–5
Inventor group, 124, 129